Praise
A Cross of

T0165806

"Mr. Castillo tells a story of which far too many people are simply not aware, the enslavement of California Indians under the mission system. While many Americans know of the Trail of Tears and other Indian atrocities, most do not know of the atrocities perpetrated on Indian people in California. *A Cross of Thorns* sheds light on this period in history."
—**Ben Nighthorse-Campbell**, U.S. Senator, retired

"*A Cross of Thorns* pulls back the veil of lies, deceit, and cover-ups that has been perpetuated for nearly two hundred years."
—from the Foreword by **Valentin Lopez**, chair of the Amah Mutsun Tribal Band of the Costanoan/Ohlone Indians

"A scholarly magnum opus . . . a highly readable historical work, filled with battle stories and previously unchronicled narrative."
—**Dan Pulcrano**, *Metro Silicon Valley*

"An extraordinary work of historical scholarship and a compelling read from beginning to end. As informed and informative as it is thoughtful and thought-provoking,"
—**Paul T. Vogel**, *MBR Bookwatch*

"Adds immeasurably to our understanding of a complicated and contested chapter of California's history . . . fascinating in its detailed accessibility."
—**Jim Van Buskirk**, *San Francisco Examiner*

The saga of unholy injustice detailed in A Cross of Thorns left me feeling kicked in the gut, with my sense of moral outrage boiling over. Yet it is presented in subdued and sober terms, with fact after fact and story after story, building a sure case against the canonizing of Franciscan Friar Junipero Serra."
—**Matthew Fox**

A CROSS OF THORNS

The Enslavement of California's Indians by the Spanish Missions

Elias Castillo

CRAVEN STREET BOOKS

Fresno, California

Published by Craven Street Books
An imprint of Linden Publishing
2006 South Mary Street, Fresno, California 93721
(559) 233-6633 / (800) 345-4447
CravenStreetBooks.com

Craven Street Books and Colophon are trademarks of
Linden Publishing, Inc.

ISBN 978-1-61035-304-5

First paperback edition

Printed in the United States of America
on acid-free paper.

Library of Congress Cataloging-in-Publication Data on file.

Contents

Acknowledgments

I most gratefully acknowledge the endless patience and support I received from my wife Cathy and the invaluable guidance of my agent, Michael Hamilburg. Encouragement and help was received gratefully from Michael Cronk and Diane McNutt, Joanne Jacobs and John Wakerly, Linda and Robert Faiss, Ron and Darla Miller, Daniel Bauer, William and Kathie Briggs, Dennis Rockstroh, and Peter Unsinger.

I also owe a debt of gratitude to the University of California's Bancroft Library, Mexico's *Archivo General de La Nación*, and the Santa Barbara Mission Historical Archive for their dedication in preserving the documents, records and letters of the mission era, providing the critical proof and insight that was needed to complete this book. Finally, my heartfelt appreciation goes to Stanford University's Cecil H. Green Library, as well as to the California Room of the San Jose State University Dr. Martin Luther King Jr. Library for its magnificent collection of books documenting California's mission era.

Foreword

U ntil now, the true and full history of the California missions has never been told. When visitors tour the missions, they are usually presented with stories and images of peaceful, loving priests and soldiers who treated the Indians as adored children.

These stories belie the truth of the missions, where Native Americans suffered under harsh and brutal conditions. As a young boy, I listened to stories from my elders about the cruelty of the missions. There were tales of how native women were captured—with their thumbs tied together with leather straps to form human chains—and marched forcibly from their tribal lands to the missions. If the Indians did not cooperate, the soldiers, at times, killed them. In one incident, more than two hundred women and children of the Orestimba tribe (living near what is now the town of Newman) were being taken to Mission San Juan Bautista. When, after passing the summit at the Orestimba Narrows, these women refused to go any farther, the Spanish commander ordered the women and children killed with sabers and their remains scattered.

The oral traditions of our tribal band, the Amah Mutsun, taught us stories of how certain Spaniards would appear when the Indians were first brought into the missions so they could get their pick of the young girls and boys for their perverted appetites, always with the tacit approval of the priests. Our elders told us that because the soldiers at the Monterey Presidio were raping so many of the Indian women and girls at Mission Monterey, the priests moved the compound to Carmel.

While many California Indians were raised knowing the history of the missions from the Native perspective, we were unaware of the history of the Franciscan priests or the Spanish and Mexican governments. *A Cross of Thorns* tells us, in a comprehensive way, how the priests conspired to enslave the Indians and ignore the goals of the Spanish Crown and, subsequently, the Mexican government. This book documents how the Roman Catholicism of that era viewed the Indians of the New World as heathens whose faith was based on entities it considered demonic. The Spaniards who went to the New World were initially only interested in obtaining wealth and then returning to Spain. But as the empire's regional power grew, the Spanish crown wanted to protect its land and thwart Russian expansion into California. Therefore, the Spanish (and, later, Mexican) government sought to use the Indians as a labor force to support their various goals, not the needs of the church. But in time it was the church which had the greatest impact on the lives of the Indians.

A Cross of Thorns pulls back the veil of lies, deceit, and cover-ups that has been perpetuated for nearly 200 years. It provides irrefutable evidence, which the author, Elias Castillo, has painstakingly footnoted so there can be no question as to its veracity. It is this evidence—this truth—that California's church-owned missions must address in order to publicly confront the terrible deeds that were committed.

Each year at Mission San Juan Bautista, more than forty thousand fourth graders take field trips to see the historical site. The children learn, incorrectly, that the missions treated the Indians with love and warmth. To this day, nothing at the mission describes how over eighty-four tribes were taken to this mission and how very few survived. Records show that thousands of Indians died there during the mission era.

The California State Department of Education helps perpetuate these lies. School textbooks covering California history, required at all elementary schools in the state, never describe fully how there were over four hundred tribes at first contact with the Spaniards. They describe inadequately how these tribes lived, how they prayed, or their special relationship with Mother Earth. Nor do they discuss how the missions were responsible for killing 40 percent of all California Indians. The history books also describe Father Junípero Serra as a loving, peaceful man with only one concern—caring for the Indians.

Rather than tell these lies, the history books should teach how Father Serra's principal goal was to baptize as many Indian souls as he could in his lifetime. In his letters, Serra described the Indians' gods as "demonic," and considered the Indians to be "barbarous pagans." He wrote that only Catholicism could save the Indians from evil, believing that punishment was important to rid the demons from their souls. For this reason, natives were lashed regularly, sometimes so severely that death followed.

Father Serra also believed that for him to successfully save the Indians, he had to suppress their culture. The result is a profound and lasting trauma stemming from the Spanish period, as well as from the Mexican and early American periods. It is an illness that persists in many of our tribal members today. Issues of alcoholism, drug addition, suicide, and poverty among our people are directly linked to this history. These conditions have hampered our people from giving their children a strong sense of identity, raising them to be optimistic, or having love for all things. How, then, can we pass along the thousands of years of indigenous knowledge that originally came from our ancestors?

A Cross of Thorns offers a comprehensive look into the thinking of the mission system's Franciscan friars and vividly describes their scant regard for the Indians' traditions and culture. We look forward to the day when the Roman Catholic Church, the state of California, and the Franciscans tell the true story of the missions. We are grateful to Elias Castillo for writing this very important book.

Valentin Lopez

Chair, Amah Mutsun Tribal Band of the Costanoan/Ohlone Indians

Preface

For more than a century, the terrible reality of California's twenty-one Catholic missions has been obfuscated by a myth that portrays those compounds as sites where Franciscan friars and Indians peacefully existed, sharing a mutually loving and near-idyllic existence—despite mission records and letters written by the founding friars *themselves* describing a completely opposite reality. The mission myth continues unabated, ignoring the suffering and deaths of thousands of Indians within those walls. Visitors entering the majority of restored missions, cared for by Catholic organizations, stroll through ancient colonnades, chapels, carefully trimmed gardens, and walls covered by flowering vines. No mention is made of the darkness that enveloped those sites from 1769 to the 1830s.

Across California, streets, playgrounds, and even schools have been named after Padre Junípero Serra, the Franciscan leader who led the effort to found the missions, and who advocated that only by using "blows" and holding them captives in those compounds could the Indians in the missions be civilized, a twisted viewpoint that would claim the lives of tens of thousands of California Indians. Yet Serra is revered by many in California as a gentle friar who loved and treated the Indians as if they were his children. In Sacramento, on the grounds of the state capitol, there is a bronze statue of Serra gazing at a map of California marked with the location of each mission. San Francisco has a gigantic statue of Serra overlooking the entrance to its famed Golden Gate Park. In Washington, D.C., in the National Statuary Hall of the nation's Capitol Building, there is a statue of Serra holding a model of a mission in one hand and a large cross in the other.

For decades, the California State Department of Education has required every elementary school in the state to teach fourth grade pupils of the supposed contributions of not only Junípero Serra, but of the missions themselves. Many Californians recall building a model of a mission as a school assignment.

A Cross of Thorns delves into the reality of mission life, the brutal punishments suffered by mission Indians, their captivity, and the forced labor they endured as "neophytes." Letters residing in Californian and Mexican archives, accounts of travelers, and scholarly studies have provided the detailed accounts and analyses needed for this book. It is my hope that this work will put an end to a myth that has existed for far too long.

I was first prompted to consider writing this book nearly eight years ago, when I wrote an op-ed article for the *San Francisco Chronicle* criticizing a proposed U.S. Senate bill to provide $10 million in matching federal funds to help restore the missions. The Senate version of the bill mistakenly described the missions as places where the Indian and Spanish cultures lovingly melded to create California's early way of life. In that article, I described the missions as little more than death camps run by Franciscan friars where thousands of California's Indians perished. My goal was not to oppose the restorations. It was to advocate that, if the bill was approved, the truth regarding the treatment of the Indians, including the great numbers who died, be presented at each of the missions.

The reaction to the article astounded me—numerous readers emphatically supported what I had written. One elementary school teacher told me she had refused to teach her pupils anything about the missions because she knew how the Indians had suffered within them. Others praised my piece, telling me it was about time the truth was told about the missions.

Shortly after the article's publication, I learned it had been read in its entirety into the United States *Congressional Record* by then-Congressman Jim Gibbons of Nevada, who cautioned that, in the wake of my article, care should be taken in the wording of the Senate bill in view of the Indians' suffering. All language praising the missions was removed when the House passed the bill subsequently signed into law by then-President George W. Bush. Having my article read into the *Congressional Record* was the final factor that solidified my resolve to write this book.

1

Saving Souls

Earth is the Center of the Universe. All planets revolve around it, pushed by powerful angels.
—Friar Junípero Serra (despite scientific proof to the contrary, Serra clung to that belief all his life)

Six years after founding the first California mission in San Diego, Friar Junípero Serra wrote a letter requesting that four Indians who had dared flee from Mission Carmel be severely whipped two or three times.

That little known request was made to Spanish military commander Fernando de Rivera y Moncada on July 31, 1775. In the letter, Serra cavalierly describes the search party that recaptured the runaways as going to the mountains "to search for my lost sheep." The request that Rivera flog the Indians is a chilling contrast to the pervasive image of Serra as a gentle and kind priest who never mistreated the mission Indians. In reality, Serra, a respected theologian who considered Indians subhuman, had hurled a cloak over the entirety of California's coast, enveloping it in a darkness filled with death and suffering. Not only does Serra ask Rivera to lash the Indians, he also inquires if the commander needs shackles to punish them further: "If your Lordship does not have shackles, with your permission they may be sent from here. . . ."[1]

That single revelatory sentence from Junípero Serra's own pen is indicative of the horrors that befell the Indians that Serra and his fellow Franciscans had enticed into those first missions. What were shackles and

---

1. Serra to Governor Fernando Rivera y Moncada, 31 July 1775, in *Writings of Junípero Serra*, Vol. IV, ed. Antoine Tibesar (Baltimore: Furst, 1966), 425.

chains doing in a mission where friars and Indians supposedly worked together in a loving atmosphere? Additionally, what authorization was given to Serra and the friars to enslave not only the Indians, but also their children and their children's offspring and impose forced labor on them? Serra's mandate from the Spanish king was to educate the Indians and then release them. Instead, he took it upon himself to effectively imprison them for life and use the Native Americans as forced labor.

Underlying the Franciscan friars' disdain of the Indians was the fact that they valued the souls of their captives far more than their material existence on earth. The Friars' utmost goal was to ensure that upon death those souls, kept free of sin, ascended to heaven, thereby fulfilling their Franciscan vows to Christianize the Indians. The Franciscans thus tightly restrained the Indians' ability to enjoy life or engage in amorous adventures. It mattered little if the Indians suffered. Their deaths were not mourned by the Franciscans, but were, rather, rejoiced as another soul sent to heaven and God.

Indians who grieved and wept over the loss of a loved one were ordered whipped. Likewise, Indian mothers who suffered a miscarriage were not allowed to grieve over losing their child. Instead, they were accused of committing abortion and at times whipped. The Franciscans would punish these women by having them cradle a grotesquely carved figure of an infant and, humiliated, stand outside the mission church. This harsh treatment was aimed at preventing Indian women from aborting their pregnancies in an attempt to spare their infants from suffering the intolerable conditions of existence within the missions.

A robust birth rate was considered critical by the Franciscans to counter the terrible death rate that developed in each compound. Friars harangued Indian women to have more babies. Yet despite these efforts, the death rate within the missions was so appalling that more Indians died than were born annually, crippling an Indian population that was already reeling from disease, malnutrition, depression, and physical abuse.

Those who dared criticize Serra and his Franciscans for their treatment of the Native Americans risked being crushed by the power of the Roman Catholic Church, with its power of excommunication, or being literally torn to pieces by the Inquisition, which could conduct an investigation using horrendous means of torture against anyone who dared challenge the church or its hierarchy.

Despite that threat, the Spanish military commanders and governors of California opposed the friars' use of the Indians as forced labor to work the missions' enormous tracts of land, although they had to carefully choose their battles when it came to confronting the powerful Franciscans. Spanish officials feared that—bolstered by captive Indian labor—the missions would eventually control the economy in California by growing the power of their huge agricultural holdings, estates which covered hundreds of thousands of acres of the best land that California had to offer. Those lands provided rich pastures where mission livestock herds numbering in the tens of thousands could graze and quickly multiply.

Spanish military commanders and governors attempted to delay the founding of new missions by stipulating that the soldiers to be assigned to those compounds could not be spared to hunt runaways, or join the friars in swooping down on neighboring villages and threatening the Indians with a hellish afterlife if they did not join their missions. This tactic was effective and slowed down the missions' advance across the California coastline. Still, while Serra was himself restricted to founding nine missions, his wily successors were able to eventually entice Spanish officials into permitting them to found twelve others, stretching along the Alta California coastline from San Diego to San Francisco Bay.

Cruelty toward the Indians was a common denominator in each mission. One friar, Gerónimo Boscana, who studied the Indians' beliefs, wrote they "... may be compared to a species of monkey ...."[2] Others, including Serra's successor, Friar Fermín Francisco de Lasuén, held similar thoughts, calling them ungrateful liars who were never to be trusted.

The mission Indians, called neophytes by the friars, had terrible, sadistic punishments inflicted on them by the Franciscans. In one incident, the leader of a group of recaptured runaways had his hands and

---

2. Gerónimo Boscana, *Chinigchinich; A Historical Account of the Origin, Customs, and Traditions of the Indians at the Missionary Establishment of St. Juan Capistrano, Alta California; Called The Acagchemem Nation; Collected with the Greatest Care, from the Most Intelligent and Best Instructed in the Matter. Translated from the Original Spanish Manuscript by one who was many years a resident of Alta California.* New York: Wiley & Putnam, 1846. In Alfred Robinson, *Life in California During a Residence of Several Years in that Territory: Comprising a Description of the Country and the Missionary Establishments.* Unabridged republication of the first edition published in New York, 1846 (New York: De Capo, 1969), 335.

legs bound, then had the skin of a newly slaughtered calf tightly wrapped around him and sewn shut. He was tied to a post and left to suffocate under a hot sun that slowly shrank the calf skin. The description of that nightmarish event was provided by a Russian seal hunter, Vassili Petrovitch Tarakanoff, who had been captured on the coast in 1815 and held for several years in mission San Fernando before being released.[3]

There were other similar incidents of great cruelty. At Mission San Francisco, the captain of a trading ship came upon Franciscan friars using a red hot iron to burn crosses into the faces of a group of men, women, and children who had tried to escape from the mission. In Southern California, thugs appointed by friars from the ranks of their Indians at Mission San Gabriel used a bullwhip, nearly ten feet long, to beat the natives.[4]

One distinguished visitor to Mission Carmel was shocked at the fetid squalor in which the Indians were forced to live. Jean-François de Galaup, Comte de Lapérouse, a French admiral leading a major expedition ordered by King Louis XVI to explore the Pacific Rim, arrived at Monterey in 1786 amid pomp and circumstance. He commanded two ships carrying many of France's renowned scientists.[5]

Escorted to Mission Carmel, Lapérouse was appalled at what he saw. Bedraggled Indians, some in shackles and stocks, were being walked to a work site accompanied by Indian guards who swung whips to ensure their staying together. The sight, he wrote in his log, was no different than the slave plantations his expedition had visited on the islands of the Caribbean. He described the policies of the Franciscans toward the mission Indians as "reprehensible," adding they were beating the Indians for violations that in Europe would be considered insignificant.

As the first non-Spanish European to visit the mission, Lapérouse had expected more from the Spanish settlement. Instead of cathedrals and beautiful Spanish colonial buildings and courtyards, he found

---

3. Tarakanoff was interviewed by Ivan Petroll in Alaska for Hubert Howe Bancroft's *History of California*.

4. James J. Rawls, *Indians of California: The Changing Image* (Norman: University of Oklahoma, 1984), 62. P. 232 provides a full description of the incident.

5. Jean François de la Pérouse, *A Visit to Monterey in 1786, and a Description of the Indians of California*. In *California Historical Society Quarterly* 15:3 (1936), 218. In *Documentary Evidence for the Spanish Missions of Alta California (The Spanish Borderlands Sourcebook Vol. 14)*, ed. Julia G. Costello (New York: Garland, 1991), 1–8. The French expedition and Pérouse's notes are detailed in this book, 169–189.

only crudely made adobe huts with roofs made of branches and twigs (the design of the missions would be greatly improved years later). For Lapérouse, it was a sordid sight. The French admiral wrote how much better it would be if the Franciscans treated the Indians in a manner that gave priority to their individual human rights, rather than ensnaring them with a rigid and relentless set of rules.

Serra and his fellow Franciscans obviously did not share this attitude. For them, the mission Indians were to be treated more like mere chattel. They were to be fed, encouraged to marry and reproduce, kept free of sin, provide forced labor, and ultimately give up their souls to God. Serra's and the friars' lack of compassion for the Indians stemmed from their minds being mired in the dark ages, suffused with the attitude that Spanish Catholicism was to be rigidly followed and that Spaniards were members of a master race—all others and non-Catholics were beneath them. The innovations in philosophy and technology wrought by the Renaissance meant little to them.

Even advances in science were ignored by Serra. The diminutive friar stubbornly maintained, even in the eighteenth century, that earth was the center of the universe, with all the planets revolving around it, pushed by angels using great powers. To him, witches were also a reality, trailing evil as they flew through the night.[6] Serra felt it was his duty to defend those beliefs that the great thinkers of his time had declared utter nonsense.

This insight into Serra's thinking raises the question of what other beliefs and factors motivated the Franciscans to act in such a savage manner toward the Native peoples of California? For answers, one must become cognizant of the great maelstrom that Spain unleashed on the New World after its discovery by Cristóbal Colón in 1492, a period that spanned more than 300 years.

---

6. *Palou's Life of Fray Junípero Serra*, annotated and translated by Maynard J. Geiger (Richmond, Academy of American Franciscan History, William Byrd Press 1955), 361 (see footnote 37, detailing Serra's work with the Inquisition.) Regarding Serra's belief that the universe orbited earth guided by Angels, see Sandos, James A., *Converting California: Indians and Franciscans in the Missions* (New Haven, Yale University, 2004), 80. A description of his belief regarding the universe can be found on pp. 109–110 of this book.

2

Conquest

We came to serve God and the king, and also to get rich.
—Bernal Díaz del Castillo, an officer with Hernán Cortés, explaining in 1568 why the Spanish *conquistadores* had traveled to the New World.

In 1767, Spain sought to protect and bolster its flagging empire. King Carlos III, an enlightened monarch, had ordered his emissaries in Mexico to populate Alta California in the most immediate and efficient manner possible.

The monarch feared it would only be a matter of time before Russian fur hunters in Alaska, who were successfully hunting seals and sea otters for their expensive pelts, would move down the coast to begin hunting on California's beaches and lay claim to the region. Yet Spain had few resources for such a massive undertaking. Its once powerful army and bountiful wealth had long ago disappeared, squandered on expensive European conquests from which the nation had gained little or nothing.

California was a remote land in the outermost reaches of Spain's domain in North America. No Europeans had ever settled in that region, a land shunned by early Spanish maritime explorers who had found there nothing of value. Without gold, of which none was evident to them, the area was worthless. Despite that assessment, the king could ill afford to lose the region to Russia, which would threaten the rest of Spain's New World, a vast domain weakened by poverty and the oppressive trading policies set by earlier Spanish rulers.

Had the year been 1550, Spain could have easily organized an expedition to Alta California, launching galleons filled with thousands of soldiers to guard its lands. The nation's treasury was then brimming with the conquered riches of the New World, and across Mexico, Central and South America, and in Europe, Spain was financing its enlarging armies and navy with its newly found fortunes in gold and silver.

The Iberian Peninsula was basking in the golden afterglow of the discovery of the New World by Cristóbal Colón (Christopher Columbus) in 1492. Spain had used the booty from the New World to rebuild the exhausted forces of its monarchs, Isabel I and Fernando II, *Los Reyes Católicos,* who had led the final bloody battles that destroyed the 800-hundred-year-long Moorish reign over their country.

The conquest of the Moors had begun in the northern region of Castile, where Spaniards had established a stronghold against Arab invaders from North Africa. Spain's Catholic armies, in battle after battle, had slowly and methodically pushed the Moors southward until the only Muslim outpost left was the grand city of Granada in southern Spain. It finally yielded on January 2, 1492.

Aiding the royal couple in their final push to Granada had been the church, which hailed the conquest as a means of forcing all Muslims out of Europe. In the wake of the reconquest, and bolstered by their Roman Catholic faith, the Spaniards considered themselves invincible warriors.

Yet scarcely had the queen and king taken a deep breath before the problem of financing their reign began looming. As they sought to find sources of revenue, Columbus, the Italian seafarer turned Spaniard, appeared before the court with a proposition that had the potential of solving Spain's money problem. Columbus believed a new, shorter trade route across the ocean would allow Spain to reap the riches of Asia and fill its vaults with gold. He proposed to sail westward across the Atlantic to reach China and India, instead of following the arduous, dangerous route around Africa. Isabel listened with rapt attention.

In the end, the Queen agreed to finance Columbus's voyage. In early August, 1492, just months after the Spanish monarchs had brought Moorish Granada to its knees, the Italian sea captain set sail from Palos, Spain, commanding three ships: the *Pinta,* the *Santa Maria* (his flagship), and the *Niña.*

It took Columbus and his crews thirty-three days before they became the first Europeans to set foot on the western part of the New World. After spotting land, they dropped their anchors off an island Columbus named San Salvador. Rowboats were lowered from the ships and on October 12, Columbus, with banners and Spain's flag flying, claimed the land in the name of *Los Reyes Católicos*, Isabel and Fernando.

Columbus was ecstatic. He believed he had found an outlying Asian island and that China was just over the horizon. But the island natives who greeted him did not appear to be Asian. Their tools and weapons were made of obsidian and other stones, whereas in India and Southeast Asia steel was commonly used for such objects. Columbus brushed aside that fact and reveled in establishing Spain's dominion over a new part of Asia—a land teeming with wildlife, massive forests, rivers and lakes, untold mineral wealth, and Indian nations. In that initial voyage, he also laid claim to other islands, including Cuba and Hispaniola, the latter of which would later be divided into the Dominican Republic and Haiti.

Columbus returned to Spain in early 1493 with a few trinkets of jewelry and gold nuggets, gifts from the natives who greeted his expedition on the beach. His statements were enough to convince Isabel and Fernando that he had discovered a new Asian trade route. The rejoicing monarchs welcomed him with open arms and showered him with titles. Soon, Pope Alexander VI conferred on Spain its right to ownership of the New World by issuing the papal bull *Dudum siquidem* on September 26, 1493. The decree supplemented an earlier bull, *Inter caetera*, which had commanded Spain not only to Christianize all the indigenous peoples of the New World, but "that barbarous nations be overthrown and brought to the faith itself."[1] Both bulls also delineated the territories where Spain would prevail.

Columbus, stubbornly claiming Asia was a few leagues away from his initial discoveries, managed to launch three other voyages to the New World. In his second trip, he was ordered to take 1,200 settlers, among them carpenters, blacksmiths, farmers, masons, sailors, and shipbuilders, to Hispaniola. They would establish the way station that Spain would need on its new route to Asia. In that voyage, Columbus ordered one of his officers to slice off the ears and noses of any Indians caught stealing the Spaniards' supplies.[2] Meanwhile, Columbus continued seeking the

---

1. Francis Gardiner Davenport, *European Treaties Bearing on the History of the United States and its Dependencies to 1648* (Washington, D.C.: Carnegie Institution of Washington, 1917), 75–78.

2. Hugh Thomas, *Rivers of Gold: The Rise of the Spanish Empire from Columbus to Magellan* (New York: Random House, 2003), 140.

route he believed would lead him to the Asian mainland. Finding neither Asia nor gold, he instead promoted Hispaniola as a bountiful source of slaves. In 1499, the explorer estimated the island could provide 4,000 slaves for export annually.[3]

Columbus's dreams of a new route to Asia never materialized. In May of 1506, he died a broken man, clinging to his belief that he had found the outermost part of the Indies. He had been stripped of all his titles and even jailed briefly, accused of incompetence in administering the new Caribbean colonies.

Almost immediately after Columbus's monumental discoveries, the Spanish monarchs slammed a wall down around Spanish America. Only Spanish ships could sail into the ports of their new dominions. No other nation could bring goods for sale or trade to the new lands. With those restrictions, Spain guaranteed itself ownership of whatever wealth it found in the New World. It sent more troops and settlers, mainly craftsmen, to establish colonies in *Nueva España*. Aboard the emigrants' ships were cattle and pigs that were set free to roam the forests, where they thrived amid the lush, bountiful flora.

For nearly thirty years, the Spaniards settled in the Caribbean, conquering the Indians through massacres and the spread of European diseases to which the natives had little or no immunity. The Indians died in alarming numbers, unable to survive measles, mumps, smallpox, and chickenpox. Others collapsed from the brutal labor and dangerous conditions they suffered under in Spanish mines and plantations. Noble David Cook has described the period from 1492 to 1642, "in terms of the number of people who died, (as) the greatest human catastrophe in history."[4]

In 1519, in violation of Spanish policy, Hernán Cortés, a Spanish adventurer commanding several hundred well-armed men, sailed to the east coast of Mexico and pushed inland to the majestic Aztec city of Tenochtitlan, now known as Mexico City. Once there, they were greeted by Aztec Emperor Moctezuma, draped in brightly colored cloaks of cloth and feathers and gold jewelry. Cortés and his men had entered a vast, beautiful city built on man-made islands, unlike anything the Spaniards had seen. So glorious was the sight, that it prompted Captain Bernal Diaz

---

3. Ibid., 244–251.

4. Noble David Cook, *Born to Die: Disease and New World Conquest, 1492–1650* (Cambridge: Cambridge University Press, 1998), 13.

del Castillo to praise its "great towers and temples, and other edifices of lime and stone which seemed to rise out of the water. To many of us it appeared doubtful whether we were asleep or awake . . . never yet did man see, hear, or dream of anything equal to the spectacle which appeared to our eyes . . . ."[5]

Within the walkways and plazas of the city, paved smooth with stone, they found Aztec jewelers using gold and silver to fashion intricate jewelry, drinking goblets, and ceremonial masks used by the priests and nobility. The Spaniards were soon to discover that, aside from the Aztecs, other nations within Mexico had similar wealth, living in cities where massive and elaborate stone temples and plazas had been built. Gold was used by the Indians as currency (quills were filled with the precious metal, sealed, and then used as money).

After conquering Mexico, the conquistadores wasted little time in looting the territory, melting thousands of gold artifacts into balls of gold[6] and shipping them to Spain. Gold and silver mines worked by the natives were also seized and the miners enslaved, providing more gold bullion for the Spanish galleons returning to the Iberian Peninsula.

The conquistadores crushed the Indian nations, stripped them of their most valuable possessions, and destroyed their complex cultures. Nothing of those New World cultures was considered sacred. Temples were ransacked, then turned over to Catholic priests who quickly burned priceless libraries containing the history of the Indian nations, including their literature, science, and knowledge of medicine. The Indians were often forced to renounce and smash the sacred statuary of their gods.

Spain had launched its settlement of *Nueva España* in as barbaric a manner as can be imagined. The bloodshed that had started in the Caribbean and then Mexico spread to South and Central America. In 1513, to provide legal justification for their conquest of the Caribbean,

---

5. Bernal Diaz del Castillo, *The True History of the Conquest of Mexico*, trans. Maurice Keatinge (New York: Robert M. McBride, 1927), 160.

6. During this period, the Spanish did not pour molten gold into the now familiar brick-like ingots, but instead cast it into small balls. The Tarahumara Indians of Mexico's Copper Canyon in the state of Chihuahua at one time referred, in Spanish, to the gold balls as "*bola, naranja, fierro*" or orange balls of iron. Supposedly, the Tarahumara Indians had been told by the Spaniards, probably in the late sixteenth to eighteenth centuries, that death would befall them if they divulged the location where they had hoarded their gold balls. Legends in that area tell of stockpiles of gold balls being found in the graves of Spanish miners who died within the canyon and were buried by the Indians along with their gold.

Spain drew up the *Requerimiento* (Requirement), a document aimed at the subjugation of all New World Indians to the Spanish monarchy and Catholicism. The *Requerimiento* spelled out the consequences of death, destruction, and enslavement if resistance was offered. It was read to all Indian leaders with whom the conquistadores had contact, whether or not they understood Spanish. For any Indian monarch or tribe who defied the Spaniards, ignored the Spanish king, or refused to accept Catholicism, the *Requerimiento* had dire warnings:

> . . . if you do not comply, or maliciously delay obedience to my injunction, then, with the help of God, I will enter your country by force, declare war on you with the utmost violence, subject you to the yoke of obedience to the church and king, seize your wives and children and make slaves of them, and sell or dispose of them according to His Majesty's pleasure; I will seize everything you own and do everything within my power to bring misery to you as rebellious subjects who refuse to acknowledge or submit to their lawful sovereign. I declare that all the resulting bloodshed and calamities shall be blamed on you and not His Majesty, or to me, or the gentlemen who shall serve under me.[7]

Near the end of the sixteenth century, Spaniards abandoned the practice of reading the statement. All new land they explored and any natives found in those areas simply became part of the growing Spanish empire.

As the Spanish monarchs opened their new lands to settlement, conquistadores and adventurers streamed into the New World, jostling for berths on the Spanish galleons that left Spain almost monthly. They were joined by masses of settlers, among them farmers, carpenters, blacksmiths, and the other craftsmen needed to develop the vast newly conquered lands. These immigrants quickly established their presence on Cuba, Hispaniola, and other Caribbean isles. Many abandoned their trades to seize gold and silver, wrest land from the Indians, and establish sprawling sugar, hemp, and coffee plantations. Nothing could keep them from this newfound wealth. By the beginning of the seventeenth century, more than 600,000 Spaniards had flocked to *Nueva España*.

The majority were men who, by and large, were failures in their own country. Most were illiterate; some were convicts granted clemency by the Spanish crown on the condition that they sail to the New World. Only a handful were educated Spaniards, who typically came seeking adven-

---

7. David J. Weber, *Bárbaros: Spaniards and Their Savages in the Age of Enlightenment* (New Haven: Yale University Press, 2005), 17–18.

ture and wealth. The remainder were fortune hunters or career soldiers. Brutish louts would be an apt description of the conquistadores. Del Castillo, Cortez's captain, bluntly stated: "We came here to serve God and the king, and also to get rich."[8]

Spanish historian Gonzalo Fernández de Oviedo y Valdez, who lived in that era, provided this description of the conquistadores:

> They are the sort of men who have no intention of converting the Indians or of settling and remaining on this land. They come only to get some gold or wealth in whatever form they can obtain it. They subordinate honor, morality, and honesty to this end and apply themselves to any fraud or homicide and commit innumerable crimes.[9]

The conquistadores all had one thing in common—the goal of achieving great wealth quickly and ruthlessly. There are no known conquistadores who came to the New World seeking freedom of religion or political reform (something the Spanish crown would have forbidden), or seeking trade with the natives. They carried with them only beads and worthless trinkets to trade with New World nobility. Accompanying them were priests, charged not only with maintaining the souls of the adventurers, but also with forcibly converting the natives to Catholicism.

Within the Caribbean, the Spaniards considered the island tribes to be primitive solely because their social and political culture, mode of dress, and customs were far from Spanish culture. On the mainland, in contrast to the Caribbean tribes, the major nations of the Aztecs, Maya, Incas, and other smaller groups were far more complex in their government, dress, weapons, tools, architecture, and customs. It made no difference to the Spaniards. They vanquished and destroyed all equally.

As they sought to enrich themselves, the Spaniards, while not averse to killing natives, were nevertheless shocked by the Indian nations' widespread use of human sacrifice as offerings to their gods or emperors. The Aztecs were particularly bloody, killing thousands atop their temples, literally ripping out their victims' hearts and then hurling the lifeless bodies to tumble down the steep stairs amid throngs of cheering Aztecs. The practice appalled the conquistadores who, after crushing the Aztecs

---

8. Jonathan Kandell, *La Capital: The Biography of Mexico City* (New York: Random House, 1988), 89.

9. Thomas, *Rivers of Gold*, 137.

and the other Indian nations, quickly ended that practice in the sixteenth century.

While the Spaniards rightfully considered human sacrifice abhorrent, it never occurred to them that the European practices of burning victims at the stake, skinning them alive, breaking them on the wheel,[10] garroting, and other forms of torture were equally appalling. The pogroms against Jews and the persecution of Protestants and Moors in Spain and other parts of Europe led to horrific, bloody excesses in which tens of thousands died—the 1572 St. Bartholomew's Day massacre of some 30,000 Huguenot Protestants in Paris being a prime example.

As former conquistadores settled into the vast royal land grants, they used Indians as forced labor, but ran into unexpected problems. The natives, if whipped enough, could be worked virtually to death. But it was the difficulty in training the forced laborers that frustrated the conquistadores and plantation and mine owners. The Indian slaves were inefficient laborers, tending to sink into such a deep depression that they seemed to welcome death rather than work for their Spanish overlords.

Underlying the forced labor was the Spanish use of the *encomienda*, which had been first applied to Spain's conquered Moors. It allowed landholders in the northern region of Castile to require peasants to provide labor for them. The practice was exported to the New World and allowed conquistadores and settlers to collect taxes or tributes from Indians entrusted to their care. A settler had simply to apply to the governor's office to become an *encomendero*. He was usually granted his request and the lands he sought, along with the accompanying Indians. In return for being granted free Indian labor, the natives were to be assimilated into Catholicism and eventually into Spanish colonialist culture—something that rarely occurred.

Spanish priest Bartolome de las Casas, who denounced and sought to end the cruel treatment of the Indians, was the primary mover in having the *encomienda* abolished. It was replaced by the *repartimiento*, which

---

10. Breaking on the wheel was a heinous practice in which a prisoner was spread-eagled on a large wheel. Executioners wielding large iron clubs would systematically smash all the bones of the victim's limbs. The limbs, their bones broken, were then wound through the spokes of the wheel which was then raised on a pole with the mutilated victim still alive and strapped onto it. The prisoner was left to die an excruciatingly slow death.

allowed a grantee to obtain forced, free Indian labor for a set period of time only. But this new policy did little to curb the abuse of Indian laborers by landholders.[11]

Eventually, the treatment of the Indians so horrified Spanish King Carlos I that in 1530 he forbade enslavement, a ruling generally ignored in the New World. Thousands of miles separated the king's palace in Madrid from his new realm, and officials who enforced the king's decrees found it difficult to carry out their tasks because of that distance. In the New World, Spanish inhabitants easily ignored those orders that threatened their personal enrichment.

Seven years later, with no improvement in the treatment of the Indians, Pope Paul III was prompted on June 2, 1537, to issue *Sublimus Dei*, a papal bull seeking an end to the massacre and enslavement of the Indians. His decree established that Indians had souls, could reason, and were equal to all other men. Sadly, this effort, too, had little effect.

Throughout the sixteenth century, Spain continued expanding its hold on the New World, using campaigns that can only be described as genocidal against the indigenous people. The conquistadores marched across Mexico, Central America, and South America, destroying the Incas, Maya, and Aztecs. Many of the great cities and temples of those Indian nations were dismantled stone by stone,[12] and Indian emperors tortured and killed. These nations had built astronomical observatories, and maintained libraries filled with historical, scientific, and medical manuscripts, as well as books of poetry and legends. But such structures were all obliterated within three decades, as Spanish priests declared any vestige of Indian culture the work of demons requiring total destruction.

The end for those Indian nations came swiftly because, despite armies numbering in the thousands, their weapons—mainly flat clubs, their edges studded with razor-sharp obsidian—simply shattered against Spanish armor and swords made of steel. Other Indian weapons,

---

11. Lesly Bird Simpson, *The Encomienda in New Spain: The Beginning of Spanish Mexico* (Berkeley: University of California Press, 1950); John Francis Bannon, *Indian Labor in the Spanish Indies: Was There Another Solution?* (Boston: Heath, 1966).

12. In Mexico City, the precursor to the city's enormous cathedral was built entirely of stone ripped from an Aztec temple, a project that was ordered by Hernán Cortés and launched in 1524. The present *Catedral Metropolitana de la Asunción de María* (Metropolitan Cathedral of the Assumption of Mary) was built over the smaller, original cathedral beginning in 1573. It was completed in 1813, reusing some of the original stone blocks from the Aztec temples.

including powerful darts, lances, slingshots, bows and arrows, clubs, and knives, also proved ineffective. The Indian ranks were decimated by Spanish *arquebuzes*,[13] cannon, lances, horses, and crossbows. And the relentless epidemics of European diseases also greatly weakened the Indian nations.

Following their conquest in the early sixteenth century, the former conquistadores built *haciendas* on land awarded to them by the Spanish crown. They thus became *hacendados* (owners of the *haciendas*) who had wealth and importance, and zealously guarded their aggrandizement. Their use of slave labor eliminated the need to consider using advanced technology in developing their colonies' resources. They cared even less about education or its benefits. Why should they? Indian forced labor was all they needed to prosper in this fertile land, replete with gold and silver mines.

The *hacendados* considered Indians much like disposable machinery. Once an Indian died, there was little problem in replacing him or her from the nearest village of terrified natives. While machinery that could do many jobs better than manual labor was being developed in Europe, there was never any need for it in *Nueva España*.

The enslaved natives of the plantations were subjugated by fear of severe punishment. When they asked visiting priests what sin they had committed that God should punish them in such a terrible manner, the padres' answer was soothing and simple: Do not commit the sin of questioning God's will, suffer what God has ordained for you, and you will reap your reward in heaven, where you will forever be joyous and free from want.

Fatalism, the belief that life is preordained by God and nothing can change it, swept across Latin America's poor and Indian populations. For nearly 500 years, fatalism stymied progress across Latin America. Anyone who challenged *Nueva España's* social inequality was not only sharply rebuked by both priests and the *hacendados*, but powerfully constrained by the strict differences between social castes.

In sharp contrast to Latin America, English colonists thousands of miles to the north did not accept the dogma of fatalism. Those settlers had sailed across the Atlantic Ocean in search of a better life, with the ambition to lift the yoke of oppression—both political and religious—

---

13. Spanish for arquebus, a firearm with a smoothbore, long barrel that was muzzle-loaded and fired by using a matchlock. It was the forerunner of the rifle.

from their shoulders. Creativity blossomed in those northern colonies. Mechanical ingenuity was needed to increase industrial and agricultural production and led, eventually, to improved designs for plows and the construction of textile factories, foundries, and the great engines needed for those industrial plants.

For the Spanish colonies, by contrast, increasing efficiency simply meant increasing the number of Indians assigned to a task. *Nueva España* was virtually devoid of new ideas to improve production. With the exception of the very wealthy, the struggle to survive the region's grinding poverty left little opportunity and few resources for those who shunned fatalism and sought mercantile or mechanical innovations that could improve their lives. In addition, Spanish regulations strictly restricted what could be manufactured in its New World, forbidding the production of high quality fabrics, precision tools, and machinery.

Life in *Nueva España* remained unchanged for centuries. The *hacendados* maintained an iron grip on their status and wealth at the expense of the poor. Priestly visits to those estates generally followed a pattern of first consoling the Indians while reinforcing their sense of fatalism, then joining the Spanish family beneath the shaded colonnades of the *hacienda's* mansion to sip sweetened hot chocolate spiced with cinnamon. It was the perfect time for the padre to provide a report on the Indians' behavior and attitude toward the *hacendado*.

Sundays, the Christian day of rest, was the great equalizer; all could attend Mass in the cathedrals, cooled by thick, insulating stone walls. In those splendid services, priests, cloaked in chasubles[14] heavily embroidered in glittering gold thread, chanted in Latin, a language that few could understand. Altar boys rang tiny bells while the priests held up sacred chalices made of gleaming gold and unseen choirs sang heavenly songs. All the while, aromatic clouds of burning incense wafted through the interior, cloaking the Mass in a mysterious, perfumed, smoky veil.

The rituals had some similarities to native customs. Before the Spanish conquest, high priests of the Incas, Maya, and Aztecs, draped in brightly colored fabrics, wearing gold ornaments and elaborate feather headdresses, had slowly ascended the steps of their towering temples. As drums, rattles, flutes, marimbas, and whistles created traditional music, plumes of white incense smoke swirled from atop the temples, and other Indians chanted or danced below. As mentioned previously, human

---

14. The chasuble is the outermost vestment worn by Catholic priests during Mass.

sacrifices were often part of those rituals, so the Indians could still relate somewhat to a priest turning wine into blood, then drinking it, and eating a blessed wafer representing the body of Christ.

In Europe—with the exception of Spain—economic development blossomed. The Dutch, English, and French, banned from commerce with New Spain, launched an era of trade by forging sea routes to Asia. Their fast merchant ships carried mechanical goods, firearms, and equipment relished by India and China. They returned laden with rare, fragrant spices, exotic silks and other fabrics, delicate china, and tea, items that sold at high prices across Europe.

The colonies of New Spain, meanwhile, slowly began decaying. Across *Nueva España*, with Catholicism on their side, the progeny of the conquistadores developed their newfound wealth and basked in the prestige bestowed upon them by grateful Spanish kings. Slavery, as in America's Southern plantations, was the key to maintaining the affluence of the sprawling *haciendas*. But it was also a stone wall blocking full economic development. The *hacendados'* reluctance to engage in entrepreneurship or encourage technology was mirrored by Spanish craftsmen who abandoned their skills in favor of being granted land and the subsequent free Indian labor to work their mines and plantations. The entire situation was exacerbated once African slaves were shipped across the Atlantic Ocean to work in the *haciendas*.

Spanish settlers in the New World never fully exploited the mining of useful metal ores, other than gold or silver. Consequently, huge deposits of ores remained undiscovered until the late nineteenth and early twentieth centuries, a failing which further delayed the nascent industrialization from taking hold. *Nueva España* also did not have sufficient numbers of master craftsmen who could work what metals were available into large quantities of useful implements, or design new and more efficient tools that could have been exported across the world.

The social castes established by the Spaniards in *Nueva España* were another hindrance to progress. The complex system involved sixteen levels approved by Spanish viceroys, and created totally unnecessary social stratification determined by one's ancestry. Social positioning in that restricted system—heavy with racism—depended on whether one had been born in the New World, and also on the number of one's Negro or Indian ancestors. The principal castes included the *peninsular, creole, mestizo, castizo, mulatto,* and *negro* (Spanish for black). *Peninsulares* were persons born and reared to adulthood in Spain before coming to the New World; *creoles* were persons of Spanish ancestry born in the New World; *mestizos* had both Spanish and Indian blood; *castizos* were offspring resulting from a marriage between a mestizo and a peninsular; and *mulattos* had Spanish and African blood. *Negro* identified any person who was brought as an African slave to the New World beginning in the mid-1500s until 1716, when Spain abolished the enslavement of Africans in the New World (with the exception of Cuba and Puerto Rico, where slavery was allowed to continue until the 1860s).

The caste system fixed a person's social position, although in later years the attainment of personal wealth could allow one to improve one's social status. If a *creole* learned a particular skill that brought him wealth, it would elevate him in society, but he would still be a *creole,* someone who was not to be paid much attention by the *peninsular.* Certainly, a young *creole* might find great difficulty in entering a university. Progress was hindered by the presence of the New World's elite class, composed of families that owned the vast *haciendas,* whose position in society was firmly established and who wielded the most power. Those in this highest level of Spanish society had no reason to listen to a *mestizo,* even if the lower-caste member had a better idea to improve their economy.

Outside of Spain, the thinking that spawned the Industrial Revolution was not hampered by rigid social stratification. In England, France, Germany, and other like-minded nations, anyone who conceived of a better process or way to increase profit, no matter what their social level, could, at the very least, catch the attention of entrepreneurs and people with money. Imagination, creativity, and technical expertise blossomed in Europe and in the English colonies as the Industrial Revolution created new cities, machinery, and armies of salaried workers. Those traits were sadly lacking in Latin America, where slavery or forced labor dampened the incentive to develop better manufacturing equipment and processes.

While technology in Spain was lagging, it was racing at breakneck speed in the English colonies and Europe. In Paris, Frankfurt, Rome, Geneva, London, Boston, New York and Philadelphia, master craftsmen were busy designing and building clocks and pocket watches—precision instruments that required exacting machinery. In European cities, engineers and scientists were also beginning to painstakingly design tools with the precise tolerances needed to build the first crude prototypes of steam engines and harness hydropower, the linchpins of the Industrial Revolution. Compasses became more accurate, improving navigation, and telescopes had such finely ground lenses that distant stars, whose exact locations were necessary for navigation, came into clear view. Improvement in the design of ships' hulls and complex sail and mast supports made vessels faster and provided stronger protection against storms.

Thus merchant ships arrived in *Nueva España* laden with the advanced products manufactured by other Europeans, and returned to Spain carrying sugar, coffee, tobacco, hemp, and cocoa from the sprawling plantations. The money Spain realized from its New World commerce was quickly spent to purchase goods produced outside the Iberian Peninsula. Dependence on foreign goods, plus the cost of maintaining Spanish armies that stood ready to enforce the orders of the king's viceroys in the New World, crippled Spain's economic growth.

The empire suffered a tremendous blow with the defeat of the Spanish Armada in 1588. Spanish King Felipe II, the religious zealot ruler of Europe's largest empire and its most powerful army, sought to oust English Queen Elizabeth I and restore Roman Catholicism to England. In launching his doomed fleet, Felipe II was confident his forces would easily rout the English, despite the fact that English admirals had developed superior naval strategies and warships.[15] In comparison, the sluggish Spanish galleons were more suited for hauling cargo than for battle on the open seas.

To ensure victory, Spain assembled a fleet of 130 vessels, most of them merchant carriers, to protect the flanks of a Spanish army of approximately 20,000 men that would board barges in Flanders and then cross the English Channel to invade England. Felipe II believed that just the sight of the powerful naval force might prompt the English to surrender and that any English warship insolent enough to challenge the Spanish flag would be devastated by the sheer might of the Armada.

The outcome was a military disaster for Spain. Crippled by incompetent leadership and logistical failures, the Armada had little chance of victory. The English admirals coupled superior tactics with highly maneuverable

---

15. Neil Hanson, *The Confident Hope of a Miracle: The True History of the Spanish Armada* (New York: Knopf, 2005), 36.

warships, and also took advantage of a fortunately timed storm, to defeat the Spanish fleet. England's highly trained cannoneers swept the galleons' decks with accurately aimed volleys which killed and wounded Spanish sailors, ripped sails to shreds, and toppled masts. English cannon left the galleons helplessly adrift and burning, their decks awash with blood from the dead and dying beneath a tangle of splintered masts, ropes, and canvas. Many ships sank slowly to the bottom of the English Channel.

Felipe's folly had squandered his nation's fortune. The Spanish economy foundered, its treasury virtually emptied by the cost of the Armada and crippled by a restrictive culture in which the ruling elite sneered at commerce, industry, and trade.[16] By the mid-seventeenth century, Spain's economic and military might had virtually disintegrated, while its European rivals continued to explore, innovate, and prosper.[17] Intellectually, Europe—with the exception of Spain—was the world's center of Enlightenment. God, the universe, the laws of science, and even the reality of one's own existence were being questioned. Roman Catholicism, with its philosophy and history of intolerance toward new thought, was brusquely shoved aside.

Nueva España was crippled by poverty, illiteracy, and despotism that continues even into the twenty-first century. Education, or rather the lack of it, was another of the fallen dominoes that doomed Latin America. Knowledge, whether studying the universe or mere introspection, was not considered necessary. In the minds of the conquistadores and priests, God, along with brutal raw power, had willed that Catholicism should overwhelm the heathens just as it had conquered the Moors. Education was irrelevant.

In Europe, spreading literacy had paved the road to the Renaissance and the Age of Enlightenment. Literacy, powered by Gutenberg's press, supported the mass printing of the Bible and eventually led to creating books on an endless range of topics, allowing new ideas to blossom, which in turn promoted advances in technology, medicine, philosophy and science. Literacy blossomed across Europe.

However, in Spain and *Nueva España*, illiteracy was the norm. The population's general inability to read was a boon for the Spanish upper classes. It kept the lower masses from reading books that could lead to their absorbing ideas that might pose a threat to the stifling rules and

16. T.R. Fehrenbach, *Fire and Blood: A History of Mexico* (New York: Macmillan, 1973), 36.
17. Ibid., 249.

order of the land. The rights of humans to life, liberty, and the pursuit of happiness, as eventually set forth in England's North American colonies, applied in the Spanish New World only to the powerful nobility and the wealthy.

The Catholic Church tightly controlled whatever books were available. Essays on philosophy, religious reform, or the inalienable rights of man were denied to the common man, who would have been unable to read them anyway. Any author of a questionable book was in danger of being summoned for interrogation by the Inquisition. The Church ensured that its dogma was inviolable. It had eyes everywhere, making sure that everyone followed Church-sanctioned rules.

And yet, we must consider what the outcome would have been if commoners in Latin America had been universally taught how to read and write, and that its ports had been opened to members of all religions. It is very likely that, as occurred in the English colonies, the commoners would have realized that human rights were above the Divine Right of Kings or any religion. Eventually democracy would have flourished.

Instead, the combination of *hacendados*, Catholicism, fatalism, a rigid caste system, illiteracy, and trade restrictions strangled full development of Spain's empire and depressed the human spirit. It was the empire's indigenous people who suffered the most from this harmful combination of factors.

3

Servants of God

By what right and by what justice do you keep these Indians in such cruel and horrible servitude?
—Friar Antonio de Montesinos in 1511, scolding Spaniards for their treatment of the Caribbean Indians.

In the wake of the *Conquista*, convents and cathedrals rose across Mexico and South and Central America. From within their thick stone walls, many housing gilded altars, the Christianization of the Indians accelerated across *Nueva España*. Spain was acting under the authorization of the *Real Patronato*, issued in 1486 by Pope Innocent VIII, giving Fernando of Aragon the responsibility of introducing Catholicism abroad. That decree, along with the papal bull *Inter Caetera*, issued in 1493 by Pope Alexander VI, opened the door for hundreds of priests from all Roman Catholic orders to flock to *Nueva España*. Dominicans, Jesuits, Franciscans, and others priestly orders from Spain boarded ships and sailed across the Atlantic to, in effect, destroy Indian cultures, baptize the survivors, establish churches, and require the indigenous populations to attend Mass or suffer punishment.

The Catholic missionaries began arriving in villages, where they built churches and then forced the Indians to move near them. In most cases, except in the California missions, the Indians were not confined within church grounds but could continue to hunt and tend their farm fields. Swift whippings were meted out to those unfortunate Indians who violated stringent rules established by the missionary priests. T. R. Fehrenbach has written that in the padres' minds, the "*indio* might be human . . . but he had to be ruled with an iron hand . . . generations of priests came to believe with passionate sincerity that *indios* could only be taught the curse of Eve with the whip."[1]

During initial encounters, the process of Christianizing the natives began with a display aimed at showing the power of the priests, as Spanish soldiers knelt before the priests and sometimes kissed their feet. This illustrated to the watching Indians the power and importance of the padres. The Indians next witnessed demonstrations of Spanish weapons, a move aimed at cowing them into accepting the strangers into their land. As Spain continued expanding its reach, "Missionaries resorted to force and fear. Force, to be sure, invited counterforce so that missionary and Indian alike often lived in a climate of fear."[2]

The final step in converting the Indians involved construction of a permanent church filled with Catholic paintings and statues of Jesus, the Virgin Mary, saints, and an altar set in front of massive and complex carvings gilded with glittering gold leaf. All statues were lifelike, with those depicting the crucifixion of Christ carefully carved and painted to ensure that the beholder was fully aware of the wounds and suffering endured by Jesus.

In later years, as Spain began mining vast amounts of precious metal, some churches replaced those gilded artifacts with ones made of solid gold or silver, a move aimed at impressing the Indians with the power and glory of the Christian God. If such displays or a reading of the *Requerimiento* failed to win the Indians over to Christianity, the conquistadores resorted to terror.

In the Caribbean, the conquistadores moved relentlessly from isle to isle in search of gold and silver, killing those Indians who, having escaped earlier epidemics of European diseases, tried to defend their lands. Across the whole of Spain's New World, the pattern was similar. Priests accompanying the soldiers could do little to prevent the deaths of the Indians and simply looked away. The padres were an integral part of any expedition within the New World, carefully recording what they saw and heard, initiating the first steps towards transforming the Indians into devout Catholics, and ensuring that the adventurers never deviated from their devotion to Catholicism.

---

1. T.R. Fehrenbach, *Fire and Blood: A History of Mexico* (New York: Macmillan, 1973), 115.
2. David J. Weber, *Arts and Architecture, Force and Fear: The Struggle for Sacred Space in the Arts of the Missions of Northern New Spain, 1600–1821* (Mexico City: Mandato Antiguo Colegio de San Idelfonso, 2009), 4.

Bartolomé de las Casas, who in 1512 had become the first priest ordained in the New World, was a lone voice who spoke out courageously against the horrific treatment of the Indians. He was born in 1484 in the Spanish city of Seville. At the age of 18 he had come to the New World as an adventurer, but joined the church after becoming appalled at the atrocities committed against the Indians. Ten years after being ordained, he joined the Dominican order of priests to try to end the shocking treatment of the Indians. In 1513, he was present when the conquistadores killed approximately 3,000 men, women, and children during a single afternoon in Caonao in Cuba.

The Caonao massacre is described in his book, *Brevisima Relación de la Destruccion de las Indias* (*A Very Brief Account of the Destruction of the Indies*), published in 1552. Widely circulated in Europe, the book strongly criticized Spain for its extreme cruelty toward the natives and was published in an effort to counter outright lies in reports being sent to Spanish King Carlos I regarding the treatment of Indians. While those reports whitewashed the brutality toward the natives, de las Casas wrote that his book would provide "the very great and final need to make known to all Spain the true account and truthful understanding of what I have seen take place in this Indian Ocean."[3]

In the Caonao incident, de las Casas described how, as their chaplain, he accompanied a group of conquistadores to supposedly "claim" part of a native settlement. When he and the armed men arrived at the site, a large gathering of Indians greeted them with a "bounteous quantity of fish and bread and cooked victuals." There was no indication, according to the priest's description, of any threat from the Indians.

What happened next shocked and horrified de las Casas:

> On one occasion, when the locals had come some ten leagues out from a large settlement in order to receive us and regale us with victuals and other gifts, and had given us loaves and fishes and any other foodstuffs they could provide, the Christians were suddenly inspired by the Devil and, without the slightest provocation, butchered before my eyes, some three thousand souls—men, women and children—as they sat there in front of us. I saw that day atrocities more terrible than any living man has ever see nor ever thought to see.[4]

---

3. Bartolomé de las Casas, *A Short Account of the Destruction of the Indies*, ed. trans. Nigel Griffin (New York: Penguin, 1992), xxxii.

4. Ibid., 29.

In other incidents, de las Casas described that when Spaniards attacked villages their primary goal was to kill all the inhabitants:

> . . . slaughtering everyone they found there, including small children, old men, pregnant women, and even women who had just given birth. They hacked them to pieces, slicing open their bellies with their swords as though they were so many sheep herded into a pen. They even laid wagers on whether they could manage to slice a man in two at a stroke or cut an individual's head from his body, or disembowel him with a single blow of their axes. They grabbed suckling infants by the feet and, ripping them from their mothers' breasts, dashed them headlong against the rocks.[5]

While de las Casas's book shocked Europeans, it did not compel Spain or other European nations to fully reform their opinion that America's Indians or natives of other countries then being explored were less than human beings—an unshakable attitude that led to the terrible atrocities committed against native populations in North America and across Latin America.

While he campaigned tirelessly against the brutality of the Spaniards, de las Casas, in addition to preserving what remnants of Indian culture he could, sought also to end the hardships of the Indians enslaved within the plantations and mines of Mexico, especially on the Yucatan Peninsula. Although there are no figures to record how many Indians died on the sugar cane and hemp plantations, and in the mines of Mexico, we can infer from de las Casas's descriptions of life on those vast holdings that hundreds of thousands of Indians perished during Spanish rule, which lasted until the early nineteenth century. De las Casas went on to become the first bishop of Chiapas, Mexico, and is immortalized as a defender of Indians and their rights.

De las Casas was not the only Spaniard to decry the treatment of the Indians. Another Dominican priest, Antonio de Montesinos, had earlier protested the treatment of the indigenous people in Santo Domingo in the Caribbean. During a sermon on December 4, 1511, he chastised churchgoers, accusing them of being in "mortal sin" because of the:

> . . . cruelty and tyranny which they impose on these innocent peoples. By what right and by what justice do you keep these Indians in such cruel and horrible servitude? By what authority have you imposed such

---

5. Ibid., 15.

detestable wars against these peoples who have lived peacefully in their lands . . . ? Are they not human?[6]

Despite de Montesinos's sermon and the subsequent uproar, the government did little to ease the tortured life of the Caribbean Indians under Spanish rule. Spanish King Fernando did enact the Laws of Burgos and Valladolid to provide some relief in the treatment of the natives, although its enforcement was lax.

One of the first things that both priests and conquistadores stopped were the penchant of some Indian nations for human sacrifices. Gone were the bloody rituals and carefully arranged skulls of their victims that the Maya and Aztec used to instill fear in their neighbors. Instead, priests, who busily baptized Indians into the Catholic faith, intoned humility, love, kindness, and charity with one important caveat: no one could question the will of the Christian God. He was all-powerful, all-knowing, and all-seeing. Heaven awaited those who were meek and obedient to God and did not question his ways. Ferocious punishment was meted out to those who did not heed the teachings of the priests.

The Catholic Church and its belief in fatalism was exactly what the conquistadores and their progeny needed to ensure that no one threatened their positions and wealth. Priests could be satisfied with healthy donations from the *hacienda* owners, while government officials could be controlled with bribes. Both priests and officials were invited to lavish fiestas at the sprawling estates. The poor, be they Indians, *creoles*, *mestizos*, or *negros*, would not challenge the ruling class so long as Spanish soldiers enforced both secular law and religious dogma. Catholicism took care of their souls, and *La Santisima Inquisición* stood ready and willing to burn or torture those who challenged God's will or Catholicism.

Spanish priests, scattered across the whole of Latin America, ensured the creation of devout Catholics within the Indian nations. They were also the eyes and ears of the hierarchy, ready to report any signs of rebellion among the masses. Additionally, the padres became responsible for educating the children of the *hacienda* owners, teaching them first in classrooms within church grounds or convents, then later in Catholic universities established across Latin America.

---

6. Hugh Thomas, *Rivers of Gold: The Rise of the Spanish Empire, from Columbus to Magellan* (New York: Random House, 2003), 294–295.

Within the halls of the universities, the children of the *hacienda* owners were taught how to manage their families' vast lands. And those schools had one additional goal: to guarantee that the children and grandchildren of the conquistadores would remain devout Catholics, defending not only their faith, but their status and wealth, ready to crush anyone who dared challenge them or the church. Only the sons of the highest social classes, with some rare exceptions, were enrolled in those campuses.

Their curriculum was not geared to create thinkers, scientists, or artists, or encourage curiosity, intellectuality, creativity, or entrepreneurship. Consideration of human rights, introspection, or questioning the role of humanity outside of Catholicism was anathema to the universities of Spain's New World. The lessons learned within those universities indirectly instilled in students a belief that God's will had placed the progeny of the conquistadores at the uppermost level of Spanish society.

In contrast, the children of Spain's working class, both on the Iberian Peninsula and in *Nueva España*—the bakers, carpenters, masons, blacksmiths, farmers, cooks, and clerks—by and large were schooled at home unless their parents could afford to send them to parochial schools, where lessons instilled the doctrine of fatalism.[7] Any contribution from the Indian culture to Spanish knowledge was shunted aside, thereby ignoring, as an example, a vast lore of medicinal herbs and other treatments.

European discoveries or theories that challenged Catholic teachings, such as the belief the earth was the center of the universe, were banned both in Spain and its New World. During the seventeenth century, Diego Rodriguez, a priest in Mexico City and a mathematician astronomer at the Royal and Pontifical University there, spent thirty years in an unsuccessful effort to bring the works of Galileo and Kepler (forbidden in Spain) to the New World. He also was never permitted to separate theology and metaphysics from science.

Rodriguez and like-minded academics were forced to meet in secret to discuss the latest scientific and astronomical advances in Europe. Under the threat of a fine and excommunication, booksellers in Mexico City, all six of them, had to obtain permission from the Inquisition for any book they offered for sale. Any author, seller, or owner of a questionable book was in danger of being summoned by the Inquisition.

---

7. Fehrenbach, *Fire and Blood*, 249.

The attitude of rejecting not only new knowledge, but also ignoring all aspects of Indian culture, was bemoaned by scholarly Franciscan priest Bernardino de Sahagún. He took it upon himself to study and preserve as much of Indian life as he could find. He had sailed to Mexico in 1529 and was stunned by the scope of destruction of the Indian culture, history, and, especially, languages.

Almost immediately, Sahagún began studying Nahuatl, the Aztec language, eventually mastering it. His knowledge and work with the surviving elders of the Aztecs and other tribes allowed him to compile and translate a collection of hieroglyphics and literature that provided a scholarly, anthropological view of Indian knowledge. In his work, he hired Indian scribes to portray their history in the style they had used customarily before *La Conquista*. It was all to little avail. Sahagún's work was condemned by the Holy Inquisition and Spanish King Felipe II on the basis that it would perpetuate pagan beliefs and delay the forced Christianization of the Indians. Sahagún's greatest work, the twelve-volume *Historia General de las Cosas de Nueva España* (*General History of the Things of New Spain*)[8], written in Nahuatl and illustrated by Indian scribes, remained unpublished until the nineteenth century. His work, albeit delayed in its dissemination, earned him the title, "father of American ethnography."

Understanding the policies of Catholicism and the culture it forged in the New World requires looking back at what transpired near the end of the Spanish campaign against the Moors and Islam. As the court of Isabel and Fernando rejoiced and gave thanks to God for their victory over the Moors, uneasiness still resonated across the Iberian Peninsula. There was a fear, a near paranoia, that while the remaining Moors had been vanquished, they could still threaten the new monarchy. In fact, Niccoló Franco, the *nuncio* (papal ambassador) of Pope Sixtus IV, had earlier warned of the supposed threat posed by any surviving member of those religions.

If Catholicism was to flourish in Spain and replace Judaism and Islam, any menace to that goal, however slight, needed to be eliminated quickly and harshly. The victorious king and queen eventually gave the

---

8. A well-preserved copy of Sahagun's *Historia General* can be found in the Laurentian Library of Florence in Italy. Another version is in Madrid's Library of the Royal Palace. The volumes in Florence and Madrid are copies of the originals that are believed to have been destroyed by Spanish censors. Sahagun's work is also known as the Florentine Codex.

non-Catholics little choice—either convert to Catholicism or leave the country, which meant abandoning any wealth they had accumulated. Many Spanish Moors and Jews who had established an intellectual culture superior to the rest of Europe during the Dark Ages were, under royal decree, either forced to renounce their religion or were compelled to flee. What remained in Spain was a population seething with intolerance toward any remnant of their former rulers. To guarantee a complete elimination of the Muslim and Jewish culture, the monarchs also ordered the destruction of all Moorish and Jewish libraries, considered Europe's most advanced in science and literature.[9] [10]

To ensure compliance against Judaism and Islam, in 1477 Isabel authorized Spain's Catholic Church to investigate anyone suspected of practicing the outlawed religions.[11] *El Tribunal del Santo Oficio de la Inquisición* (The Tribunal of the Holy Office of the Inquisition) or simply *La Santisima Inquisición* (The Most Holy Inquisition) was born. In Rome, the Spanish Inquisition's intolerance in its first year alarmed Pope Sixtus IV, who realized it could be wielded as a political tool by the Spanish monarchs. He subsequently issued a message urging the king and queen to eliminate it, stating his fear that it could do more harm than good:

> Many true and faithful Christians, because of the testimony of enemies, rivals, slaves, and other low people—and still less appropriate—without tests of any kind, have been locked up in secular prisons, tortured and condemned like relapsed heretics, deprived of their goods and properties, and given over to the secular arm to be executed, at great danger to their souls, giving a pernicious example and causing scandal to many.[12]

Unfortunately, the pope abandoned his efforts to rein in the Inquisition. Spanish King Fernando threatened to withhold military aid to Rome when it needed as many allies as possible to counter the Ottoman

---

9. Daniel Fogel, *Junípero Serra, the Vatican, and Enslavement Theology* (San Francisco: Ism, 1988), 14.

10. Underlying the call to oust the Moors in the mid-fifteenth century was a fear that the Ottoman Empire's conquest of Constantinople in 1453 posed a Muslim threat to all of Christian Europe.

11. The Spanish Inquisition followed the original Inquisition begun in 1233 by Pope Gregory IX.

12. Henry Kamen, *The Spanish Inquisition* (New York: New American Library, 1965), 53.

Empire. With little choice, Pope Sixtus issued a bull granting the Spanish monarchs control over the Inquisition.

On October 17, 1483, Isabel and Fernando, further empowered the Inquisition by appointing Bishop Tomás de Torquemada to direct it using Dominican priests as enforcers. Under his direction, torture became the Inquisition's favorite method of forcing confessions from helpless suspects who may or may not have committed "sins" against the church. Many of the lucky few who were tortured but eventually released nevertheless suffered a double blow by losing their estates. Individuals were accused of such acts as practicing Judaism or Islam; of heresy, witchcraft, or blasphemy; pacts with the devil, polygamy, perjury, usurping priestly powers, violation of celibacy, and maltreating the Holy Eucharist. From 1480 to 1530, *La Santisima Inquisición* of Spain ordered at least 2,000 victims burned alive at the stake.

Those dreadful displays of religious intolerance— called *autos-de-fé*[13]— involved long and solemn rituals attended by nobles and the church hierarchy. These officials were ensconced on platforms draped with fine cloths and seated on ornate chairs. Below them, unruly crowds of sightseers turned the death sentences into near carnivals as the victims screamed for mercy and writhed in pain. In addition to its victims, the Inquisition's dark legacy was to stifle and censor the progressive and creative thoughts that were at that time leading to scientific discoveries, new philosophies, and the acceptance of basic human rights in England, France, Germany, and other European nations.

By 1571, *La Santisima Inquisición* had crossed the Atlantic Ocean,[14] where it would remain a bloody tool of Spanish Catholicism for more than 200 years. The number of its New World victims has never been determined exactly. The Spanish monarchy finally abolished it in 1834 after a Spanish teacher was executed for stating that religion was not necessary to believe in God.

Intolerance of any religion other than Catholicism had become a mainstay of Spain and *Nueva España*. Spanish faith in God was what had inspired them to defeat the Moors and instilled in them a sense of invincibility and intense devotion to Catholicism. In their view, they

---

13. Spanish for "acts of faith."

14. The Inquisition was located in Mexico City on the present-day corner of Republica de Brasil and Republica de Venezuela streets, now the location of the Museum of Mexican Medicine.

had become the master race of the world. Yet, after 274 years of Spanish rule, *Nueva España* was riddled with extreme poverty and illiteracy, and Spanish colonies were little more than impoverished stepchildren of a nearsighted monarchy. Compounding that failure was a society in which the wealthy zealously protected their status and prohibited the common man from seeking political, economical, and social reforms.

The church cared little about the living conditions of the poor in the Spanish colonies, instead focusing on ensuring that their souls ascended to heaven. Meekness, devotion, and unquestioning acceptance of authority were the keys to heaven for the wretched. It would take 200 more years before Catholicism in Latin America reversed its goals and began campaigning for a better life on earth for those who were at the bottom of a highly stratified social culture that essentially ignored human rights.

By 1768, Spain's Latin American subjects lived in a society that was split into two economic sections. Workers labored in near slavery on the colonies' sprawling plantations, providing sugar, cocoa, coffee, tobacco, and hemp in huge quantities, although still not enough to rescue Spain's impoverished and stunted national economy.

At the same time, Spain was also facing the loss of its lands in California. The crown feared that Russian fur traders in Alaska would migrate down to Alta California and challenge its vast North American territory. To counter that move, King Carlos III ordered his viceroy in Mexico City to take immediate steps to ensure that all of California remain under Spanish control. Under the king's plan, *presidios* (forts), missions, and settlements would be established along the Alta California coastline. The presidios would protect the missions and settlements and prevent incursions by any foreign power into the remote land. In turn, the missions would Christianize the Indians and educate them for ten years, transforming them into Spanish subjects loyal to the king.

Alta California at the time was devoid of Europeans. Spain had explored the region minimally and, finding neither gold nor silver, had ignored it for more than 200 years. The stage was thus set for the once-powerful nation that had brutally conquered *Nueva España* to assert its rule over the coastal Indians of California—in the name of God and Carlos III. Those California natives, bystanders actually, would fall victim to a Spanish strategy aimed not at conquering Indian nations and looting them, as had happened in the rest of Latin America. Instead, the goal was to protect Spanish land and, in so doing, accommodate the zealous faith of a particular Franciscan friar—Junípero Serra.

On May 16, 1768, José de Gálvez, the Visitor General of New Spain and a man well acquainted with the science of his era,[15] met with his staff in a newly constructed government building in San Blas, a new Spanish port located on the west coast of Mexico. Outside, torrid temperatures mixed with high humidity, but inside the building the officials were protected from the heat by thick, insulating stone walls and floors. Seated at the head of a long rustic table, Gálvez opened the meeting at which he and his staff would seal the fate of California's Indians. Their discussion would center on analyzing the reports and maps of previous expeditions into Alta California to determine the most efficient method to keep it from Russian expansion.

The Visitor General knew that the task assigned to him by the king and Francois Charles de Croix, the Viceroy of Mexico, was virtually impossible. As Visitor General, appointed by King Carlos III, Gálvez was similar to an inspector general and had far-reaching powers to ensure that the king's money was being well spent in *Nueva España*. Spain, however, had neither the soldiers nor the money to properly fulfill the royal decree. Gálvez and his staff had to use what was available and then determine the strenuous logistics needed not only to found the California sites, but to keep them supplied along a coastline they knew only by the ancient charts unrolled before them.

Gálvez was determined to become thoroughly knowledgeable about what lay ahead. The Spanish official, after conferring with de Croix and determining in Mexico City what was needed for the monumental task, had turned to the church to help keep California in Spanish hands. He selected Franciscan missionaries who were close at hand, readily available and experienced in controlling Indians at little expense. Spain would thus have to depend on a virtual handful of friars to launch a strategy that the king, his viceroy, and Gálvez hoped would protect the monarch's claim to California.

The eventual plan involved establishing presidios, missions, and pueblos along Alta California's coast, where ships could supply them with everything they needed—chocolate, linen tablecloths, communion wafers, or statues of saints. A secondary source of supplies would be carried by mule trains along a lengthy arduous trek from Mexico. Ironically, histo-

---

15. David J. Weber, *Bárbaros: Spaniards and Their Savages in the Age of Enlightenment* (New Haven: Yale University Press, 2005), 2.

rian David J. Weber has described Gálvez as a man "who had little use for missions" and who believed that church control of property not only hindered the generation of wealth, but also "the transformation of Indians into producers and consumers."16 Still, Gálvez had little other choice than to use the padres to fulfill the king's wishes.

Empowered by the king and the monarch's viceroy in Mexico City, he would send the Franciscans into Alta California led by Father Serra, their *padre presidente*, in an arduous trek that would be known as the Sacred Expedition of 1769. Serra, a fervent devotee of the Order of Friars Minor, had recently arrived in Baja California with a dozen friars. They had taken over the missions there, which had been left empty after Carlos III declared the Jesuit priests disloyal and expelled them. The king had ordered the Franciscans to educate the Indians, not a wholly benevolent effort. He believed that once literate, no other nation could deny that educated, Spanish speaking Indians were Spanish subjects.

Once Gálvez briefed Serra on the colonization plans, the *padre presidente* began seeking volunteers from his group of Franciscans and procuring supplies for the venture. To the diminutive friar, the new adventure was a godsend, aiding him in reaching his goal of baptizing as many souls as he could during his lifetime. Serra would be bolstered in his great endeavor by the combination of a keen intellect and the fervor of his dedication to Catholicism. Those two factors would allow him to develop the influential arguments he would need to keep the missions independent of California's Spanish government, albeit with almost constant friction between him and the territory's governors.

Traveling with Serra would be squads of soldiers to protect the friars, a handful of hardy pioneers, and small herds of livestock. The priest and those around him would be trailblazers into a land where three previous expeditions had found nothing to attract Spanish conquistadores.

While Hernán Cortés had first discovered the Baja California peninsula in 1535, it was not populated by Spaniards until the late seventeenth century when Jesuit priests, bereft of government support, traveled to the arid land and established a series of missions to save Indian souls. It was a disastrous effort that resulted in the extinction of Baja California's Indians by the early nineteenth century. They had fall victim to European diseases, and had also perished from maltreatment administered first by the Jesuits and later by the Franciscans.

16. Ibid., 242.

In 1542, seven years after Cortés's discovery, Juan Rodríguez Cabrillo, leading the first coastline exploration of Alta California, sailed northward along the west coast of Baja California and continued past the peninsula, discovering two bays that he named San Diego and Santa Monica. He then reached the vast Monterey Bay before beginning a return journey in which he suffered a serious leg fracture aboard his ship. Gangrene from the injury claimed his life on January 3, 1543.

It took fifty-one years before another major expedition sailed to Alta California. In 1594, Portuguese Captain Sebastián Rodríguez Cermeño discovered what is now called Drake's Bay north of San Francisco Bay. He mapped entrances to the bays of Monterey and Santa Monica before returning to Mexico. His findings encouraged Spanish Viceroy Gaspar de Zúñiga y Acevedo, Conde de Monterey, to organize a new expedition to chart California's coast.

An expert sea captain named Sebastián Vizcaíno was appointed to lead the third expedition. He had first sailed along the east coast of Baja California in 1596 and helped chart it. Vizcaíno was so encouraged about his initial findings that he petitioned the viceroy to explore the west coast of the peninsula. Finally, after six years, Vizcaíno was charged by the viceroy to sail to Cabo San Lucas, at the tip of the Baja California peninsula. From there he was to proceed north nearly 2,000 miles to Cape Mendocino, mapping all the rivers and bays along the way, exploring as many as he could, and giving them the names of saints. He was to make only minimal contact with any natives lest they become Spanish enemies. The last thing the Spanish officials wanted was to be overwhelmed by superior numbers of angry Indians.

Vizcaíno finally set sail on May 5, 1602, from Acapulco on Mexico's west coast. By June 11, he had reached Cabo San Lucas with three ships and 200 men. From there they sailed to San Diego, named after Saint Didacus of Alcala, Spain (the explorer's ship was also named *San Diego*). After dropping anchor, friendly Indians helped resupply the expedition's food stores. By December, Vizcaíno had reached the large bay discovered by Cermeño and named it *Bahía de Monterey* (Monterey Bay), after the viceroy's title. Vizcaíno at last reached Cape Mendocino, charting the coast before returning to San Diego on November 10, and from there returning to Acapulco.

Studying the reports of the three earlier explorations, Gálvez worked closely with Serra in developing plans to establish missions alongside the proposed presidios in San Diego and Monterey. The church and the friars could bring with them, at the Spanish government's expense, all the equipment and provisions needed to establish the religious compounds.

The overall strategy hinged on using the missions and forts, after they were established, to encourage settlers from Mexico to journey into Alta California. And while pioneers from Mexico settled in Alta California, Gálvez hoped the Indians being educated in the missions would become faithful members of the new society. Eventually, under the Spanish official's plan, Alta California would have numerous towns populated by both Indians and settlers from Mexico who would worship God inside immense churches and cathedrals, equal to the finest in Spain and other parts of *Nueva España*.

Yet, two years after San Diego and Monterey were founded, there were forebodings that the project could collapse. The Father Superior of the College of San Fernando in Mexico City, Rafael Verger, oversaw Serra's responsibilities. In an August 3, 1771 letter to Manuel Lanz de Casafonda, he lamented that the only reason he had approved Serra's and the Franciscans' involvement was that Gálvez had requested it. He was also disturbed by Serra's enthusiasm and wrote that it was "necessary to moderate somewhat his ardent zeal." Verger openly predicted the missions could never succeed, arguing they were under-financed. He also worried that if the project failed the Franciscans, not Gálvez, would be blamed. Additionally, he feared that if the Indians allied themselves into an overwhelming force they could easily destroy all of the missions.[17]

Four years after Verger's letter, Serra voiced similar worries regarding an Indian attack. In a letter written July 24, 1775, to Verger's successor, Fray Francisco Pangua, he wrote, ". . . God save us if at any time they should come out victorious or that many should unite against us: were that to happen, who knows what would become of us, or how we would pass through their country."[18] Verger's and Serra's fear of a united Indian attack was justified, given Spain's relatively small army in the New World.

---

17. Charles E. Chapman, *The Founding of Spanish California: The Northwestward Expansion of New Spain* (New York: MacMillan, 1916), 103–111. A transcript of the full version of Verger's letter in Spanish, dated Aug. 3, 1771, can be found in the University of California Berkeley's Bancroft Library collection of letters "concerning missions in Alta and Baja California." BANC MSS M-M 1847.

18. Serra, *Writings of Junípero Serra*, 295.

Spain could not afford expensive conflicts that took a toll on its treasury and in human lives.

In 1519, when Cortés launched his terrible campaign against the Indian civilizations of Mexico, the indigenous population was estimated at 25 million.[19] Seventy-four years later, only a small fraction of that population remained.[20]

In 1768, the beginning of a parallel tragedy, albeit smaller in scope, was about to unfold. Along Alta California's coast, indigenous people went about their daily tasks, fishing, gathering clams on the beaches, checking their stores of acorns and other foodstuffs gathered for the winter, and tending fires for warmth and cooking. California's Indians were blissfully unaware that the Spaniards were preparing to seize their lands and violently end their way of life.

19. *The Cambridge History of Latin America*, ed. Leslie Bethell (Cambridge: University of Cambridge Press, 1997), 4.
20. Robert McCaa, "Was the sixteenth century a demographic catastrophe for Mexico: An answer using non-quantitative historical demography." Paper presented at the *V Reunión Nacional de Investigación Demográfica en México*, Colegio de México, Mexico City, June 5–9, 1995.

4

Los Indios

Chinigchinich . . . created man, forming him of clay found upon the borders of a lake. Both male and female he created.
—Friar Gerónimo Boscana[1], describing, in his study of Indians at Mission San Juan Capistrano, their belief in a powerful deity who created man and woman.

No one knows exactly when the first humans arrived in the New World or in California. What we do know is that they have been in the Americas for thousands of years. In Chile, scientists have found artifacts at least 14,000 years old.[2] Humans spread across the sprawling continents of the New World, settling in lands that often teemed with game, nut-bearing trees, berries, and wild vegetables. Others found a way to survive in sweltering deserts that offered little in food.

At sites throughout the hemisphere, groups established villages, allied with neighbors to form tribes with defined borders, refined their languages, and zealously guarded their lands against all intruders. The process was repeated across North, Central, and South America until the continents were dotted with indigenous nations that developed the skills and tools to survive in regions as disparate as the torrid deserts of North America and the lush, humid, jungles of South America.

Along the California coast, stretching from San Francisco Bay to Baja California, the inhabitants were blessed with a temperate climate.

---

1. These words were written during the period of years (1812–1826) in which Boscana, a Franciscan friar, served at Mission San Juan Capistrano.

2. Tom D. Dillehay, M. Pino, C. Ramirez, M.B. Collins, J. Rossen, J. D. Pino-Navarro. "Monte Verde: Seaweed, Food, Medicine, and the Peopling of South America," *Science* (320, no. 5877, 2008), 784-786.

From San Diego to Santa Barbara, summer temperatures generally ranged from the high seventies to the eighties in degrees Fahrenheit, with cooler temperatures north of Santa Barbara. Inland, just west of the coastal mountain range, temperatures could soar into the nineties and one hundreds. Winter daytime temperatures measured between the low sixties and fifties. In the region of the San Francisco Bay, spring and summer were sometimes as much as ten degrees lower than areas to the south, as a cool offshore current moderated temperatures and created fog that swirled toward shore.

Food was bountiful all along the coast. The ocean supplied fish, mollusks, and crabs. Many beaches were breeding grounds for seals of all types, including massive elephant seals with their long, dangling noses, and the fur seals later sought by the Russians. Salmon and trout were also plentiful in the many rivers and streams that wound their way westward from the coastal mountain ranges to the Pacific Ocean. The land was filled with small game and deer. Grizzly bears and mountain lions, the largest predators, abounded.

Spanish military commander Pedro Fages's brief but elegantly detailed description of California—written after he was ousted from his command following disputes with Friar Junípero Serra—was published in Mexico City in 1775. It offered the first depictions of the land and its potential, and of the Indians, their customs, religions, culture, implements, and weapons. Fages's work is valuable because many of the Indians he described had not yet been influenced by European customs, food, culture, or religion, unlike those who became subjects of scholarly study from the late nineteenth century onward.

Fages was amazed at the bountiful variety of wildlife he saw in the region:

> . . . there are to be seen, besides a number of other land animals, deer, antelope, conies, hares without number, wildcats, wolves, some bears, coyotes and squirrels of three kinds. Among the birds there are various kinds of thrushes, and a few birds of prey. There are also quail, sparrows, mocking birds (sic), woodpeckers, vultures, and buzzards. The aquatic birds are pelicans, herons, ducks, divers, mud hens and other kinds.[3]

---

3. Pedro Fages, *A Historical, Political and Natural Description of California by Pedro Fages, Soldier of Spain.* First published in Mexico City in 1775. Tr. Herbert Ingram Priestley, 1937 (Ramona, Calif.: Ballena, 1972), 12.

Fages also described the land as having elk, wild sheep, buffalo, panthers, and foxes, and reported that seals and otters could be found inland along the major rivers flowing into San Francisco Bay.

Adaptation was the key to human survival. In the warmer inland areas, small rivers, streams, and lakes could disappear in droughts that could last for years, creating hardships for those first inhabitants. Where the weather was bitter and harsh during specific seasons, or where the land required careful tending to produce crops from previously wild plants, the Indian nations crafted skilled technology that allowed them to thrive.

Indian living in the south, past Santa Barbara, developed the means to grapple with land that was more desert-like, with thick brush and sparse forests filling the flat areas along the coast. Those living in the Los Angeles and San Diego regions faced inland summer temperatures that could soar past 100 degrees Fahrenheit. Further inland, over the San Gabriel, San Bernardino, and San Jacinto mountains, was the Mojave Desert, where tribes such as the Kitanemuk, Tataviam, Serrano, Cahuila, Chemehuevi, Kawaiisu, Mojave, Mono, and Koso lived. In this harsh land, neither oaks nor game were plentiful and the inhabitants faced a constant struggle to survive the searing summer temperatures that climbed past 110 degrees Fahrenheit. Winters, however, were mild.

The rugged Sierra Nevada mountain range with its soaring peaks rose in eastern California. Snow blanketed the mountains in winter, but summers were mild, allowing a relatively few Indian communities to make the place their home. In the cool, mountainous northern half of California dwelled more than twenty tribelets, the largest being the Wintu, Nomlaki, Konkow, and Pomo. Northern coastal Indian small nations included the Chimariko, Mattole, Hupa, Yurok, and Wiyot. Due to their remoteness, most of these groups escaped captivity within the missions.

Beginning from the southernmost coastal area to San Francisco, California's coast was inhabited by various ethnolinguistic groups, each of which spoke a distinct language and formed tribelets within themselves. These groups included the Kumeyaay, Luiseño, Gabrieliño, Chumash, Salinan, Esselen, Costanoan, Ohlone, Coast Miwok, Wappo, and Lake Miwok Indians. The coast was dotted with the many villages of these hunter-harvesters, some of whom had mastered boat building and could live off both the ocean and land.

Small mammals were hunted, acorns and edible plants and roots were harvested, and fish, clams, oysters, and crabs were taken from the sea. Men focused on making tools, such as weaving nets and finely made bows and arrows. Fish hooks were carved from bone fragments. Antlers shed by deer were carved and ground into sharp-edged wedges, or made into chisels that cut wood by hitting the blunt ends with a rock.[4] Bones of beached whales were commonly used to make tools. String for fishing and hunting was woven from hemp or milkweed.

Coastal inhabitants had no need to build elaborate homes that required cutting down trees. The only material needed was tules (rushes), or even branches from bushes. These were bundled and tied together to build a hollow, conical shelter over a frail framework of a few thin, pliable branches. Smoke from fires rose through the center and out the top. These shelters provided adequate protection in the mild coastal climate.

In times of plenty, the coastal Indians thrived from resources gathered or hunted along the coast. But they established seasonal customs that helped ease the occasional droughts that reduced the amount of food available. During seasons with little rainfall and food scarcity, neighboring villages joined to increase the efficiency of food gathering.

Many of the coastal tribes were skilled in making boats of rushes. Their assembly was simple. Boat builders gathered bundles of long rushes, bound them tightly together, and added more bundles until a section perhaps nine or ten feet long was completed. Those sections were then tied together and the ends folded or worked to make the bow and stern.

The tule boats were satisfactory for rivers, lakes, and shallow waters off the coast, but only the Chumash of the Santa Barbara region had the skills needed to build wooden boats that could venture far out to sea. This tribe and the Gabrieleño speakers just to the south were the only known groups in California that had mastered the ability to cut wood into long planks by splitting it with bone wedges.[5] Bone tools were also used to drill the holes in the planks, allowing them to be lashed together. The spaces

4. Alfred L. Kroeber, "Elements of Culture in Native Culture," in *The California Indians: A Sourcebook*, 2nd ed., ed. Robert F. Heizer and Mary Anne Whipple (Berkeley: University of California Press, 1971), 23.

5. University of California linguist Kathryn Klar and Terry Jones, an archeologist at California Polytechnic State University San Luis Obispo, believe there may have been Polynesian contact with the Chumash region because of the similarity between Polynesian and Chumash words for boats and a fishhook believed to be of Polynesian design. Their findings were published in *American Antiquity* (70, no. 3, 2005).

between the planks were sealed with fiber and tar. These large, seaworthy boats (*tomols*) were used for both fishing and to travel along the coast, including visits to the outlying Santa Barbara Channel Islands for trade with their indigenous inhabitants.

The asphaltum, or tar, the Indians used to seal their boats was gathered in clumps that washed onto the beaches. Even to this day, asphaltum is still washed up onto shores along the same coastline or, more rarely, found in surface pits, the most famous being the La Brea Tar Pits. Asphaltum was also used to waterproof woven baskets.

Communities that ate shellfish dumped the shells into mounds, Indian garbage dumps that can be found all along the coast. Those piles of refuse became the subject of a detailed analysis begun in 1913 by Edward Winslow Gifford, who analyzed their exact contents to determine what food resources were most popular with the Indians. Gifford found that the mounds were composed mainly of the remains of oysters, clams, and other mollusks, along with fish, ash, and the bones of small mammals.[6] He described one of the biggest mounds, measuring sixty feet high and 350 feet in diameter at Emeryville in the San Francisco Bay area, as having been created over a period of 3,300 to 3,700 years.[7]

Mountain ranges that ran parallel to the coast separated California's coastal Indians from its inland inhabitants, who lived in a vast valley made up of the Sacramento Valley in the north and the San Joaquin Valley in the south. This inland valley stretched 300 miles from north to south and was forty to fifty miles wide. In the center flowed the Sacramento and Feather rivers, home to numerous Indian villages. Along the eastern edge were the American and Yuba rivers, fed by tributaries from the rugged Sierra Nevada mountain range. A number of settlements flourished along these distant river banks and remained relatively undisturbed by European settlers until the Gold Rush of 1849.

Like all of California at that time, the great valley were filled with wildlife, which supported eighteen tribes, including the largest tribe, the Yokuts, plus the Patwin, Konkow, Miwoki, and Nomlaki. Sherburne F. Cook has estimated the population of the Sacramento Valley in the second half of the eighteenth century at 76,100 persons, covering 22,700

---

6. Edward Winslow Gifford, "Composition of California Shellmounds," *University of California Publications in American Archaeology and Ethnology* 12, no. 1 (1916):4.

7. Ibid., 13.

square miles, while in the southern San Joaquin Valley the number was 83,800 natives living on 33,400 square miles.[8]

The inland Indians depended on rainfall to nourish the plants and roots they gathered for food. When rains were plentiful, plants thrived and provided food for the animals the Indians trapped and hunted, such as birds, rabbits, squirrels, and other small mammals. Oak trees provided acorns, a food staple for the Indians, who carefully harvested and stored the fallen nuts. The Indians made soup from pine nuts and sugar from "an olive-like fruit on a very heavy tufted shrub, described as six feet high with reddish stems and leaves like that of the mangrove."[9] Making the sweetener involved separating the pulp from the seeds, then pressing and drying the sugary pulp in baskets.

The Indians of the valleys lived in conical shelters that were dug half underground. The round depression was covered with a framework of thick branches covered with reeds that were then plastered with clay for insulation. If a shelter became infested with fleas, it was simply burned and replaced.

Prior to the missions, the Indian population was estimated at 26,100 in the northern area from San Francisco Bay to San Luis Obispo, while the central area that stretched from the Santa Barbara Channel to Mission San Buenaventura was home to 18,500 Indians. The third sector, from San Fernando to San Diego, is believed to have been populated by 20,000 natives.[10] Overall estimates of the state's indigenous population prior to the mission period (1769 to the 1830s) range from a low of 133,500 to a high of 350,000.[11] The figures are derived almost exclusively from records kept by the missions.

Those pre-Hispanic communities were separated into small nations that anthropologists now call "tribelets" or "tiny nations," ranging in population from 100 to 500 members, usually averaging about 250 individuals. Scholars have estimated that approximately 500 to 600 tribelets

---

8. Sherburne F. Cook, *The Population of the California Indians, 1769–1970* (Berkeley: University of California Press, 1976), 19.

9. Rupert Costo, "The Indians Before Invasion," in *The Missions of California: A Legacy of Genocide*, ed. Rupert Costo and Jeannette Henry Costo (Ann Arbor: Braun-Brumfield, 1987), 12.

10. Ibid.; Heizer and Baumhoff, *California Settlement Patterns*, 42–43.

11. Ibid., 1.

existed in California.[12] While the boundaries of the tribelets varied in size, they generally were less than several hundred square kilometers, and "people could walk from the principal village to the tribelet's boundary within one-half to one day."[13] There are estimates, based on archaeological and anthropological excavations, that as many as 50,000 village sites existed in all of California.[14]

Certain technical and cultural aspects of life were common to most of the Indian tribes in California. For example, baskets that could hold and store food supplies were needed, prompting the development of the fine basket-weaving tradition that came to be noted for its high degree of efficiency and beauty. Some baskets—tightly woven and then sealed with asphaltum—could hold hot water. In addition to basket-making, soapstone, a soft rock, was carved into pots. In Southern California, pots were made from fired clay.

Women and children were responsible for gathering acorns, roots, seeds, and edible plants on the land that their individual tribes claimed. Edible seeds such as pine nuts were stored in baskets. Acorns were gathered and processed to make them edible, then patted into round, thick cakes, and cooked on hot rocks beside fires. In grassy plains areas, the Indians burned the meadows annually to keep brush and tree seedlings from sprouting, or to clear the land of dead growth, allowing new plants to flourish. The controlled burning allowed grass and seed bearing plants to thrive, attracting deer, elk, antelope, and rabbits that could then be hunted.

Powerful bows that combined layers of sinew and wood made hunting easier and found widespread use throughout the tribes. Sinew, shredded into long, threadlike strands by chewing, was used because of its high tensile strength of 28,000 pounds.[15] Boiled hides provided a glue with the same composition as sinew and was used to apply the sinew to the back of the bow (the side away from the archer). The combination of sinew,

---

12. Kent G. Lightfoot, *Indians, Missionaries and Merchants: The Legacy of Colonial Encounters on the California Frontiers* (Berkeley: University of California Press, 2005) 3, 43.

13. Ibid., 42–43.

14. Robert F. Heizer and Martin A. Baumhoff, "California Settlement Patterns," in *Prehistoric Settlement Patterns in the New World*, ed. Gordon R. Willey (New York: Wenner-Gren Foundation for Anthropological Research, 1956), 32.

15. Vernard Foley, George Palmer, Werner Soedel, "The Crossbow," *Scientific American*, (January, 1985), 106–107.

wood, and hide glue required a strong pullback. This in turn increased the velocity of the arrow, making it far more deadly. The making of these bows was complex, requiring precise skill to produce a valued hunting instrument that, although not as long as European bows, could propel an arrow with great force and accuracy up to 200 yards.

Similarly, arrow-making was another skill which required precision. The arrow shaft had to be straightened by scraping it with an obsidian knife and rubbing it on sandstone. Sinew and hide glue were then used to attach the feathers that stabilized the arrow in flight. The carefully chipped arrowhead, made of obsidian or a hard rock, was attached into a notch at the tip of the arrow shaft, again by using sinew and hide glue.

A common hunting method involved teams of men beating the grass to corner wild rabbits or other game, and then clubbing them to death. Some of the tribes used carved wooden clubs, and in Southern California some of the coastal Indians crafted boomerang-like throwing sticks.

War against other tiny nations was common, with the conflict usually centering on raids for food or the kidnapping of women and children. The chief of each village was the only person who could condone war for causes such as a violation of boundaries by a neighboring tribelet. Revenge was also a common reason for combat, stemming from the kidnapping of a wife or child, an insult to a chief, or the use of "witch-craft" to kill a member of a village. If an enemy was thought to be too strong, a village chief might travel to neighboring communities of the same tribelet to seek allies. Such alliances did not come cheap. Village leaders whose help was sought required payments of pelts or blankets before agreeing to an allegiance. If an alliance was formed, large-scale mobilizations were launched, including the stockpiling of large inventories of bows and arrows and the organization of a small army.

Once enough weapons were stockpiled an attack was launched, led by a chief or a revered tribal leader skilled in combat strategy, who determined the plan of attack and could not be disobeyed. The attackers formed a long column led by the strategic leader and followed by teenage soldiers, then by adult men. Trailing the war column were the village women, carrying extra bundles of bows and arrows and food for the march. The women's responsibilities included gathering arrows shot by the enemy and taking care of the wounded. If successful, the war party would sometimes capture children and women from the opponent's tribe to be used as slaves or forced into marriage. Otherwise, they were killed.

Little quarter was given, and any men captured were killed and sometimes dismembered. Facial skin, including the scalp, was taken in battle by some tribes and displayed in post-combat celebrations. However, such prizes were not revered afterward or displayed as permanent trophies.[16] Prisoners were tortured horribly before being killed.

How often these conflicts arose is not known. Certainly they were not constant, or else a warrior class would have been created, such as those found among the Incas, Mayans, Aztecs, and other nations. Perhaps they were sporadic, with long time periods separating each incident. When the tribelets were not warring with each other, they traded arrows, bows, obsidian knives, fur blankets, and seashell jewelry.

While villages within a tiny nation may have had a common language and culture, they did not generally recognize a central government. The chief's position was hereditary, as far as is known, and was passed from father to son. The chief also was the only village member allowed to have multiple wives. Although most coastal Indians followed this pattern of leadership, variations existed in Northern California and within the Santa Barbara Channel Islands. Leaders, in cooperation with a shaman, had the responsibility of identifying the specific seasons for village members, who then began the numerous activities needed to prepare for each period. Villages also paid homage to a deity, usually an elderly member who was honored at celebrations. He was selected by acclamation and protected during war.

Village chiefs did not exert influence in daily living and did not get involved in family feuds, even in the case of homicide. Village members had virtually unrestricted freedom to do as they pleased as long as their activities did not impose on others. Only in the event of war or a major hunt would the men converge to cooperate on behalf of the village or tribelet.

Alliances to guard against raids were often created by the marriage of one tribelet member to a member of another tiny nation or village— marriages that were sometimes sealed when the future couple was still in infancy. In a normal wedding in which an alliance was not involved, the future husband made his desire of his future bride known to her family.

---

16. Kroeber, *California Indians*, 37.

If her parents approved, a ceremony was held, with the entire village celebrating for up to three days.

Among the mid-coastal villages reaching up to San Francisco, a more common method of marriage involved having a couple appear in their village in the morning with scratches on their bodies. This was all that was needed for the couple to declare themselves married. Fages wrote:

> ... when a single man and a single woman are seen together at dawn savagely scratched, it is a sign that they have contracted matrimony during the night, and with this sole proof they are considered publicly and notoriously as man and wife by the entire village.[17]

The Spanish commander, astonished by the Indians' ecstatic love making, adds that couples scratching each other was not limited to a single night. It occurred frequently. Fages does not fully explain how he verified that custom in the following description:

> ... they never think of making legitimate use of the faculty permitted by marriage, without at the same time making use of the nails, repeating on such occasions the same cruel and barbarous expression of love and conjugal affection. This will seem an incredible thing, perhaps without parallel so far as is known of other nations, however untaught and savage they may be. There is no doubt, however, that this happens, and I write it after exact verification of the fact.[18]

If marriage scratches or any type of wound became infected, Indians resorted to shamans to heal the injury (or any other disease). The Indians believed sickness stemmed from the presence of a "foreign or hostile object." "Singing, dancing, and smoking tobacco ... Manipulation of the body, brushing it, and blowing of tobacco smoke, breath or saliva," were the usual efforts made by shamans to cure an illness.[19] Effective herbal potions for minor illnesses were also known and used, along with splints to immobilize broken bones.

In their social lives, Fages wrote, the Indians frequently organized dances, games, and joyous gatherings at dawn to greet a new day. Almost every village also had a sweat hut or *temescal*, where Indian men could refresh themselves with sauna baths once or twice daily. Fires were stoked inside to heat rocks and raise the temperature. One at a time, men would

17. Fages, *Description of California*, 58.
18. Ibid., 58–59.
19. Ibid., 39.

enter the hut and use a shaped bone with an edge to wipe off sweat before coming out and dousing themselves with cold water—a bracing and enjoyable daily habit.

Games were common among the Indians, including one that was played only by women. They would seat themselves in a circle with a highly decorated tray in the middle. The women would take turns throwing sea snail shells filled with asphaltum onto the tray while bets were made. The winner was decided by how many of the shells landed face down.

Men enjoyed a contest in which ten sticks, each marked with crossed lines on one side, were thrown onto a level circle of sand with a long wooden dowel in the middle. The players took turns throwing the sticks all at one time, trying to have them all land with the marked side up. The dowel in the middle made it more difficult for a player to win.

Another game required great skill in spear throwing. It involved two players who entered a smooth and level rectangle about ten yards long. Each player was given a long pole sharpened at one point. The object was, while remaining inside the rectangle, to spear—while it was still in the air—a small circle made of rolled up leather straps, with a hole the size of a dime in the middle. The game began when the leather was thrown into the air, and the player who speared the wheel most often was declared the winner.

The Indians also enjoyed dancing, especially at the onset of spring when dances sometimes lasted for days. For such celebrations, men donned elaborate feathered headdresses and skirts and painted their faces with black or white stripes. Women, while they did not wear such elaborate dance garb, were enthusiastic participants in the festivals. They were also in charge of organizing them. In those dances, the men lined up single-file, stamped the ground in exaggerated steps, and let out a resounding whoop or whistle suddenly. Meanwhile, women danced parallel to the men or in circles adjacent to the men. Rattles and slapsticks accompanied the dancers. The Indians also used dances to celebrate the onset of puberty for girls, and initiation rites into manhood status for boys. Other dances were held to celebrate victories in war.

In 1816, a Russian expedition visited Mission San Francisco (now Mission Dolores), where Franciscan friars told the expedition's artist, Ludovik Andrevitch Choris, that seventeen different nations were represented among the Indians at the mission. The large number of different small nations present at a single mission leaves no doubt as to the extent of the influence each of the twenty-one mission wielded. Those tribelets identified as being from the Sacramento River would have been found more than forty miles from the Mission San Francisco compound. (By 1810, the friars were sending out parties as far as the eastern edges of the San Joaquin Valley to search for new Indians, having depleted the number of natives immediately surrounding the missions.) The identification of so many of these groups at Mission San Francisco indicates that, although the majority of large tribelets were recognized, there may have been dozens of other tiny nations of which little or nothing is now known. They simply vanished during the nineteenth century, victims of European diseases, the devastating policies of the Spanish missions, and reorganizations in which members of a separate tribelet, unable to exist on their own, melded into neighboring small nations. Later incursions by Mexicans and the American prospectors during the 1849 Gold Rush were also to blame for those disappearances.

Anthropologists, sociologists, and archaeologists who have studied the history of the major tribes and tribelets have determined that at least one hundred languages were spoken in California, "as mutually unintelligible as English and Chinese. No area of comparable size in North America, or perhaps in the world, contained a greater variety of native languages and cultures than did aboriginal California."[20]

Anthropologists have theorized that these unique languages resulted from the fact that members of each tribelet rarely ventured beyond the boundaries of their group. Robert Heizer believed that: "California . . . was a region holding a large number of societies that had limited knowledge, understanding, experience and tolerance of neighboring peoples." Members of a tribelet lived and died within a small area with a boundary not more than ten or fifteen miles from their village. Their "whole life must have made one's world small, familiar, safe and secure."[21] That world was so tightly knit that early anthropologists, according to Kent Lightfoot, likened it to an "image of many multicolored billiard balls glued onto a landscape, their hard, almost impenetrable bodies containing a homog-

---

20. James J. Rawls, *Indians of California*, 6.

21. Robert F. Heizer, "Natural Forces and Native World View," in *Handbook of North American Indians: Vol. 8, California*, ed. R. Heizer (Washington, D.C.: Smithsonian Institution, 1978), 649.

enous population" that did not venture outside the shell of that imaginary billiard ball.[22]

By the time linguistic research occurred in the late nineteenth and twentieth centuries, many of the languages had sadly disappeared. Those tribelet members who had spoken them had either died from European diseases or perished in the mission environments. Others simply left the missions when they were secularized and scattered across California, unable to return to their ancestral lands that had been seized by the Spanish and Mexicans. Their original languages had long been usurped by a mixture of Spanish and other languages spoken by neophytes from the different tribe within the confines of the missions.

Adding to the erosion of specific languages was the Spanish attitude that Indian culture was unworthy of study or preservation, although some mission friars did learn at least one Indian language. Fages described the Indians as "savages so untaught and uncivilized in all else which concerns their intercourse and customs."[23] His description of their physical features was just as negative: "The natives throughout the tract described are, generally speaking, rather dark, dirty, of bad figure, short of stature, and slovenly . . . ."[24]

However, Fages had a surprisingly different attitude toward Indians living in the San Gabriel mission area. "These Indians," he wrote, "who live near the *Rio de los Temblores* (Santa Ana River), on its banks and the adjacent beaches . . . are fair, have light hair, and are good looking."[25] Interestingly, Fages does not state whether the Indians' skins approached the lightness of the skin of northern Europeans and the level of their color of hair. Were these Indians an aberration from the normally brown skinned and black haired Indians of California, or the result of some long ago and forgotten intrusion of white Europeans into the area who inter-married with Indian women?

Common to all groups was an oral tradition in retaining their history. It not only explained their origins, beliefs, and culture, but also provided entertainment around village fires at night. That tradition—rather than

---

22. Lightfoot, *Indians, Missionaries, and Merchants*, 48.

23. Fages, *Description of California*, 21.

24. Ibid.

25. Ibid.

the use of written symbols—sufficed to bind members of each tribelet to each other.

The Indians' tales of creation were complex and elegant. Among those stories is that of Chinigchinich, who created mortals, and was revered by the Indians surrounding Mission San Juan Capistrano. It was recorded by Gerónimo Boscana, a scholarly friar who, like Fages, had little regard for the Indians:

> The Indians of California may be compared to a species of monkey; for in naught do they express interest, except in imitating the actions of others, and particularly in copying the ways of the "*razon*," or white men, whom they respect as beings much superior to themselves; but in so doing, they are careful to select vice, in preference of virtue. This is the result, undoubtedly of their corrupt and natural disposition. The Indian, in his grave, humble and retired manner, conceals a hypocritical and treacherous disposition. He will deceive the most minute observer, as has been the case with many, or with all, who have endeavored to learn his character, until time has revealed his true qualities. He never looks at any one, while in conversation, but has a wandering and malicious gaze. For benefits received he is never grateful and instead of looking upon that which is given, he beholds only that which is withheld. His eyes are never uplifted, but like those of the swine, are cast to the earth. Truth is not in him, unless to the injury of another, and he is exceedingly false.[26]

Although the Franciscan friar unjustly considered the Indians despicable and ignored their complex culture, he did record their beliefs during the early nineteenth century. Boscana questioned the elders of the Acagchemem, who lived in the vicinity of Mission San Juan Capistrano, who explained to him that at one time "there was no earth. Instead, there was the heaven above and the ground below and these two were also brother and sister; neither the heaven nor the earth however, was as we now know it." The Acagchemem could not explain the bodily forms of the brother and sister, only that they existed:

> Below, there was only darkness. The sun was created when the brother brought it to his sister and asked her to be his wife. Thus wed, the pair produced earth (which grew southward), sand, and rocks that included the flint needed for their arrow tips. The soil was a white clay that was used as an ornament atop their heads. Plant and animal life

---

26. Boscana, *Chinigchinich*, 335.

were next, followed by the birth of Ouiot. Eventually Ouiot, a being of unexplainable existence, grew up and eventually bore children—the first family, but not mortals. They were of an ethereal nature.

Ouiot's family grew and aged. Then his offspring treacherously conferred and determined that he was too old to rule and must die. They poisoned him, but his mother became aware of the plot and mixed a potion that would have saved him, had it not been for Coyote, who, attracted by the fragrance of the potion, overturned it. With Ouiot dead, the next step was to arrange a funeral pyre, but the Coyote, named Eyacque, escaping from a trap set in his retreat, lurked awaiting a chance to eat from Ouiot's body, but he also determined that he would die with Ouiot. As the pyre was ignited, Eyacque, the Coyote, leaped upon the body, tore a piece of flesh from it and ate, earning the name Eno, the name used by the Indians for thieves and cannibals. Eventually the name became Eyoton, a derivation of Eno and Ouiot. In the wake of Ouiot's funeral, a spectre appeared and was summoned by Ouiot's children as they conferred on what to eat in place of the clay on which they normally fed. When they called on the spectre to identify himself, he declared that his name was Chinigchinich and asked the subject of their debate. When they told him, Chinigchinich stated that he was the creator of all things and would 'make you another people, and from this time one of you shall be endowed with the power to cause it to rain, another power to influence the dews, another to produce the acorn, another to create rabbits, another ducks, another geese, another deer.'[27] To each of these new beings he distributed a specific power, ordaining that they should be consulted and simultaneously presented with gifts.

Next, Chinigchinich used clay from a lake to create man and woman, whose descendants became the Acagchemem tribe. Not only was Chinigchinich the creator of man and woman, he was also "ever present and in all places," seeing all and rewarding the good and punishing the wicked.

In their villages, the Acagchemem built temples to Chinigchinich. These were the centers of worship for the tribe members and also provided sanctuary for anyone who had committed a serious crime, such as adultery, homicide, or theft. The temples, about six feet high, were

27. Gerónimo Boscana, *Historical Account of the Belief, Usages, Customs and Extravagancies of the Indians of this Mission of San Juan Capistrano Called the Acagchemem Tribe*, version from *Chinigchinich*, trans. Alfred Robinson, revised and annotated by John P. Harrington (Banning, Calif.: Malki Museum Press, 1978), 27–30.

huts, somewhat oval in shape, containing a figure of Chinigchinich.[28] The rationale for providing sanctuary was that because their god was "friendly to the good and punished the wicked, he also would not permit anyone to be molested who sought his protection."[29]

Boscana's record of the Acagchemem's religion allowed anthropologists to later determine that other California indigenous nations held similar beliefs about a higher being, imbued with supernatural powers as the creator of earth and all its life. Like many people around the world, the Acagchemem believed in a god who watched over them eternally and established the social norms in which good was rewarded and evil was punished. Chinigchinich was the highest authority for the Acagchemem, with the village leader next in line.

The daily living of California Indian groups at the time of the arrival of the Spaniards was guided by the norms established by leaders, who in turn followed the rules established by their predecessors. California's Indians did not live day-to-day, in which tribal members had no idea where they would find their next meal. Instead, their lives were strictly governed by their leaders. These men, labeled *capitanes* (captains) by the Spanish, determined punishments when warranted, and also settled disputes between village members. They determined when to hunt and when to gather and stockpile food, ensuring there were always provisions in plentiful quantities to support their followers.

A spiritual life or belief in supernatural beings, as described above, shaped individual behavior and reinforced the cohesiveness and efficiency of the tribelets. Technologically, the Indian nations developed only those tools needed to live in a land where food was readily available and the climate did not threaten their existence. In an almost Eden-like environment, California's Indians had adapted splendidly to the bountiful resources of the land and ocean, and so thrived for thousands of years.

---

28. Ibid., 37.
29. Ibid., 39.

5

Friar Junípero Serra: The Beginning

That the spiritual fathers should punish their sons, the Indians, by blows appears to be as old as the conquest of these kingdoms.

—Friar Junípero Serra (July 7, 1780), justifying his flogging of mission Indians to Governor Felipe de Neve by maintaining it was the customary policy used since the conquest of the New World by Spain.

Junípero Serra was born at one o'clock on the afternoon of November 24, 1713, in Petrá, a village on the island of Majorca, about 130 miles off the east cost of Spain.[1] He was baptized as Miguel Joseph Serra on the day of his birth. Later, he would change his first name to Junípero. Having his baptism on the same day he was born may have been prompted by the fact that newborns who appeared frail, as Junípero did at his birth, were quickly baptized for fear they might die without the holy ceremony. The midwife who had delivered him returned home from the baptism, cradling him in her arms and leading a procession of relatives. She handed him to his mother, Margarita, still in bed, uttering words in the Majorcan dialect: *Ja'l vos tornam cristiás* (I return him to you a Christian). As was usual, his mother probably had not kissed Junípero until after his baptism, following the Majorcan custom that an unbaptized child was *un moret* ("a little Moor").[2] Serra was the third of five children born to

---

1. The house in which he was born, 6 Calle Barracas, is still preserved, and a plaque identifies it as the Franciscan friar's birthplace. The narrow street, lined with ancient two-story stone residences, was renamed Calle Junípero Serra in his honor in 1949. Even the font where he was baptized on the day of his birth is preserved in a side chapel of St. Peter's parochial church in Petrá.

2. Maynard Geiger, *The Life and Times of Fray Junípero Serra, O.F.M., or The Man who Never Turned Back (1713–1784)* (Richmond: William Byrd, 1959), 6.

Antonio Nadal Serra and Margarita Rosa, middle-class farmers. It was a humble beginning for the future priest.

In his childhood years his parents, devout Catholics, took him to the Franciscan friary and school of St. Bernardine in Petrá, only a block from his home. There, under the guidance of the priests, he received his elementary education. He won praise from the friars for his work in Latin, mathematics, reading, and writing, and developed a gifted voice in singing Gregorian chants.

At the age of 16, after he made it known that he wanted to become a priest, his parents enrolled him at the *Convento de San Francisco* in Palma, the capital of Majorca, to begin his studies. Serra's desire to become a Franciscan was initially denied by the Very Reverend Fray Antonio Perelló Moragues, who considered him far too young to be admitted based on Serra's small stature. The priest quickly reversed his decision when told the young man's actual age.[3] After a year of study, Serra was admitted into the Franciscan Order of Friars Minor (O.F.M.) and on September 14, 1730, entered the *Convento de Santa Maria de Los Angeles de Jesús*, which neighbored Palma.[4] There, he astonished his teachers with a mind so disciplined that he excelled in all his studies.

During his time as a novitiate, Serra remained small, just a bit taller than five feet.[5] When he was 17 years old, he was still not tall enough to turn the pages of books placed on a lectern during recitals—but he did grow a bit while attending the Convento.

At the time that Serra joined it, the Franciscan order—which had been proposed by St. Francis to Pope Innocent III in 1209 and given verbal approval at that time—had been in existence for just over 500 years. Later, St. Francis gained formal, written approval from Pope Honorius III, who confirmed this new order of priests (along with that of the Dominicans) on November 29, 1223. Honorius III had a specific purpose in recog-

---

3. Ibid., 18.

4. Ibid.

5. His eventual height of five feet, three inches, was determined by an exhumation of his burial site in 1943 at the sanctuary of Mission Carmel in Carmel, California. It was undertaken as part of his beatification process by the Vatican. Earlier exhumations to identify his grave had occurred in 1856 and 1882. The remains were definitely identified as those of Serra in 1943 by Theodore McCowan of the University of California at Berkeley and Mark Harrington of the Southwest Museum of Los Angeles. His remains, after they were positively identified, were placed in a bronze coffin with documentation and reburied at the same site.

nizing the two orders: He needed enforcers from within the church who would hunt down heretics and crush any reformist movements. Both Franciscans and Dominicans would fulfill this need for him.

Under the strict rules written by St. Francis, members of the Order of Friars Minor promised to live a life of poverty, devoid of property save for a few worldly goods, and to rid themselves of virtually all their possessions. They were required to wear a tunic with a hood, bound at the waist with a thick white rope. The twelve rules of St. Francis also stipulated that the friars wear sandals and not travel on horseback "unless forced to do so by obvious necessity or illness." Unlike many other Catholic orders, the Franciscans were not bound to live cloistered lives in a monastery, but were permitted to travel and spread Christianity. Their needs would be met by donations or alms given to them.[6] However, centuries later the Franciscans, while not living in monasteries, did erect centers called *conventos* (convents) where they lived, taught, and set out on proselytizing ventures.

Serra readily accepted the life of poverty required by the Franciscans. Amid the quiet cloisters and colonnades of the *convento*, he spent his days in prayer, study, and meditation. While there, he developed the fervent spirit and devotion to Catholicism and to his fellow Franciscans that would shape the rest of his life. During this period, Serra first experienced and adopted the practice of self-punishment known as mortification of the flesh, something that is still sanctioned by the Roman Catholic Church.

After completing a two-year probationary period, Serra was admitted into the Franciscan order on September 15, 1731, at *Convento de Santa María*. It was in that ceremony that he changed his first name to Junípero after St. Junípero, a companion of St. Francis. Once admitted to the Franciscan order, he began his studies for the priesthood at the *Convento de San Francisco* in Palma. Serra was 18 years old and his admission into the order was one of his most joyful days, so much so that he would renew his vows every year. It was also the beginning of a career that would take him thousands of miles from Spain to Mexico and finally to California. Serra's attention came to focus on two things: the propagation

---

6. Bookkeeping was important to the friars, who kept meticulous records of their expenses. An example is the account outlining stipends that still exists today in Petra. It lists the dates and amounts paid when Serra was invited to preach in towns outside of Palma.

of Roman Catholicism and the baptism into that religion of as many souls as he could find in his lifetime. In complying with those goals, he vowed to live a chaste and humble life free of sin.

In his education for the priesthood, Serra, as he had before, excelled academically. At the end of six years of study, he was ordained a priest in December 1737. Earlier, in November, he had completed a difficult examination and was appointed a lector of philosophy. He was later named professor of philosophy at the Pontifical Imperial Royal and Literary University of Majorca, commonly known as the Lullian University.[7] While there, he also completed studies for a doctorate in theology and was eventually honored by being named professor *de prima* of the Chair of Scotistic Theology.

Eventually, Serra's teaching and expertise became renowned both within and outside the university. His sermons were considered of such high caliber that they attracted Palma's best intellectuals. One retired professor remarked, after listening in rapt attention to one of Serra's sermons: "This sermon is worthy of being printed in letters of gold."[8] Outside of Palma, the principal towns of Majorca eagerly sought Serra as a Lenten preacher in their churches.

As for Serra's physical appearance, it depends on which of two images one chooses. His actual visage remains a mystery because Serra never sat for a formal portrait during his lifetime. All the statues and paintings of him are based on descriptions written by other priests. Probably the most accurate image of the swarthy friar, who had dark hair and eyes, is a drawing made of him ten years before his death. That informal portrait depicts his narrow, handsome face with closed eyes and a large, possibly balding forehead. One sketch (formerly in a museum in Queretaro, Mexico, although its location is now unknown) shows him with a Franciscan cowl half-covering his head. The portrait, differing slightly from the other depiction, shows him with piercing open eyes, a thin mouth, and a straight nose.

For nearly twelve years, Serra earned fame as a professor and preacher, but in 1749, at the age of 36, he abruptly changed his life. His goal now

---

7. The name Lullian refers to Ramon Lull, a Majorcan intellectual of the thirteenth and fourteenth centuries who devoted himself to spreading Christianity.

8. Francisco Palóu, *Palóu's Life of Fray Junípero Serra*, trans. Maynard Geiger (Berkeley: Academy of American Franciscan History, 1955), 11.

was to travel to Mexico City and join the *Colegio de San Fernando*, the Franciscans' main headquarters for that part of the New World. The *colegio* prepared Franciscan priests "for the apostate of the home missions and unconverted Indian fields."[9] The influential institution controlled many Indian missions throughout Mexico.

Other orders, like the Dominicans and Jesuits, had also established missions across the New World, all of them seeking the same goal— Christianizing the Indians to save their souls. There were millions of them that needed to be saved from what the Spanish priests considered their pagan and demonic ways. Serra sought and eventually was given permission by his superior to travel to New Spain to help bring Christianity to the natives of that vast area which Spain had already ruled for more than 200 years.

Accompanying him as a devoted companion was Friar Francisco Palóu, a former student who later wrote Serra's biography. The two men had become close friends at the *convento*, and when Palóu learned through rumors that one of the friars was planning to travel to the New World, he asked Serra who it might be. Serra admitted he was the friar and then asked Palóu if he would like to join him. Palóu readily accepted the invitation.

Both apparently believed their passage to New Spain would be easily arranged, but their hopes were dashed when they sought permission from the Franciscans' commissioner general of the Indies, Fray Matías Velasco. He rejected their request to convert the "pagans" of New Spain because the order had already filled its quota of friars traveling to Mexico. Velasco wrote that he would gladly place their names on a waiting list. If any of the friars already approved to travel were to drop out, Serra and Palóu could fill their slots. But, he explained, there was a caveat. It would be difficult to place the pair, for Palóu and Serra were not from mainland Spain, and only friars from the mainland were being given first consideration. At Serra's behest, as a way out of the pair's quandary, Velasco sent a letter to other mainland commissioners, beseeching them to consider Palóu and Serra as members of a mainland friary.

Fortunately, five of the thirty-three friars destined for Mexico City dropped out, citing their fear of the sea. Velasco quickly dispatched two permits to travel, called obediences, to Palóu and Serra, but the documents never arrived. Palóu relates that a "reliable friar of the friary in

9. Geiger, *Life and Times of Fray Junípero Serra*, 91.

Palma" confided to him that the documents had somehow been lost "between the friary's portal and the cell I inhabited."[10]

A second set of obediences did reach the pair on March 30, sent by Velasco, who had not received any answer from the first mailing. Once the permits were received, Palóu quickly traveled to Petrá to inform Serra, where the friar was preaching during Lent. Serra's friend then returned to Palma to arrange for sea passage that would take them from Majorca to Cádiz, a major port on the southern coast of Spain, where the pair would leave for New Spain.

Unable to find a ship sailing for Cádiz, Palóu and Serra had to settle for a packet boat to the intermediate port of Málaga, captained by (according to Palóu) a cantankerous English captain who had no sympathy for Roman Catholicism. During their fifteen-day voyage, the captain frequently sought out Serra, arguing venomously with him and challenging him on scripture and dogma. Unaware that the friar was an expert on those subjects, the ship's master could never best Serra, who had actually sought to avoid such discussions with the captain. The captain's frustration was so vehement that at one point he accosted Serra and, holding a dagger against the friar's throat, threatened to kill him. Serra was able to free himself and reach his cabin safely, where he related the incident to Palóu.[11]

Landing at Málaga, the pair spent five days at the Friary of Our Seraphic Father St. Francis before continuing their trip, via another ship, to Cádiz, where they arrived on May 7. There they joined the other friars anxiously awaiting the sea voyage to the New World. Surprisingly, the quota of friars traveling to the New World still had three openings. Serra and Palóu relayed these obediences to Majorca, allowing three other friars to join the group.

Finally, on August 28, 1749, they embarked on what would be an arduous ninety-nine-day trip to reach Vera Cruz on the east coast of Mexico. Two weeks before reaching Puerto Rico, the ship's stores of water ran dangerously low, limiting all passengers to less than a pint of water per day. Serra, appearing unfazed by the rationing, was asked why he did not show symptoms of the thirst that was afflicting those on the ship. "I

---

10. Palóu, *Palóu's Life of Fray Junípero Serra*, 11.
11. Ibid., 12–13.

have found a means to avoid thirst, and it is this: to eat little and talk less in order not to waste the saliva,"[12] Serra answered.

Eventually, the shipload of friars and passengers reached Vera Cruz and from there continued to Mexico City on horseback. Horses were provided because the trip was considered too arduous for anyone unaccustomed to walking in the torrid tropical climate of the region. Serra, however, insisted on conforming to the Franciscan policy of avoiding travel by horse and was allowed to walk from the port city to Mexico City. En route, he apparently suffered an infection from either insect bites or a snake bite on his leg, an affliction that sporadically produced a terrible swelling of his leg which plagued him for the rest of his life. Serra, surprisingly, always rejected offers from doctors to heal the wound, maintaining he did not have time to undergo a lengthy series of treatments that might have ended his suffering.

On New Year's Day 1750, the friars reached Mexico City and crossed through the portals of the Apostolic College of San Fernando. Within five months of arriving, Serra requested assignment to the Cerro Gordo Indian missions in the mountains north of Querétaro in central Mexico. He traveled to that rugged site, where he translated and learned the Pame Indian language, and established a mission at Jalpan, Mexico, an isolated village in the mountain range located approximately 150 miles north of Mexico City. The small pueblo was the center of an effort by the Franciscans to Christianize the Pame Indians. During his time there, Serra also helped build a church. During its construction, to compensate for his small height he padded one of his shoulders so he could better carry large timbers.

Although some Indians voluntarily moved from their mountain villages to the mission, others, as was common in *Nueva España*, were forced into the settlement when Spanish soldiers burned their villages. Once the Indians were in town, Serra instructed them on farming, weaving, and using oxen and other farm animals. His efforts eventually allowed the Indians to improve their harvests to the point that they produced a surplus sold for profit.

Additionally, Serra was appointed an official of the Spanish Inquisition after he urged that the Cerro Gordo region needed an inquisitor to counter what he described as *maleficas* (witches) and other beings that flew at night to attend demonic ceremonies. As an Inquisition official, he was a main participant, albeit temporarily, in one notorious case. It

12. Ibid., 15.

involved a woman named Maria Pasquala de Nava who was being held as a suspect in the death of another woman and was accused by Serra of being a witch. After an investigation that dragged on for nearly a year, De Nava "died suddenly in the Inquisition building in Mexico City"[13] after it was determined she was a witch. One can surmise that she was either executed or tortured to death. Nava is buried at the nearby church of Santo Domingo of that city.

Along with bringing the Inquisition into the isolated mountains and destroying the local Indians' culture, the Spaniards also shattered the natives' veneration of a god they called *Cachum*, described as a demon by the friars. In reality, *Cachum* was a harmless deity whom the Indians thanked for a variety of things, among them bringing water to their corn-fields, granting good health, curing illnesses, and delivering victory in battles. The god also allowed couples to be married in a simple ceremony that involved presenting a blank piece of paper to the elderly keeper of the polished marble idol representing *Cachum*. Once the keeper received the paper, the ceremony was completed.

When the friars first arrived, the keeper had fled with the *Cachum* idol, attempting to hide it in a remote mountain village. The Spanish soldiers who drove the Indians from their homes and into Jalpan eventu-ally discovered a temple made of poles and a thatched roof. It was the site where the Indian priest had sought to hide the idol. The temple was burned, but the soldiers were unable to find the idol. Later, while Serra was at Jalpan, the now-converted Indians presented the idol to him.

After spending nearly a decade in the remote mountains, Serra was recalled to Mexico City in 1758. He arrived carrying the small statue from Jalpan and presented it to the *Colegio de San Fernando*, which accepted it as a trophy. It was placed in a storeroom containing documents pertaining to the missions of that area.[14]

In Mexico City, Serra was assigned to a small room, where he continued his habit of never sleeping under warm covers, using only a pillow and a blanket covering a mattress of rushes. For the next eight years, he preached at various churches, including some on the Gulf of Mexico coast and Guadalajara, demonstrating his intense and sometimes agonizing devotion to Catholicism. It was in Mexico City that his terrible and bloody self-punishment, committed during his zealous sermons from

13. Ibid., 361.
14. Ibid., 34–35.

the pulpit, both awed and shocked parishioners. At times he beat himself with a stone, or burned his chest with a torch, to encourage penance from worshipers.

In one such instance, a parishioner, overcome from watching Serra strip to his waist and beat himself with a chain, rushed the pulpit and grabbed the chain from Serra. Grasping the thick links, the man then stood before the shocked churchgoers and began thrashing his own back, shouting, amid sobs: "I am the sinner who is ungrateful to God, who ought to do penance for my many sins—and not the father, who is a saint." He suddenly collapsed and died on the church floor as Serra and others tried to revive him and administer last rites.[15]

Time and time again, as Palóu writes, Serra punished himself, "following the example of St. Francis Solanus." Serra's apparent self-loathing (he referred to himself as a "sinner") also led to his lashing himself frequently in his monastic cell. As added self-punishment, Serra wore a thin burlap undershirt interwoven with a wire mesh containing chest-piercing barbs. Palóu speculates that Serra's self-torture may have led to a pulmonary illness, because his self-inflicted injuries included seriously burning himself. This often resulted in the tearing "out [of] a piece of skin; from this practice at times he was very badly injured."[16]

At times in the friary where he lived, Serra would find an empty church choir section and there lash himself fiercely. His fellow friars, drawn by the echoing sound in the church, would gather around the site to find out who was scourging himself.[17] Franciscan scholars consider Serra's mortification extreme, going beyond "the prescribed regulations of the college."[18]

Yet in Serra's mind it was the only way to pay homage to God. Linked to that attitude was his dedication to the vows he had made to spread Catholicism, especially among the natives of the New World. His devotion to Roman Catholicism, like that of the thousands of other religious people who flocked to *Nueva España*, would be passed on to the Indians—whether they wanted it or not.

---

15. Ibid., 41–42.

16. Ibid., 274.

17. Ibid., 279.

18. Geiger, *Life and Times of Fray Junípero Serra*, 146–147.

When Serra arrived in Mexico, he brought with him an attitude that prevailed among both clerical and secular Spaniards who traveled to the new, vast empire—that the great achievements of the Incas, Maya, and Aztecs meant nothing. The culture and beliefs of all indigenous people, in the minds of the Spanish, were demonic. They had to be destroyed and replaced with the Christian belief in a single God and the complex accompanying Catholic morality, theology, and rituals. Only then would the Indians be properly indoctrinated to become part of Spanish society, albeit at the lowest level.

Catholicism would save the Indians from their sinful and evil "pagan" way of life. Any opposition by the Indians was useless against the priests, backed up by heavily armed Spanish soldiers. The goal of the Spanish clergy was to instill in the Indians a faith in which they could never question the will of God. Devotion to God and obedience to his servants on earth—the clergy—would ensure that after death the Indians would be granted an everlasting and glorious life in the Kingdom of Heaven.

Despite the heroic efforts of a handful of clergy like Bishop Bartolomeo de las Casas, who, as early as the sixteenth century had spoken out vehemently against the cruelties inflicted on the Indians, the Spanish clergy's attitude toward the Indians remained unchanged into the eighteenth and nineteenth centuries. Although Serra's keen mind dissected the complexities of Catholic theology brilliantly, he was blind to granting any human rights to the Indians. He never considered, as de las Casas had earlier, that even in the Century of Light in which Serra lived, the developing rights of European citizens could also apply to the Indians of the New World.

Although science had proved the earth revolves around the sun, Serra refused to accept those findings. In Mallorca, he had lectured: "Contrary to Copernicus, I suppose it [is] absolutely manifest that the earth remains immovable and that all the heavens . . . are moved in a circle. I say, moreover, that the Spheres are not moved by themselves but by certain Intelligences or Angels."[19]

Serra's attitude was buried deep in medieval thought, and he reveled in it. To him, God and Catholicism were the sources of all knowledge and therefore unchangeable. Science and inalienable rights were subjects to be banned from consideration.

---

19. James A. Sandos, *Converting California: Indians and Franciscans in the Missions* (New Haven: Yale University Press, 2004), 80.

Serra wholeheartedly accepted the belief of the New World Catholic orders that priests were the "parents" of the Indians. They needed to treat them as children, no matter what their age or social status, by providing guidance and administering frequent corporal punishment. That being the case, one has to then consider what type of parents would deny their offspring eventual freedom and subject them to beatings, floggings, and other punishments, such as being placed in shackles that did not allow them to bend their knees for days on end.

It is doubtful that Serra ever engaged in theological or philosophical discussions with the Indians under his care. Yet by contrast, those two subjects appear to be the only things he ever discussed with his Spanish acquaintances, both within the church and outside it. Those conversations and sermons could be so drawn out that Palóu gently chided him. In conversation, Palóu wrote, Serra:

> . . . appeared to be carried away. As a result they were longer than is usual, a fact which to many, particularly those who had little relish for the divine word, was a source of annoyance. There were not lacking those who said he did not follow the admonition[20] of Our Seraphic Father St. Francis.[21]

From 1759, when he returned from the Cerro Gordo, to 1767, as Serra trod from mission to mission, he was unaware that his life was about to change abruptly. The friar's most fervent wish—to gather new souls for Christ—was about to be fulfilled in greater measure than ever before.

On June 25, 1767, European persecution of the Jesuits reached New Spain. Spanish King Carlos III ordered the members of the Holy Society of Jesus expelled from Spain's conquered lands. In Spain, Portugal, France, and Naples, the Jesuits were accused of engaging in wholesale commerce, in violation of rigid rules delineating who could participate in commercial activity. In addition, the Jesuits were charged with being more loyal to the pope than to the kings of the various nations where they lived. The abrupt expulsion of the Jesuits from the New World left the missions of Lower California without priests.

---

20. St. Francis had admonished that the friars' "discourses be chaste and examined for the utility and edification of the people, announcing to them vices and virtues, punishment and glory, with brevity of speech because the Lord made His word short upon earth."

21. Palóu, *Palóu's Life of Fray Junípero Serra*, 282.

After founding the first of eighteen missions on October 19, 1697, those Jesuit priests and others who followed them from the mainland introduced smallpox, typhus, and plague to the peninsula, devastating the indigenous people. By 1829, the Indian population of Baja California was nonexistent and the missions collapsed, unable to continue without the labor of the Indian neophytes.

Less than a month after the expulsion of the Jesuits, the *Colegio de San Fernando* in Mexico City chose Serra to take over the missions where Indian survivors of the pandemics still lived. A messenger was dispatched from Mexico City to find Serra, who was preaching in towns and villages outside of the capital. Upon being told of the urgent need for his presence at the *colegio*, Serra returned, arriving on July 12. He was briefed on his new assignment and accepted it with enthusiasm. Within three days of his return, he and twelve other friars left Mexico City, bound for the isolated, arid peninsula off Mexico's west coast. It was an arduous trip that involved sailing across the *Mar de Cortés* (Gulf of California).

With stops in Querétaro and Guadalajara, it took the group thirty-nine days to reach Tepic, a port city on the central west coast of Mexico. They arrived there on August 21, discovering that two small packet boats designated to carry them to Baja California were still under construction and would not be ready for months. Four more friars joined them as they lingered in that sweltering city for nearly half a year, conducting missions in the area.

Finally, on March 12, 1768, the band of friars sailed at dusk for Loreto, a tiny mission and capital of the region's east coast, about 300 miles north of its southern tip. They arrived there on April 1, and by April 6 the friars, under Serra's direction, had scattered to take over the various missions the Jesuits had founded. They were under orders from the Spanish government not to make any innovations until the arrival of Visitor General Don José de Gálvez. Setting sail from San Blas on May 24, Gálvez arrived in Baja California on July 6, anchored his ship at Cerralvo Bay south of Loreto, and established his headquarters in nearby Santa Ana.

In addition to inspecting the existing missions, Gálvez, in conjunction with Serra, began the grand task of organizing the settlement of Alta California, beginning with missions at San Diego and Monterey. For his part, Serra envisioned using soldiers to keep the Indians under tight control and to protect the missions from outside attack. Other missions in the New World allowed Indians to work during the day on their own fields, but required them to attend Mass twice daily. Under Serra's plan, the Indians would live within the missions and become staunch Catholics. Unmarried women would be strictly separated from unmarried men to avoid sin. The anticipation of baptizing countless Indian souls while keeping those souls untarnished brought joy to Serra's heart.

Nearly twelve months passed before all preparations were completed for the massive undertaking that lay before them. The expedition to Alta California would be led by Gaspar de Portolá, who would, albeit briefly, become the first military governor of California before returning to Mexico. Under Portolá's direction, the expedition was separated into two parts. One part of the expedition would be transported by two ships, the *San Antonio* and the *San Carlos*, and head for Monterey Bay. Meanwhile, the second section would travel overland to the same destination. The overland group was further separated into two parties. The first party would be headed by Don Fernando de Rivera y Moncada[22], a military officer who had distinguished himself in Baja California. Portolá and Serra would lead the second overland party and would trail Rivera's group, serving as a backup in case the first party was attacked by Indians.

The *San Carlos* sailed first, carrying friars, soldiers, supplies, and ammunition, while the *San Antonio* weighed anchor a few days later. The land expeditions were expected to forage for their supplies along the way, stopping at the missions in Baja California to obtain "dried and salted meat, seeds, flour, *pinole*[23], and hardtack."[24] Portolá and Moncada would provide vouchers to the missions for what they had taken.[25]

Just before setting out, Serra's bad leg had become swollen and painful. En route, Portolá had stopped at Palóu's mission in Baja California and expressed concern that Serra's leg was not healing. He feared it might be cancerous and, if so, he doubted the friar would survive the trip. The commander had implored Serra to stay behind, but the stoic friar insisted

---

22. Rivera had formerly commanded a unit of the leather jacket cavalry in Loreto. The term "leather jackets" referred to thick leather vests with high collars worn by the cavalry, so thick that Indian arrows could not penetrate them. The riders' legs were protected by chaps of the same deer hide, not only to protect against Indian arrows but also to stave off brush when riding through it.

23. *Pinole* was corn flour used to make tortillas or a thick gruel or drink called *atole*, sometimes mixed with chocolate and sugar.

24. Palóu, *Palóu's Life of Fray Junípero Serra*, 60.

25. Ibid.

he could continue, telling Portolá to launch his part of the expedition and he would catch up with him.

Portolá's concern regarding Serra was so great he even wrote to Gálvez, warning him about the friar's condition and urging he not make the trip. Gálvez was aware of the swollen leg but, likewise, had been unable to stop Serra.

Wracked by pain, Serra eventually arrived at Palóu's Mission San Francisco Xavier after Portolá's part of the expedition had passed through. His faithful friend was shocked at the condition and appearance of Serra's limb. During the friar's three-day stay, Palóu begged the Franciscan not to make the trip, arguing that he would go in Serra's place. "I remonstrated with him over the condition of his foot and leg and about the evident impossibility of making so extended a journey . . . that he should not go with the poor health and little strength he possessed."[26]

Serra shrugged aside all concern regarding his serious condition. Astride a mule and escorted by two soldiers and a servant, he caught up with Portolá for the trip to Velicatá, a site with ample water and vegetation. Here Portolá and Serra founded Mission San Fernando Rey de España de Velicatá on May 15, 1769.

Serra was shocked when a dozen male Indians, nude as was their custom, visited the camp. Serra's account of that meeting speaks for itself regarding the friar's attitude toward the Indians' ways:

> I saw what I could hardly begin to believe . . . namely that they go about entirely naked like Adam in Paradise before the fall. . . though they saw all of us clothed they nevertheless showed not the least trace of shame, in their manner of nudity.[27]

Like virtually all of the Indians that the expedition encountered en route to San Diego, the natives arrived bearing gifts. They carried roasted agaves and four large fish which, unfortunately, had spoiled because the natives had not gutted them. The roasted agaves were the lower portion of the century plant, stripped of its fibrous branches and cooked—a common food for the Indians.

The next day, May 15, after founding the mission, the expedition continued its trek to San Diego. En route, Serra's condition worsened to the point that he could neither sit nor stand because of the intense pain in

26. Palóu, *Palóu's Life of Fray Junípero Serra*, 62.
27. Ibid., 65.

his foot and leg. Portolá halted the expedition, and blankets were spread on the ground and Serra laid gently on top of them. Portolá, dismounted and walked over to where Serra was being tended. He knelt next to the friar and told him it was impossible for him to continue the journey. Yet Serra again stubbornly refused to be left behind, declaring he would rather die en route than be taken back and abandon the expedition.

The commander resigned himself to Serra's decision and, realizing that the friar could neither ride nor walk, ordered a litter built. An Indian crew from those accompanying the group would carry Serra. The Franciscan, mortified that he would have to be carried and become a severe burden to the Indians, summoned the muleteer and asked him if he knew of a remedy for his leg.

The muleteer, perhaps exasperated with Serra's stubbornness, snapped: "Father, what remedy could I know of? Do you think I'm a surgeon? I'm a muleteer; I've healed only the sores of the animals." Unfazed, Serra quickly answered: "Well, then, son, just imagine me to be an animal, and that this wound is the sore of an animal from which I have developed this swelling of the leg and great pains I experience, which permit me neither to rest nor to sleep. Make me the same remedy which you would apply to an animal."[28]

Hearing Serra's reasoning, the muleteer and others around the stricken friar smiled. The muleteer then strode off to gather herbs, which he mixed with tallow and then ground between two stones. He then fried the mixture and, after it had cooled, applying the salve to Serra's foot and leg. Whatever its properties, the concoction allowed Serra to rise the next morning virtually free of pain and able to continue on the long journey.

Meanwhile, the *San Carlos* had finally set sail from Loreto on January 9, 1769. On May 14, nearly four months later, Rivera's expedition found it and the *San Antonio* already at anchor when they arrived in San Diego. However, they were horrified when they learned that virtually all the *San Carlos's* crew had died of thirst and from an unknown and highly contagious disease. The ship, the first to set sail, had glided past San Diego due to a navigational error, wandered too far north, and its badly-made water barrels had leaked out their precious supply. The ship's captain had immediately made toward land to refill the casks, but the only water they could find was so brackish it made all of the crew ill. One by one, the crewmen

---

28. Ibid., 67–69

died of thirst and "scurvy."[29] Those who survived were so weak they were unable to even lower boats and search for water.

On July 1, 1769, after six weeks of traveling in four-hour stretches (and sometimes only two hours) with the ailing Serra, the second land expedition arrived at San Diego. Climbing over a hill, Portolá's party spotted the camp that had been set up near the shore of the bay. Portolá's men immediately began firing wildly into the air to greet Rivera's men and the sailors from the two vessels. Soldiers in the camp, startled at first by the gunfire, rejoiced as they quickly heard the cheers from the arriving group. They raced to their stacked rifles and also began cheering and firing into the air, some waving their hats wildly. Soon the cannons from the *San Antonio* welcomed the arrivals by firing deafening volleys that boomed across the beach.

The air filled with thick clouds of acrid white smoke while both groups shouted greetings to each other. Indians who had visited the group with fish to trade for clothes, cowered, flinched, and grimaced at the incredible blasts of rifle and cannon fire. For the natives of Alta California, the event was a bitter taste of things to come.

---

29. While Palóu writes that the crew died of scurvy, it is more likely they died of a combination of illnesses caused by the brackish water and, perhaps, scurvy.

6

An Ordeal of Tears

*. . . and two or three whippings which Your Lordship may order applied to them on
different days may serve, for them and for the rest, for a warning may be of spiritual
benefit to all.*
—Friar Junípero Serra, on July 31, 1775, requesting that Spanish Governor
Fernando de Rivera y Moncado flog four mission Indians as punishment for
attempting to escape from Mission Carmel.

Fifteen days after arriving in San Diego in 1769, Serra founded Mission
San Diego de Alcalá (Mission San Diego), the first Spanish mission of
Alta California. The date was July 16, the day Spaniards celebrated a 1212
victory over the Moors in Spain called the Triumph of the Most Holy
Cross. Serra felt that the date was fitting, as he would use the Holy Cross
to drive out "the whole army of hell and subject to the sweet yoke of our
holy Faith the barbarous pagans who inhabited this New California."[1]

Curious Indians, unaware of what was to befall them, flocked to the site
and gathered around the Spaniards, listening to the sounds of a language they
could not understand. They had looked on with awe as Serra celebrated a
Mass of thanksgiving on a rudimentary altar with the faint sound of crashing
surf in the background. Resplendent in gold-embroidered vestments, Serra
intoned the Catholic Mass melodiously as he handled the glittering gold and
silver artifacts used in the service. Small bells rang softly, and the perfumed
white smoke of incense swirled across the altar and the kneeling worshipers.
Within days, the Indians were led to understand that Serra, as a priest, was
transforming wine into blood, and that the round white wafer that Serra delicately swallowed had also been changed into the body of Christ.

1. Palóu, *Palóu's Life of Fray Junípero Serra* (Richmond, Academy of American Franciscan
History, William Byrd Press 1955), 75.

The founding ceremony was held seven days after the *San Antonio* had sailed for San Blas to pick up sailors to replace those who had died aboard the *San Carlos*. Misfortune, however, did not escape the *San Antonio*. Nine of its crew died within the time it took to reach San Blas, apparently infected with the same disease that had wreaked havoc with its sister ship. Serra and friars Juan Vizcaíno and Fernando Parrón, while waiting for the return of the *San Antonio*, turned to nursing the sick men. A makeshift hospital was set up at the San Diego encampment, along with crude huts made of branches and bushes.

When not nursing the sick, Serra and the two friars held Mass daily and followed their Franciscan routine as closely as they could, including rising at midnight for matins, their nighttime prayer. Whenever Serra had a few minutes to himself, he spent it mending his now-ragged undertunic. He would eventually prepare a note requesting a replacement "of the thickest wool" to help ward off the cold.[2] His letter would be carried on the return trip of one of the vessels supplying the outpost. Work on the new mission, to be located at a site with a view of the port and suitable for an adjacent future town, was postponed until the expedition had recovered from the deadly epidemic that had crippled its numbers.

On July 14, two days prior to the founding ceremony, Portolá had set out leading a land expedition of nearly 100 men to Monterey. He left behind Serra, eight soldiers, and the two other friars to await the return of the *San Antonio*. Portolá's company consisted of sixty-six men, including his second-in-command Captain Rivera; twenty-five leather-jacket soldiers; and friars Juan Crespí and Francisco Gómez. Muleteers, servants, and Indian guards from Mexico made up the rest of the group.

Within the San Diego camp, Indians, who now visited almost daily, became bolder and sought to filch tools and supplies, and even the Spaniards' own clothing. On August 14, the Indians launched an attack that killed one Spaniard, although the Indians were quickly driven off in the short-lived skirmish.[3]

The violence prompted one of the soldiers, Sergeant José F. Ortega, to write a foreboding letter to Palóu in Baja California, advising him that "a strong guard is needed at every establishment for only force can conquer the avarice and duplicity of the Indian." He added, gloomily, "there is

---

2. Serra to Friar Prades, San Diego, 3 July, 1769; Junípero Serra Collection, document 185, Santa Barbara Mission Archive Library.

3. See Chapter 10 for a full account of the attack.

little hope of converting the Indians of San Diego."[4] Nevertheless, some Indians did eventually join the San Diego mission, though not as many as the friars desired. Some sought alliance with the powerful Spanish, while others were enticed with the promise of three meals a day and joining a religion which, they were convinced, had a powerful God.

In the aftermath of the attack, Serra was able to persuade several young Indians to become Christians and prepared them for baptism. Young Indians would make up the first converts in every mission, curious to join the Spaniards with their steel weapons, and enthused by the friars' promises of an easier life. Older Indians kept their distance. Although Serra could not speak the Indian language, he did have an Indian boy in the expedition whom he ordered to learn the native tongue. With help from the youth, Serra was able to communicate somewhat with the Indians. It is doubtful, however, that the Indians were able to fully understand Catholicism, including the centuries-old traditions of Western Europe. Most likely, the friars taught the Indians to simply mouth the sounds of the Spanish words in the liturgy. Although the Indians did not know what the words meant, it was sufficient for Serra to baptize them as Catholics.

For the next six months, during which the expedition celebrated Christmas and the New Year, the Spaniards at San Diego heard nothing from Portolá. Finally, on January 14, 1770, his expedition straggled back, weary from their long journey and low on food and supplies. Portolá reported that they had missed finding Monterey, but had discovered the huge San Francisco Bay. However, after poring through maps stored at San Diego, Portolá realized the site where they had planted a cross was, indeed, Monterey. Depressed and weary because he had not recognized Monterey and fearful that their supplies would run out, Portolá made a fateful decision: Unless the supply ships San José or San Antonio returned by mid-March with fresh supplies, the entire expedition would abandon San Diego and return to Mexico on March 20.

Serra, realizing that his hope of baptizing the Indians of California would be shattered if they turned back, met with the captain of the San Carlos, which was still anchored at the port. Inside the captain's cabin, he and Serra reached a secret agreement. If Portolá returned to Mexico by a land route, Serra and the friars would come aboard the vessel and await the arrival in San Diego of either the San José or the San Antonio.

---

4. José F. Ortega to Francisco Palóu, 2 February, 1770; Junípero Serra Collection, document 199, Santa Barbara Mission Archive Library.

The friars would embark on whichever ship arrived first and sail north to found a mission at Monterey.[5]

The agreement turned out to be unnecessary. Just one day before Portolá planned return to Mexico, the *San Antonio*, laden with supplies, hove into view off San Diego. Cheering expedition members spotted the ship as Serra and his friars were celebrating St. Joseph's Day in their ramshackle church. Serra was overjoyed. With fresh supplies, he could continue north to Monterey to found the second mission in California, where he intended to establish his headquarters as president of the missions. This step would greatly further his goal of "harvesting" as many pagan souls as he could.

Within a few days, Serra was aboard the *San Antonio* sailing to Monterey Bay. Friars Vizcaíno and Parrón stayed in San Diego while Friar Juan Crespí traveled overland to Monterey with Portolá, the Spanish officer now confident of the location of the bay. Under Serra's plan, Crespí, upon arriving in Monterey, would then travel to San Buenaventura, nearly 200 miles south of the new presidio and roughly halfway between Monterey and San Diego, to found a third mission.

After what Serra described as a "distressful sea voyage of a month and a half,"[6] the *San Antonio* arrived at Monterey on May 31, 1770. Portolá's expedition was waiting for them, having arrived eight days earlier. On June 3, 1770, amid cannon blasts and musket fire, Serra celebrated Mass for the first time in the area. This was followed by the planting of a large cross and the unfurling of the Spanish king's royal standards, signifying formal acquisition of the land. Mission *San Carlos Borromeo de Carmelo* (Mission Carmel), Serra's headquarters in Alta California, had become a reality. Adjacent to it was Spain's seat of government, *El Presidio Real de San Carlos de Monterey*. The Franciscan relayed the good news to his friend Palóu in Baja California, along with a request that he send incense and church candles to Monterey.

Serra considered his arrival in California to be a moment of monumental importance, given the scope of the project before him. He was energized by the attitude that the spirituality of religion was far more important than carnal earthly life. Death was the important step toward reaching heaven, an event meant for rejoicing, not bereavement. The diminutive

---

5. Palóu, *Palóu's Life of Fray Junípero Serra*, 87.
6. Ibid., 92–93.

friar's fanatical zeal to serve the Christian God would lead him to establish a policy of packing each mission with as many Native Americans as he could, heedless of the quality of life within those compounds. For the sake of possibly saving their souls, his actions most certainly did make material life difficult and often miserable for the Indians, through the forced daily attendance of Mass, the separation of boys and men from girls and unmarried women, and the severe punishment meted out to those who violated mission rules and restrictions.

As *padre presidente* of the missions, Serra began his task of having his fellow friars Christianize as many souls as they could, either forcibly or by gentle persuasion. The king's command that the friars educate the Indians and turn them into loyal and free Spanish subjects apparently fell by the wayside as religious goals were instead prioritized. Realizing that more Indian attacks were possible, Serra ordered the building of a strong wooden wall around Mission Monterey, protecting the initial crude huts that had been built to serve as living quarters, workshops, and the first church.

Portolá soon returned to Mexico, and Don Pedro Fages became the commanding officer of the Monterey complex, albeit with only a handful of soldiers. One of his first decisions was to tell Serra he could not spare any soldiers for a journey to San Buenaventura, where the friar sought to found the third California mission.[7] Fearful of an Indian attack, Fages did not want to risk dispersing his main force. The founding of Mission San Buenaventura would have to wait until the Spanish reinforcements were sent from Mexico.

That setback, however, did not dismay the Spanish viceroy in Mexico City, Don Carlos Francisco de Croix. He rejoiced when told that Spain now had missions and presidios in San Diego and Monterey. Almost immediately, on the viceroy's orders, the pealing of church bells echoed across Mexico City, while printers hurriedly issued notices announcing Spain's success in Alta California.[8] As fast as the notices were printed, government workers raced to bundle them, then scurried to paste the notices on walls and doors. Crowds quickly gathered to read the exciting news and share the euphoria that Spain had once more expanded its borders. Across the city, the news spread from mouth to mouth in the homes of the ruling elite. Hot chocolate was brewed, port and red wine

---

7. Palóu, *Palóu's Life of Fray Junípero Serra*, 132.
8. Ibid, 97–98.

bottles were uncorked, mugs and fine crystal glasses were filled, and the king was toasted by his loyal subjects, honoring his vision for a still-expanding empire.

As part of the celebration, the viceroy ordered the founding of five new missions in Alta California—to be named San Francisco, Santa Clara, San Gabriel Arcangel, San Antonio de Padua, and San Luis Obispo de Tolosa. Additionally, ten new friars were to be sent to staff another five missions in Baja California between San Fernando de Velicatá and San Diego. Those missions, not all of which were ultimately founded, were to be named San Joaquin, Santa Ana, San Juan Capistrano, San Pasqual Baylón, and San Felix de Cantalicio. Under the viceroy's authorization and budget, government workers and the *Colegio de San Fernando* quickly began assembling and crating the shipment of goods that would be needed for the new missions.

In Monterey, Serra continued the task of Christianizing the Indians. With the aid of his young Indian translator, Serra was able to entice Monterey-area Indians into baptism. The first such ceremony occurred on December 26, 1770. That event, and others that followed, involved a two-step strategy. First, an intense fear of the Spaniards was instilled in the Indians to keep them from overwhelming the Europeans' small numbers. Second, they were steeped in the Christian belief that God looked over them all and had proven his love of them by sacrificing himself.[9] Once they were baptized, the mission Indians became neophytes.

Serra abandoned an initial plan to convert the Indians to Catholicism within the missions and then settle them in nearby Catholic towns because of his fears they would fall victims to what he considered the sinful life of the pioneers from Mexico.[10] Under his revised policies, the Indians would be forced to spend the rest of their lives within the missions, as would their children and their children's children. By 1773, Serra had baptized 165 Indians.[11]

Meanwhile, Serra's plan to establish Mission San Buenaventura continued to be frustrated by Fages. At the core of their dispute was Fages's attitude that he and his soldiers should not be subordinate to the missions. Serra and the friars believed otherwise.[12] Despite Serra's appeals,

9. Ibid, 95.

10. Ibid., 102.

11. Ibid., 95.

12. Theodore H. Hittell, *History of California*, Vol. 1 (San Francisco: N.J. Stone, 1897), 511.

the commander remained steadfast in his refusal to provide extra soldiers to guard yet a third mission, or to supply the mules needed to carry the supplies for it. Instead, Fages's strategy was focused on establishing an efficient Spanish fort that would be suitable for an adjacent pueblo, populated by settlers who were expected to come from Mexico. In Fages's mind, the future town in Monterey was far more important than using his men and supplies to help Serra establish a new mission.

A major divide that arose between Serra and Fages was the unruly behavior of the Spanish soldiers during their off-duty time. While Fages inflicted a stringent discipline on his men when they were on duty, he did virtually nothing to restrict them during their free time. The Spanish soldiers exercised little restraint in seeking out Indian women and abusing them. Indian complaints of rape and mistreatment quickly prompted Serra to berate Fages for not punishing his men when they committed such crimes.

An equally serious problem was the shortage of food in the missions. Serra and Fages had received pleas for help from the San Diego mission and presidio, warning they were on the brink of being abandoned because of a shortage of supplies. The problem had ensued after carpenters, masons, and blacksmiths were brought from Mexico to build and maintain the fort and mission. The mission could not produce enough food to feed the immigrants, soldiers, and Indian neophytes. The plea for help from San Diego was quickly answered by Monterey. A long pack mule train was assembled, laden with food from Monterey's own food stocks, and sent on its way to the Southern California mission. The effort, however, forced Fages to begin trading beads, cloth, and sugar with the Indians in exchange for seeds and meat, as the community awaited the arrival of the next supply ship, already three months late.[13]

At the core of the food problem was the fact that the founding friars had little or no knowledge of agriculture and the procedures needed to ensure bountiful and healthy crops. Serra had not bothered to screen the friars he had selected to determine if they knew farming techniques, let alone carpentry or animal husbandry—all critical for the successful operation of the new missions.

The combination of Fages's intransigence and the need to alleviate food and supply problems at the missions finally pushed Serra to action. The Franciscan felt he had no recourse other than to begin an arduous trek

13. Ibid., 122–123.

to Mexico City to seek Fages's dismissal and plead with the new Spanish viceroy, Antonio Mariá de Bucareli y Ursúa (who had replaced de Croix), for help in establishing San Buenaventura and other missions. Serra also planned to request that supplies to Alta California being sent via ship rather than mule train.

Serra left Monterey on October 17, 1772, on the nearly four-month journey, arriving in Mexico City on February 6, 1773. He began lobbying Bucareli to have Fages removed.[14] He also requested the missions be given full responsibility for the training, governance, discipline, and education of their baptized Indians. The only exception would be in the case of capital offenses such as murder, the prosecution of which would be the responsibility of the military commander. Bucareli ordered Fages be replaced by Fernando de Rivera y Moncada, Portolá's former second-in-command. Bucareli balked at Serra's other requests, though he sympathized and said only that he would give them serious consideration.

His mission completed successfully, Serra returned to Alta California and reached Mission Carmel on May 11, 1774. The new commander, however, would not resolve Serra's problems. Rivera, like his predecessor, was an enlightened man who had little time for missions. The development and founding of secular towns in California was foremost in his mind. Rivera was adamant that he did not have enough soldiers and supplies to carry out his goal of developing California while simultaneously caring for Serra's missions. Like Fages, Rivera informed Serra he could not spare any soldiers to guard Mission San Buenaventura.

Rivera had no patience with centuries-old Catholic rules. In one incident, the commander stormed into the San Diego mission and seized an Indian suspected of being involved in an attack on the mission. Rivera brushed aside the local friar's pleas that the Indian had fled into the church and had been granted sanctuary. When Serra learned of the incident, he fumed at Rivera's action, saying that it warranted his excommunication, the harshest penalty the church could impose on anyone. Earlier, without notifying Rivera, Serra had sent a troop of soldiers to recapture Indians who had fled from Mission Monterey. Rivera was not inclined to recapture fugitive Indians and sternly warned Serra never to use his men for such purposes without notifying him first.

---

14. Palóu, *Palóu's Life of Fray Junípero Serra*, 137–139.

Despite the animosity between the two men, Serra saw no conflict in sending a group of runaways to Rivera, requesting that he whip them. In a letter dated July 31, 1775, Serra wrote:

> Last Friday I sent out eleven adults with the servant Cypriano. They were to go to the mountains to search for my lost sheep. Last night they brought nine neophytes of this mission. I am sending four of these to your Lordship. They are Cristóbal, Carlos, Geronimo, and Ildefonso, all married men. Their wives are staying here at the rancheria. The first three have deserted a number of times, and although they have been punished at various times, there is no sign of amendment. This is the first desertion of the fourth, who is a new Christian; but he stayed away a long time. However, his character is that he could become the ringleader. Only one is missing, a companion of the first three; and when I succeed in finding him, he can take the place of the fourth. I am sending them to you so that a period of exile, and two or three whippings which Your Lordship may order applied to them on different days may serve, for them and for the rest, for a warning, may be of spiritual benefit to all; and this last is the prime motive of our work. If Your Lordship does not have shackles, with your permission they may be sent from here. I think that the punishment should last one month.

> I wish Your Lordship all health, and that God Our Lord may grant you many years in His holy grace.

> Mission of San Carlos, Fray Junípero Serra[15]

The friar's offer to provide shackles to Rivera to restrain the Indians is proof that such restraints were used by Serra's mission (and throughout the California missions) to imprison—in chains or stocks—any neophyte who violated mission rules or habitually attempted to run away. Whether Rivera actually lashed the Indians, as the Franciscan requested, is not known.

Much to Serra's pleasure, Rivera stayed in Alta California for only a year before being promoted to lieutenant governor of Baja California. The friar's rejoicing at Rivera's promotion was, however, short-lived. The governor's replacement, Felipe de Neve, became Serra's nemesis. Neve ruled California as governor from 1775 to 1782, first from Loreto in

---

15. *Diario del Capitan Comandante Fernando de Rivera y Moncada*, Vol. I, *Coleccion Chimalistic*, ed. Ernest J. Burrus (Madrid: José Porrua Turanzas, 1967), 165.

Mexico, and then from 1777 to the end of his term from Monterey. Serra and Neve quarreled bitterly during the governor's entire tenure.

The new governor, like Rivera, considered the development of secular towns his primary goal in California. Likewise, he believed that all human beings, including Indians, had basic rights that could not be denied. One of those rights was personal freedom, something that Serra simply could not condone. Men like Neve believed that religion was neither sacrosanct nor necessary to guarantee a moral society. Serra, in contrast, was mired in church dogma, which he had twisted into a terrible, dark benevolence. He maintained that the baptism of Indians granted him the responsibility to deny them liberty, based on his belief that only by shielding the baptized Indians from what he considered the coarseness of normal human life would they ascend to heaven upon their deaths—which was a tragically frequent outcome.

Without the looming threat of punishment, it is likely the Indians would have quickly abandoned the missions once they determined that their freedom was being denied. Serra's defense of maintaining the neophytes in a state of captivity is aptly illustrated in an exchange of opinions with Neve, who was seeking authorization from Spanish officials in Mexico City to grant self-government to the California mission Indians. In 1779, Neve made the request in accordance with the order by Spanish King Carlos III that all Indians were to be freed from the missions and allowed self-government after ten years of education. In seeking improvement for the neophytes, he did not hide his opinion that the mission Indians' fate was "worse than that of slaves."[16]

Neve, as part of his policy to help the neophytes, had ordered Serra to have the mission Indians elect their own leaders in an effort to prepare them for self-government. (Prior to Neve's edict, the friars had selected certain Indians to be *alcaldes*, who acted as quasi-mayors and represented the interests of the Indians before the friars.) The governor's action was aimed at breaking the stranglehold the missions had on delaying the Indians' full participation in the development of California.

Almost immediately, Serra, in a letter dated March 29, 1779, to Friar Fermín Francisco de Lasuén, his eventual successor, schemed to sabotage Neve's orders and deny the Indians any form of self-representation. In a strategy that can only be described as Machiavellian, Serra sought

---

16. Edwin A. Beilharz, *Felipe de Neve: First Governor of California* (San Francisco: California Historical Society, 1971), 52; Sandos, *Converting California*, 71.

and obtained Lasuén's support to pretend to comply with Neve's orders. They would accept the letter of decree from the governor but withhold its details from the Indians, informing them only that the action was aimed at preparing them for self-government. The elections would be held, but because the friars were to count the votes and declare the winners, they could easily rig the results to elect only Indians that could be counted on to obey their orders.

In a letter to Lasuén that outlined the conspiracy, Serra wrote: "Be prudent as the serpent and simple as doves, but the serpent was more cunning for it . . . what more could we ask for?"[17] The friar had outwitted the California governor's effort to improve the mission Indian's lives.

The *padre presidente*, adamant in his belief that the Indians were incapable of self-government, insisted in a January 7, 1780, letter to Neve that he and his friars could not free the Indians, relinquish their authority to use "blows" to punish and control them, or relinquish directing the future elected mayors:

> That the spiritual fathers [friars] should punish their sons, the Indians, by blows appears to be as old as the conquest of these kingdoms, and so general, in fact, that the saints do not seem to be any exception to the rule. Undoubtedly, the first to evangelize these shores followed the practice, and they surely were saints . . . In the life of Saint Francis Solano, who has been solemnly canonized, we read that, while he had a special gift from God to soften the ferocity of the most barbarous by the sweetness of his mission in the province of Tucumán in Peru—so we are told in his biography—when they failed to carry out his orders, he gave directions for his Indians to be whipped by his *fiscales*.
>
> Now the *alcaldes* are likewise sons to the missionary fathers, and as such they are likewise under their care. Seeing that they are not less in need of direction, correction, and training, I do not see by what law, or what line of reasoning, it can be argued that they should be exempt.[18]

Simply stated, Serra had no reluctance to harshly punish the Indians. He argued that if a Catholic saint like Francisco Solano used such methods, he and his friars should be similarly able to whip the Indians,

---

17. Serra to Friar Fermín Francisco Lasuén, Monterey, 29 March 1779, in *Writings of Junípero Serra*, Vol. III, 294–297; Junípero Serra Collection, document 266, Santa Barbara Mission Archive Library.

18. Serra to Governor Felipe de Neve, Monterey, 7 January 1780, in *Writings of Junípero Serra*, Vol. III, 413-415; Junípero Serra Collection, document 278, Santa Barbara Mission Archives Library.

using the friar-appointed *alcaldes* for that purpose. Serra, in the same letter, also shrugged off excesses in Indian corporal punishment:

> I am willing to admit that in the infliction of punishment we are now discussing, there may have been some inequalities and excesses on the part of the fathers and that we are all exposed to err in that regard.[19]

Sadly, Serra's arguments prevailed, and the friars continued authorizing the use of whips, sharpened prods, shackles, and stocks by the *alcaldes* to punish their flock.

Death came quickly to the Indians in the California missions. Epidemics, mainly of European diseases for which the Indians had no immunity, were almost continuous, and were aggravated by horribly over-crowded and filthy living conditions. Rather than express grief over the deaths, Serra rejoiced. And, according to his biographer and close friend, Friar Francisco Palóu, Serra frequently proclaimed, "Thanks be to God that by now there is not a mission that does not have sons in heaven."[20]

Even the many deaths of Indian children did not faze Serra's dark joy. In a report dated July 24, 1775, to Friar Francisco Pangua, his Franciscan superior at the *Colegio de San Fernando* in Mexico City, Serra wrote:

> In the midst of all our little troubles, the spiritual side of the missions is developing most happily. In [Mission] San Antonio[21] there are simultaneously two harvests, at one time, one for wheat, and of a plague among the children, who are dying.[22]

Indian deaths created for the friars a more earthly concern about the diminished manpower needed to run each mission. Their solution was to use harsh means, including threats and outright kidnapping, to induce fresh groups of Indians to leave their villages for the missions, replacing those who had died.

The goal of Christianizing the Indians was a failure, due largely to the Franciscans' belief that it was unnecessary to teach the Indians proper Spanish, or for the friars (with a few exceptions) to learn the natives'

---

19. Ibid.

20. Palóu, *Palóu's Life of Fray Junípero Serra*, 277.

21. Mission San Antonio de Padua was founded on July 12, 1771, about sixty miles south of Mission Carmel.

22. Serra to Francisco Pangua, Father Superior of the College of San Fernando in Mexico City, Monterey, 24 July, 1775, in *Writings of Junípero Serra*, Vol. II; *Cartas de Junípero Serra*, Fol. 64–65, Biblioteca Nacional de Mexico.

tongues so they could fully explain Christian doctrine to the neophytes. When, decades later in 1833, the Indians were freed, many of them manifested their resentment and anger toward the friars by immediately casting aside their Catholicism. Further, the Spanish government, in an effort to erode Indian culture, required the teaching of Christian doctrine only in Spanish and not in any native language. They also said Mass, including the sermon, only in Latin, which to Indian ears must have been gibberish.

Not all Indians welcomed the friars or joined the missions. In the fall of 1775, six years after its founding, the Indians surrounding mission San Diego, angered that the Spanish invaders were usurping their land, attacked the mission with 800 to 1,000 warriors, destroying it and killing a priest, a blacksmith, and a carpenter. In the aftermath of the conflict, Spanish military reinforcements arrived and quelled any further uprisings by the Diegueños.[23] The uprising in San Diego was just one of several that shook the California missions during their existence.

As the nonnative population of Alta California began to expand in the late 1700s, the ongoing dispute between Serra and Neve was emblematic of the general conflict between the Franciscans and secular authorities.

In 1779, two years after taking office, Neve issued a set of regulations regarding the development of California. The founding of secular towns or pueblos was the prime goal of the government. Missions were last on the list, and were not to be given allowances for supplies or funds. He decreed that of the eight missions already founded, only those near the presidios would be staffed by two priests, and one of them would have to serve as chaplain to the presidio. The other missions could not increase the number of priests serving at each site. Neve made clear that his policy was to educate the Indians so they would be "fit for future citizenship and self-reliance."[24]

Neve, using the authority conferred on him as governor, also forbade Serra to administer the Sacrament of Confirmation, the Catholic cere-mony in which a person is accepted into the Roman Catholic Church.[25]

---

23. "Diegueños" is the Spanish description of somebody from the San Diego area. The Indians there were the Kumeyaay.

24. John Steven McGroarty, *California, Its History and Romance* (Los Angeles: Grafton, 1911), 131.

25. Palóu, *Palóu's Life of Fray Junípero Serra*, 210–212.

Although Serra maintained that he had been authorized by the pope to administer the rite, he could not produce proof. Without that proof, Neve issued his restriction against Serra, forcing Serra to undertake a lengthy process in which he first had to write to the *Colegio de San Fernando* in Mexico City and have a copy of the papal authorization sent to Monterey. It is very likely that Neve issued the restriction simply to harass and frustrate Serra in his efforts to Christianize the Indians. Eventually, Serra obtained the necessary document and Neve lifted his ban.

Much to Serra's dismay, the governor forged ahead with his major goal. One of his first actions, on November 29, 1777, under orders from Spanish Viceroy Antonio Maria de Bucareli y Ursúa, was to have Lieutenant José Joaquin Moraga establish *El Pueblo de San José de Guadalupe* at the south end of San Francisco Bay. The settlement's purpose was to supply food for the pueblos and presidios in Monterey and San Francisco. Five years later, the town and its Mexican settlers were wholly self-sufficient, producing enough surplus to feed the other two settlements, as well.

In 1781, four years after founding San José, Neve ordered the formal establishment of *El Pueblo de la Reyna de los Angeles* (the Town of the Queen of Angels). It gave stature to a tiny settlement that had been there since 1771, and would later become the sprawling metropolis known as Los Angeles. No mission was founded there, only the pueblo. As with San José, the new Southern California town was created to produce food for the presidio and town in San Diego and the surrounding region's future population.

Neve's decision not to have missions near the new towns was indicative of the strong differences that existed between him and Serra throughout the Spanish official's administration in Alta California. One of the stormiest incidents occurred in the mission at Carmel, where Neve had entered to speak with Serra prior to Mass. The specific subject of their angry encounter, while not known exactly, may have involved Neve's order to Friar Fermín Francisco de Lasuén, then head of Mission San Diego, that mission *alcaldes* be elected at each mission to prepare them for self-government. Lasuén had countered that the friars were not parish priests but missionaries, and that the missions were not pueblos, referring the matter to Serra.[26]

---

26. Serra, *Writings of Junípero Serra*, Vol III, 457n185.

Serra wrote to Lasuén and described his argument with Neves. In the letter, he disputed something Neve had told him. Serra wrote on March 29, 1779, that the governor ". . . brought up something so flatly contrary to the truth that I was shocked, and I shouted out, 'Nobody has ever said that to me, because they could not say it to me!'" Neve then smiled, stating "that he too was a logician and gave me thereby to understand what he was telling me was inferred, even though in itself it was not."

Angrily, Serra countered that Neve's logic "was very faulty, because such an inference was not there but leagues away from it." The stormy meeting ended with Neve telling Serra that he should not worry, that the subject was entirely confidential and only between the two. That evoked another outburst from Serra, who told him he was outraged "even if only a single individual knew of it."[27]

The friar's irate response may have been a catharsis that allowed Serra to vent his feelings toward Neve's continued efforts to diminish the importance of the missions and grant the Indians their freedom. And, on Neve's part, whatever the subject of the encounter, he may have baited Serra into an outburst because the Franciscans insisted on keeping the Indians in a state of abject misery, something Neve knew was wrong but could not change due to the power of the church in New Spain.

The Franciscans' opposition to Neve's plans reached all the way to Mexico City, where the friars launched strategies to sabotage the governor and maintain the missions' status quo, and lobbied the viceroy to keep them supplied at the expense of his Mexico City office. By the time Neve was promoted in 1782 to a new position outside California, the friars had successfully postponed his orders, but had not defeated his policy toward the missions.

Serra labored as best he could to keep alive the goal of having the missions become the central points of California, rather than the secular cities of San José, Los Angeles, or the other presidios and towns that Neve was supervising. When Pedro Fages, Serra's old nemesis, replaced Neve, the renewed relationship was not as stormy as before. Perhaps Fages realized that Serra was 69 years old and the combination of time and the hardship of life on the Spanish western frontier would favor the younger governor's longevity. Within two years of Fages's arrival, Serra would be dead.

---

27. Ibid., 293–294.

Beginning in 1783, one year before his death, Serra launched what would be his last effort to convert thousands of Indians at the missions. He left Carmel for a lengthy journey that would take him to the nine missions that then existed to confirm Indians prepared by the friars. It was all part of his plan to confirm as many neophytes as he could before his ten-year authority to administer the sacrament expired.

When he returned to Carmel in mid-summer, 1784, he fell ill with what was apparently an upper respiratory disease. Beginning on August 19, his condition deteriorated while he valiantly tried to continue his daily work—attending Mass and even singing with the same neophytes he had trained to perform during the services. Serra, at age 70, realized he was dying and wrote to the missionaries, asking them to visit him before he died. The letters, however, were misplaced and did not reach their destinations in time.

Neophytes faithful to Serra stayed by him. Palóu, his faithful friend, was summoned from San Francisco and chronicled the friar's last days. Finally, on August 28, 1784, Serra lay down on his rustic bed of planks, covered by a thin blanket, and asked that he be left alone. He died peacefully, still cradling the foot-long crucifix he always carried. One of his last wishes was that he be buried in the chapel of Mission Carmel.

Records show that during Serra's time at Mission Carmel, 1,014 Indians had become Catholics in Monterey. Overall, he single-handedly baptized more than 5,000 California Indians before his death.[28]

In the wake of Serra's death, the Franciscans at the *Colegio de San Fernando* launched a public relations campaign, portraying the missions as idyllic sites in which the friars and their Indian charges lived in harmony and love. Palóu's *Relación Histórica de la Vida y Apostólicas Tareas del Venerable Padre Fray Junípero Serra*, the *padre presidente's* biography, was written as part of an effort to ensure that Neve's secular policy of establishing presidios and towns did not sweep away the missions. The campaign was successful. It allowed the missions to operate independently of California's Spanish governors and to continue enforcing Serra's restrictive policies, ensuring that the neophytes' forced labor provided the support needed for the compounds to flourish.

---

28. Palóu, *Palóu's Life of Fray Junípero Serra*, 241.

7

The Missions

A few days later the expedition moved to a pretty plain about a rifle shot from the beach, and there established the presidio and the Mission to it.
—Friar Junípero Serra, June 12, 1770, in his account of the founding of Mission San Carlos de Monterey, the second of the California missions.

In the early 1800s, in the soft gray light just before dawn, a barely audible pealing of bells could be heard each morning along the coast of California stretching from San Francisco Bay to San Diego.

Riders on horseback, just a mile or two inland from the crashing surf, could stop their horses and, if they listened carefully, hear the faint bells in the distance. It didn't matter where on the coast they were, the bells could always be heard. They echoed across the isolated coastal stretches of California, ringing in the morning, at noon, and in the evening.

The source of the bells was the Roman Catholic missions that ranged up and down the coast, each only a day's ride on horseback from the next. They were the legacy of Friar Junípero Serra. Linked by a series of dirt roads named *El Camino Real* (the Royal Road), the missions' wealth was phenomenal. They had developed into sprawling ranch-like institutions where tens of thousands of head of livestock grazed on the best pastures available, and where vineyards flourished, producing fine wine and brandy.[1] In their prime, the missions became renowned for their hospitality, with the friars acting as welcoming hosts to merchants and visiting Spanish government officials. Rooms were always provided for visitors,

---

1. Charles E. Chapman, *A History of California: The Spanish Period* (New York: Macmillan, 1921), 386–387.

who feasted on lavish meals served with copious amounts of wine. Fresh horses, if needed, were also provided for the visitors' use.

While the friars' friends enjoyed generous hospitality, there were no such comforts for the Indians who lived and worked in the missions and their vast lands. Instead, the Indians suffered brutal punishment under a policy started during Serra's fifteen years as president of the Franciscans in California. Out of the thousands of Indians held captive in the missions, only a handful were ever taught how to read, write, understand arithmetic, or become skilled craftsmen. Under the strict regimen of the friars, most were kept illiterate and treated like children, and so became incapable of surviving in the frontier society developing around them.

The neophytes were held in mission compounds up and down the coast that were nearly identical in facilities, if not in design. Each mission had a church with either one or two bell towers. There was usually a long, one-story colonnaded building connected to the chapel where the friars had their rooms, the mission office, a dining room, a rectory, and usually a storage area for seeds and tools. Another similar building usually was built at a right angle to the friars' living space, creating a three-sided enclosure. A third building might include a kitchen for the Indians, weaving rooms, and warehouse areas for wine, grains, and hides. At most missions, that three-sided enclosure was closed off by a by a high wall that protected fruit trees and a large garden with a fountain, an area generally reserved for the exclusive use of the friars and their visitors.

Outside that enclosure were huts or adobe shelters assigned to the Indians, blacksmith facilities, a winemaking and storage area, stables, and carpentry shops. While early buildings were made of adobe covered with white plaster and protected by makeshift roofs, later structures replaced the adobe with fired bricks covered with white plaster, and roofs covered with red tiles. Stone floors were laid within the church and main structures.

The mission structures were built by neophytes who had been drawn into the missions, including many teenaged Indians from the surrounding villages. Their decision to join the missions meant that their village was stripped of much of the manpower needed for its survival. This situation typically worsened over time to such a deleterious level that the remaining Indian inhabitants had no choice but to reluctantly join the missions. Later, as waves of epidemics claimed the lives of the mission Indians, friars engaged in forays to outlying Indian villages to find new converts to replace those Indians who had died. This supplied the labor force needed to sustain the missions. Priests harangued the village Indians, warning them that great calamities would befall them and their children unless they joined the missions. Standing besides the friars were *alcaldes*, wielding whips and clubs, to ensure the Indians did not ignore the warnings. Many villages, upon becoming aware of the restrictive conditions within the missions, understandably wanted nothing to do with them. Only by threats and sometimes force could those non-neophytes be marched into the missions.

In the early years, natives who voluntarily flocked to the missions were unaware that many of those complexes were struggling to survive and were in danger of being abandoned. The Franciscans, who lacked agricultural expertise and animal husbandry skills, were facing shortages as they tried to feed themselves and their Indian novices. To allay the hunger of their Indian charges, some missions resorted to feeding them a diet consisting solely of milk. This was a disaster. Past infancy, the Indians could not digest milk, which caused dysentery and other illnesses that led to death.[2] Afterward, the friars allowed the Indians to forage for food outside the missions. Despite those setbacks, the missions did manage to survive, sustained by ships sailing from Mexico laden with food and equipment.

In time, as the missions began to flourish, the friars and Spanish officials became increasingly concerned about Indian resentment toward the Spanish intruders. In New Mexico and Arizona, the Indians had successfully forced the Spaniards from their lands, using a strategy of ambushes and terror tactics. Years later, however, the Spaniards again invaded that region with large and powerful forces that conquered the Indians. The Kumeyaay, who inhabited the area around the San Diego mission and presidio, were hostile to the Spanish. Mission San Diego survived two Indian attacks, one of them just after its founding, and the other a more serious conflict in which the mission was burned.

The Spaniards called the Indians *Diegueños*, Spanish for "people from San Diego." The Indians in that area initially showed no reluctance to steal

---

Florence C. Shipek, "California Indian Reactions to the Franciscans," The Americas 41 (4): 480-491 (1985), in *Native American Perspectives on the Hispanic Colonization of Alta California (The Spanish Borderlands Sourcebook Vol. 26)*, ed. Edward D. Castillo (New York: Garland, 1991), 184.

from the soldiers and friars and, while some Indians did join the mission, the majority rejected the Spaniards, culminating in the first attack.

The third mission Serra founded was the remote Mission San Antonio de Padua, inland from Monterey. Even in modern times, this mission remains the most isolated of the twenty-one locations. It was named after a scholarly Franciscan friar born in 1195 in Lisbon, Portugal, who was widely known across Europe. The California mission was established at a site adjacent to the River of Saint Anthony. There, Serra and his assistants hung a bell from an oak tree and rang it on July 14, 1771, calling the Indians from the surrounding area. Serra remained at the new site for two weeks before turning it over to Friar Buenaventura Sitjar, who translated the language spoken by the Indians in the area. Until his death in 1808, Sitjar directed this mission, which never developed fully like the others.

The fourth mission was established in what is now part of the sprawling Los Angeles metropolitan area. Two months after founding Mission San Antonio, Friars Pedro Benito Cambón and Angel de la Somora dedicated Mission San Gabriel Arcángel on September 8, 1771. Serra, who had earlier picked the site, was not present at the founding. Four years later, the site was moved northeast to avoid seasonal floods and to put it farther from the presidio. This move followed disputes between the friars and the local Spanish military commander which involved his soldiers' repeated abuse of the Indians. The surrounding indigenous residents were the Tongva, later named the Gabrieleños after Saint Gabriel. At the time of its dedication, the pueblo that would ten years later be formally named *El Pueblo de la Reyna de Los Angeles* was twelve miles west of the new mission.

In late August 1772, Serra, along with Friar José Cavaller and Captain Pedro Fages, trekked down the coast to a point nearly halfway between Monterey and San Gabriel. This led to the valley which had helped save Portolá's initial expedition to Monterey in 1769. Low on food, the commander had described how they had seen many bears in an oak-filled valley, which he named *La Cañada de los Osos* (Valley of the Bears). He ordered a hunt, and enough bears were killed to feed his expedition.[3] Portolá then suggested to Serra that it was an ideal spot for a mission. After visiting the site, the friar agreed wholeheartedly. A Mass of dedi-

3. Earlier the same year, the valley had also provided missions San Antonio and Monterey with enough bear meat for the winter, when food supplies at the two missions were dangerously low.

cation was held on September 1, 1772, for Mission *San Luis Obispo de Tolosa* (Mission San Luis Obispo), the fifth mission in California.

After the establishment of five missions, Spain's government turned its attention to guarding San Francisco Bay. A presidio was established at a point where the entrance to the bay could be defended. Leading the expedition that established the fort was Captain Juan Bautista de Anza, who also determined that a site next to a small lake in the area would be ideal for a mission. He named the site *Arroyo de Nuestra Señora de los Dolores* (Valley of Our Lady of Sorrows). Three months later, on June 29, 1776, Serra's faithful friend Friar Francisco Palóu and Friar Pedro Benito Cambón dedicated Mission San Francisco de Asís, named after Saint Francis of Assisi, the founder of the Franciscan order. It was California's sixth mission, and would later become known simply as Mission Dolores because of its proximity to the arroyo.

Mission San Juan Capistrano, the seventh mission dedicated under Serra, would become renowned for the swallows that to this day return to its eaves annually. It underwent two dedications, the first on October 30, 1775, and the second in the fall of 1776, and was named after a Franciscan who had achieved sainthood because of his sermons, his teaching against heresy, and his leadership against the Turks in the Battle of Belgrade. The mission had been established on the earlier date and church bells had been transported to the site, but work had hardly begun when nearby Mission San Diego was attacked by the Kumeyaay tribe. Most of San Diego's buildings were burned and Friar Luis Jayme was beaten to death by the Indians. Fearing that Mission San Juan Capistrano would be attacked next, the friars dug large pits and buried the heavy church bells with the help of the friendly Acjachemem Indians. The friars then hurried to the ruins of Mission San Diego, which had been quickly fortified after the attack. Once military reinforcements arrived, work began on replacing the charred ruins there.

In late 1776, the friars returned to Mission San Juan Capistrano, guarded by a reinforcement of Spanish troops, and resumed work on that site. With Serra presiding over the ceremonies, Mission San Juan Capistrano was rededicated on November 1, 1776. In 1806, work was completed on an elaborate church that boasted a bell tower twelve stories high. Sadly, it all came tumbling down in an December 8, 1812, earthquake. Modern seismologists determined that the temblor measured 7.0 on the Richter scale. Forty Indians inside the church were killed when the earthquake struck, entombed under tons of debris. The large church was never rebuilt and instead was replaced by a smaller one.

In the same year that work began on Mission San Juan Capistrano, an event occurred that shook the rule of kings and queens in Europe. On July 4, 1776, along the east coast of North America, colonial revolutionaries seeking to rid themselves of English taxation and oppression declared independence from England. It was the first step by the Revolutionaries in launching a full-scale war against powerful English forces over the right to be a free and independent nation. Arrayed against the ragtag Continental Army led by General George Washington were 30,000 British troops fresh from England, confident they would make short work of the upstart colonists.

Whether Serra was ever aware of the colonials' victory in the American war of independence is not known. Given Spain's continual surveillance against heresy and radical philosophies, it is doubtful that Serra's extremely conservative mind would ever have reflected on the kinds of rebellious thoughts that would soon also lead to the French Revolution.

Alta California's eighth mission was founded as part of Spanish Viceroy Antonio Bucareli's strategy to establish Spanish settlements to defend the northern and southern ends of San Francisco Bay. Initially, this eighth mission was to be located farther north in an area marked by a particular tall redwood tree which the Spaniards named *Palo Alto* (tall tree). Some 234 years later, it still stands as a carefully preserved landmark in the city of Palo Alto. That site, along San Francisquito Creek, had been picked by Friar Francisco Palóu.

The location, however, was switched when Captain Juan Bautista de Anza and Lieutenant José Joaquin Moraga identified a more southerly site for the new mission. It was about twenty miles away, on the banks of a river they discovered and named *Rio de Nuestra Señora de Guadalupe* (River of Our Lady of Guadalupe). On January 12, 1777, Friar Tomas de la Peña founded mission Santa Clara de Asís, named after Saint Clare of Asíssi, a follower of Saint Francis of Assisi, who founded the Order of Poor Ladies (known as "Poor Clares") in the thirteenth century. The location was moved two years later when the Guadalupe River flooded, destroying two years' worth of work on mission buildings. A drier and safer location was found, and Serra dedicated a temporary wooden church at the new site on November 11, 1779. Finally, on May 16, 1784, seven years after its initial dedication, with Serra, Peña, and Palóu present, the mission's church was finally dedicated. Missing from the ceremony was Friar José Murguía, who had died just five days before of exhaustion from establishing the mission. Much later, the site would become the location for Santa Clara University—administered, ironically, not by Franciscans, but by Jesuits (who had been ousted from Baja California in 1768). Founded in 1851 as a preparatory school, it later became a university and today is the state's oldest private institution of higher learning.

Prior to Mission Santa Clara's final dedication, Mission San Buenaventura, the ninth in the series, was founded south of Santa Barbara in a region populated by the seafaring Chumash tribe. It was dedicated on Easter Sunday, March 31, 1782, by Serra after a trek from Mission San Gabriel Arcángel. With Serra at the site was Friar Pedro Benito Cambón and Governor Felipe de Neve. The mission was named after Saint Bonaventure, a renowned Franciscan scholar and cardinal of Albano, Italy. It had taken nearly thirteen years to found the mission that Serra had initially sought as the third compound in Alta California.

Three weeks later, Serra dedicated Mission Santa Barbara, the tenth site, about thirty miles north of Mission San Buenaventura. The new site would also be the location of the fourth and final major presidio of California, taking its place beside San Francisco, Monterey, and San Diego. Serra, believing there was no conflict with Neve in founding this tenth mission, said Mass at the site, then began planning for what would later become "The Queen of the Missions." It gained this name for the beauty of its architecture and location, nestled in a valley facing the ocean, with a scenic mountain background.

Neve, who considered the missions a roadblock in establishing a Spanish population of Indian ancestry and was annoyed with the Franciscans, informed Serra that he could neither supply nor defend the new site. Neve bluntly told Serra that no more missions would be established while he was governor. This decision delayed the development of Mission Santa Barbara for four years. Finally, after appeals by the Franciscans to Mexico City, Friar Fermín Lasuén, Serra's successor, rededicated the new mission on December 4, 1786, two years after the deaths of both Serra and Neve.

Lasuén, as president of the Franciscans, was a guiding force in establishing the remaining eleven missions. Lasuén had little regard for California's Indians, whom he considered akin to "lower animals" and who he believed lived only for the present. "They satiate themselves today and give little thought to tomorrow," he wrote, adding that California's Indians ". . . are a people without education, without government, religion or respect for authority, and they shamelessly pursue without restraint whatever their brutal appetites suggest to them."[4] His low opinion of them never wavered during his life in California. The new *padre presidente* continued Serra's policy that corporal punishment was the only way to control the mission Indians.

Lasuén, who realized that the establishment of additional missions hinged on amicable relations with the Spanish governors of California, successfully cajoled and pleaded with them to continue their support and defense of the compounds, despite the high mortality rate of the neophytes. (On November 19, 1790, Lasuén reported to Don Jacobo Ugarte y Loyola, brigadier commandant general of the Internal Provinces of New Spain and based in Mexico City, that 4,780 Indians had died in the missions that year, with 8,528 surviving.[5] A year earlier, Lasuén had written Ugarte that just over 3,000 mission neophytes had died.)

Three years passed before the eleventh mission was added. On December 8, 1787, Lasuén dedicated Mission *La Purísima Concepción de Maria Santisima* (The Immaculate Conception of the Most Blessed Mary), in a valley halfway between Mission Santa Barbara and Mission San Luis Obispo. Within seventeen years this mission, with nearly 1,600 neophytes laboring within its vast borders, became an important production center for farm produce, leather goods, wool, soap, and candles. In 1807, a catastrophic smallpox epidemic killed more than 500 of its Indian population, fueled by the apparent failure to quarantine those who had been infected.

Four years elapsed, during which Lasuén pleaded with Spanish military commanders for support in founding Mission *La Exaltacion de la Santa Cruz* (the Exaltation of the Holy Cross). Permission was finally granted, and the twelfth mission, sitting on the north edge of Monterey Bay, was dedicated by Lasuén on August 29, 1791. Again, like Mission Santa Clara, the church had to be relocated after friars discovered that it sat in the San Lorenzo River's floodplain. In 1797, the Spanish viceroy in Mexico City,

---

4. Fermín Francisco de Lasuén, "Refutation of Charges," in *Writings of Fermín Francisco de Lasuén*, Vol. II, ed. Finbar Kinneally (Richmond, Va: William Byrd, 1965), 202, 220.

5. Fermín Francisco de Lasuén to Brigadier Commandant Jacobo Ugarte y Loyola, 19 November 1790, in *Writings of Fermín Francisco de Lasuén*, Vol. I., 216.

Miguel de la Grúa Talamanca, El Marqués de Branciforte, ordered the founding of a town across the river from the mission. Named *El Pueblo de Branciforte*, the community became a thorn in the side of the mission because of its rowdiness, as exemplified by the following account. When a privateer named Hippolyte de Bouchard raided the presidio at Monterey in 1818, the friars at Mission Santa Cruz and their neophytes at nearby Mission Carmel evacuated their compounds. Although Bouchard never raided Santa Cruz, townspeople from neighboring Branciforte, learning that the mission was temporarily empty, helped themselves to its supplies, including an extensive wine cellar. Later, when the situation had calmed down, the townspeople argued that raiding the mission was never in their mind. They had taken the supplies to safeguard them. The town of Branciforte would later change its name to Santa Cruz.

Just two months after the dedication of Mission Santa Cruz, Lasuén dedicated the thirteenth mission, *Nuestra Señora de la Soledad* (Our Lady of Solitude), on October 9, 1791. It was located approximately twenty-five miles south of what would become the town of Salinas. Lasuén was fulfilling a master plan in which the missions would be located within a day's ride of each other, following the route used by Portolá in 1769 and later named El Camino Real.

The name Soledad was chosen because Portolá and Friar Crespi, during the commander's expedition, had camped in the area. Friar Crespi, who kept a detailed journal of the trek, described an encounter with members of the Esselen tribe who had visited the explorer's camp. In trying to communicate with the Indians, Crespi thought he heard the word *soledad*, Spanish for solitude and loneliness, and thought it was a fitting description of the valley. Two years later, in 1771, Serra visited the area and was introduced by the Indians to a woman whose name sounded like soledad. The two incidents prompted Lasuén to pick that word as the name for the new mission.

Mission Soledad would be the last to be founded for six years as Spain's California governors continued to balk at providing soldiers for protection. The missions, they maintained, were simply not helping the development of California, and the military manpower they required was considered wasteful.

To bolster support for the missions, Lasuén craftily came up with an argument that had nothing to do with religion or saving souls. The Franciscan president convinced Viceroy Branciforte that if the friars were allowed to establish more missions, they could provide shelter for supply caravans escorted by soldiers traveling up and down El Camino Real. The missions could thus eliminate the cost of the caravans carrying camping equipment and food, not only for the men, but also for mules and horses. Each mission would be just a day's ride from the next. In return for those services, the missions would be free to baptize (ensnare is a more apt word) as many Indians as needed to maintain their workforces. The compounds would also retain a small number of soldiers, under the command of the friars. Branciforte readily accepted the proposal.

With the way cleared, Lasuén began the process that would lead to the creation of five more missions during his lifetime. He began by ordering the establishment of Mission San José, not along El Camino Real that had connected the earlier sites, but on the east side of San Francisco Bay, approximately fourteen miles east of the town of San José, which was by then twenty years old. Lasuén dedicated Mission San José (*La Mision del Gloriosisimo Patriarca San José*), the fourteenth California mission, on June 11, 1797. It was named after Saint Joseph, the carpenter husband of Mary. During the California Gold Rush of 1849, the mission, by then secularized and abandoned, served as an important way station for prospectors seeking the precious metal in the west-central foothills of California's Sierra Nevada mountain range.

Lasuén, in quick succession, established four more missions. The fifteenth was *San Juan de Bautista* (Saint John the Baptist), dedicated on June 24, 1797, and located about twenty-four miles inland between Mission Santa Cruz and Mission Carmel. Four weeks later, on July 25, 1797, he dedicated Mission *San Miguel Arcangel* (named for the Arcangel Michael), located between Mission San Luis Obispo and Mission San Antonio de Padua.

After swiftly appointing friars to the new missions, Lasuén traveled to other sites that had been selected by the Franciscans as far back as 1769, during Portolá's Monterey expedition. To the south, Lasuén and his friars founded the seventeenth mission on September 8, 1797—*San Fernando Rey de España* (Saint Ferdinand King of Spain), named after a thirteenth century king of the Spanish regions Leon and Castile. It was located inland, between Mission San Buenaventura and Mission San Gabriel Arcángel.

Mission *San Luis Rey de Francia* (Saint Louis King of France) was established on June 13, 1798, and named after Louis IX, who led two crusades. It was located between Mission San Diego and Mission San Juan Capistrano. This eighteenth mission would be the last one dedicated for six years and the last founded by Lasuén. Within a few years, the mission prospered, becoming a vast enterprise that supplied San Diego and the surrounding area with produce, wine, and leather products.

Lasuén died on June 26, 1803, at Mission Carmel. His work of eighteen years was continued by Friar Estévan Tapis, who on September 17, 1804, dedicated Mission Santa Inés in the Santa Ynez Valley east of Mission La Purísima. It was named after Saint Clare's younger sister, Saint Agnes of Assisi, who, on the death of her older sister in 1253, became abbess of the Poor Clares. The mission became the nineteenth in the chain.

Work on Mission Santa Inés had actually begun before its dedication, and by 1806 it featured a large quadrangle that measured 350 feet on each side. Six years later, the mission was devastated by two powerful earthquakes, each later estimated to have measured 7.0 on the Richter scale. Reconstruction quickly began, directed by Friar Francisco Javier de Uría, who also designed an aqueduct system that helped make Mission Santa Inés the leader in crop production among the missions.

It took just over a decade for another mission to be dedicated in California. The twentieth mission was actually launched as an *asistencia*, a branch of Mission San Francisco. It was a site where neophytes, stricken by the year round cold weather of that mission site, could recover. The branch was named Mission San Rafael Arcángel and was located inland on the north side of the Golden Gate, where the weather was warmer. Although it was founded December 14, 1817, it did not achieve full mission status until 1822, when Friar Vicente Francisco de Sarría, the new Franciscan president, formally upgraded it, acting under orders from the new Mexican government that had gained independence from Spain in 1821.

Mexican authorities, like the Spanish before them, were concerned about Russian incursion into Alta California and had determined it would benefit the new nation to establish a strong military presence on both sides of San Francisco Bay. They made Mission San Rafael a full mission rather than a branch of Mission San Francisco, establishing a strong foothold in that area that would eventually support a settlement.

Within months, the head of Mission San Francisco, Friar José Altamira, took it upon himself to woo the Mexican government into shutting down his mission and replacing it with a new one: Mission San Francisco Solano, to be located close to Mission San Rafael Arcángel. Mission Solano would buttress the Mexican presence in that region. Altamira, ambitious and bullheaded, no doubt considered that under the Mexican government he had no need for the Franciscan hierarchy and could thus launch his plan without approval of Franciscan President Sarría. His intentions, however, were thwarted when Sarría learned of Altamira's strategy. The *padre presidente* was subsequently able to convince Mexican officials to allow Mission San Francisco to remain open. Sarría, however, did not oppose establishing Mission San Francisco Solano.

Six months after the founding of Mission San Rafael Arcángel, Altamira dedicated Mission San Francisco Solano on July 4, 1823. Mission San Francisco de Solano would be the twenty-first and last mission to be established in California. Its namesake, Saint Francis of Solano, was the Franciscan who had earlier established a policy of whipping the Indians of Paraguay and Peru to keep them under control. He was canonized by Pope Benedict XIII in 1726. It was Saint Francis of Solano whom Serra cited as a precedent in his letter of January 7, 1780, to Governor Felipe de Neve, in which he defended his whipping of the mission Indians.

In all, Serra had established nine missions, Lasuén nine more, and Tapis, one. The last two were dedicated under Sarría. For the Franciscan friars, it was the culmination of their plan to establish a string a missions throughout Alta California, ostensibly to Christianize the Coastal California Indians. As demonstrated so far in this book, the motivation to "save souls" was undoubtedly based on deep conviction, but it is equally true that the situation soon developed into one where the Indians were little more than forced labor. This permitted the missions to thrive economically, and allowed the friars to profit personally from the sale of tallow, hides, horns, wine, and brandy to the foreign merchant ships that anchored annually off the California coast. For the Indians, it signified the beginning of brutal suffering and cultural genocide. Most died within two years, with their faith, customs, and way of life torn from them.

Fig. 1. Yokut Indians hunting near San Francisco Bay. Lithograph by Russian artist Ludwig Chloris (1795–1828). Bancroft Library.

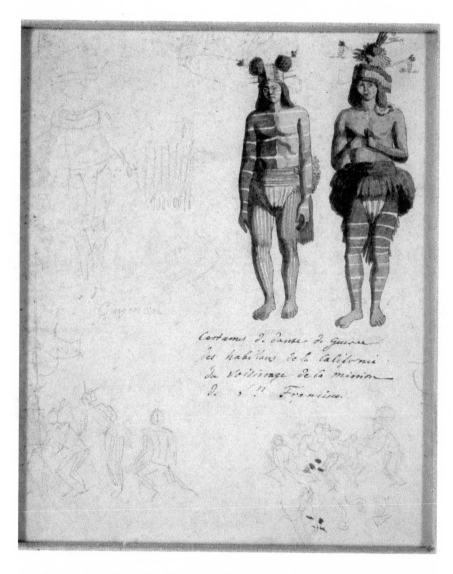

Fig. 2. Color studies of two Indians (identified in pencil as Olompoli and Sactan) in war dance costumes (headdress, body paint, and costume). Several additional pencil sketches of dancing figures (one identified as Guymon). Chloris. Bancroft Library.

Fig. 3. Native boat on San Francisco Bay. Chloris. Bancroft Library.

Fig. 4. Arms and utensils of the California Indians. Chloris. Bancroft Library.

Fig. 5. The reception of Jean-Francois de la Perouse at Mission Carmel in 1786. Spanish artist José Cardero (1768–after 1811). Bancroft Library.

303 Carmel Mission, Established 1770.

Fig. 6. Nineteenth-century postcard of Carmel Mission.

Danse des habitans de Californie à la mission de st Francisco.

Fig. 7. Danse des Californiens, San Francisco, from a drawing ca. 1815.
Bancroft Library

Fig. 8. Ein Tanz des Indianer in der Mission in St. José in Neu-Californien.
[A dance of the Indians at the mission in San José in New (Alta) California.]
German-Russian naturalist, explorer, and artist Georg Heinrich von Langsdorff
(1774–1852). Bancroft Library.

Fig. 9. View of Nuestra Señora de la Soledad Mission. American etcher Henry Chapman Ford (1828–1894). Bancroft Library.

Fig. 10. Mission San Luis Rey de Francia. French explorer Auguste Bernard Duhaut-Cilly (1790–1849). Bancroft Library.

8

Mission Life

Women are never whipped in public, but in an enclosed and somewhat distant place that their cries may not excite a too lively compassion, which might cause the men to revolt.
—Captain Jean-François Lapérouse, describing in 1826 the procedure for whipping Indian mission women.

French Navy Captain Jean-François de Galaup, Comte de Lapérouse, the leader of a major scientific French expedition, sailed into Monterey Bay on September 14, 1786. He arrived to visit the presidio and the mission founded seventeen years earlier by Junípero Serra. The visit to the bay was part of the small fleet's expedition through the Pacific Ocean, ordered by French King Louis XVI to gather detailed information on the areas bordering that vast body of water—their populations, geography, economies, and wildlife. The French captain was aboard *La Boussole*, his flagship, freshly scrubbed and painted, as was his other vessel, *L'Astrolabe*. Both displayed the billowing royal flag of France, the ensigns so large they were visible from a half-mile away.

As the ships glided silently under reduced sail into Monterey Bay, the view from the captain's deck of the *La Boussole* was enthralling: A wide, magnificent bay with beaches covered by dazzling white sand, tall pines shaped wonderfully by the wind, and verdant, steep green mountains rising in the background. Anchored in the bay were two Spanish corvettes whose crewmen lined the railings, cheering and welcoming the French.

Raising a polished brass telescope to his right eye, Lapérouse slowly scanned the beaches. Crowded around him were some of France's best scientists in the fields of botany, zoology, medicine, and cartography. Without enough telescopes for everybody, they passed the instruments around and were silent as they scanned the beaches. Adjusting his telescope, Lapérouse focused on a pair of friars running toward the beach, waving their arms excitedly, followed by a small group of Spanish soldiers waving their hats and muskets. He was surprised to see the ragged condition of the soldiers' uniforms. They were in sharp contrast to the spotless dress uniforms that he had ordered his sailors and marine guard to wear for their arrival.

The French had expected that Spain's Monterey settlement on the California coast would be bustling with soldiers, Spanish settlers, and a church with a bell tower (or at least a small version of one). Such churches and cathedrals were the major structures in the important towns and cities of *Nueva España*. Instead, they saw no substantial buildings—only a collection of weathered, crudely built adobe structures that were little more than thatch-roofed shacks set far back from the beach.

With the French ships dropping sail and anchor, Spanish cannons fired seven times in a welcoming salute that sent thick white clouds of smoke drifting across the waves. The booms of their explosions thudded into the hills beyond the beach, then echoed through the forests before fading. Lapérouse lowered his telescope and handed it to a young ensign. He turned to his first mate and ordered him to begin their answering salute. The first mate saluted. "*Oui, mon capitaine,*" he said, then turned smartly to waiting gunners below him on the main deck and shouted the order to fire.

The result was an instantaneous, ear splitting roar. One after another, the French cannon, heavier and more powerful than their Spanish counterparts, exploded in blasts of fire, noise, and enormous clouds of white smoke as they hailed the Spanish. On the beach, the Franciscan friars and the Spanish soldiers waved even more excitedly in response.

Once on land, the French commander discovered that the Monterey presidio, in its undeveloped state, had few of the expected comforts. In his journal, Lapérouse described the presidio buildings and nearby Mission Carmel as crudely made, covered with plaster and straw roofs.[1]

---

1. Not until nearly the end of the eighteenth and early nineteenth centuries would the friars receive enough craftsmen from Mexico to direct mission Indians in replacing the shoddy structures with the large and beautiful California missions that would garner world-wide renown.

Lapérouse and his entourage of officers, artists, and scientists were rowed to shore, where they were met by the soldiers and taken to the compound of Mission Carmel, about two miles inland. There, the visiting party faced another shock. Several Indians had their feet locked in heavy wooden stocks that, despite providing makeshift padding, must have horribly blistered and chewed their lower limbs.[2] They were suffering punishment meted out by the friars. Being confined to stocks, however, did not free the victims from required work. Burdened by the savage instruments, they still had to toil in the fields.[3]

The use of stocks was not the only punishment that astounded Lapérouse. In the description of his visit to Monterey, he noted the sound of whips being used against the Indians by mission overseers. Other Indians had their wrists and ankles locked by irons, heavy shackles linked by chains that prevented full movement of a victim's arms or legs.

The French captain would later describe how similar the missions were to slave plantations he had visited earlier in the Caribbean:

> The color of these Indians, which is that of the negroes; the house of the Missionaries; their storehouses, which are built of brick and plastered; the appearance of the ground on which the grain is trodden out; the cattle, the horses—everything in short—brought to our recollection a plantation at Santo Domingo or any other West Indian island. The men and women are collected by the sound of a bell; a Missionary leads them to work, to the church, and to all their exercises. We observed with concern that the resemblance is so perfect that we have seen both men and women in irons, and others in stocks. Lastly, the noise of the whip

---

2. Fernando Librado, a Chumash Indian who had been a neophyte at Mission San Buenaventura, described the stocks as "shaped of wood to cover the foot like a shoe. It was made from two pieces of wood that opened and the entire foot was placed into it from toe to heel. These pieces of wood were joined to a ring that went about the knee, and from this ring straps were attached to a belt that went around the waist of a person. Weights were fastened to the straps." In *Breath of the Sun: Life in Early California as told by a Chumash Indian*, Fernando Librado to John P. Harrington, ed. Travis Hudson (Ventura, Calif: Malki, 1979), in *Native American Perspectives on the Hispanic Colonization of Alta California*, 23.

3. Years later, other visitors and the friars themselves recorded the fact that Indians who violated the stringent regulations of the missions were left in stocks for days at a time, often without food or water. Prisoners had to urinate and defecate on themselves, because the iron straps that helped keep the stocks in place did not allow bending the knees.

might have struck our ears, this punishment also being administered, though with little severity.[4]

Although Lapérouse raised the question of why the Indians needed to be whipped, he did not explain what he meant by "little severity." Perhaps, being a ship's captain, he meant that the whipping of the Indians was not as severe as the lashing a sailor might receive on a military vessel of that era—a punishment that would rip the skin open and on occasion result in the sailor's death from loss of blood, infection, and shock. Still, it does not diminish the fact that the Indians were being whipped routinely by the gray-robed friars.

Seventeen years after the founding of the first mission, Lapérouse had become the first outsider to both visit and criticize those institutions. Although he couched his impressions in diplomatic language, his writing leaves no doubt that he was appalled at the treatment of the Indians by the Franciscan friars:

> It is with the most pleasing satisfaction that I speak of the prudent conduct of these religious men, which so perfectly agrees with the goal of their institution. I shall not conceal what I conceived to be reprehensible in their internal administration, but I must affirm that, by being individually good and humane, they temper by their mildness and charity the austerity of the rules which have been prescribed by their superiors. A friend to the rights of men rather than to theology, I could have wished, I confess, that there had been joined to the principles of Christianity a legislation which might gradually have made citizens of men whose state at present scarcely differs from that of the Negro inhabitants of our colonies, at least in those plantations which are governed with most mildness and humanity.
>
> I am perfectly aware of the extreme difficulty of this new plan. I know that these people have very few ideas, and still less stability, and that if they were to cease to be treated as children, they would escape from those who have taken the pains to instruct them. I know likewise that reasoning can produce very little effect upon them, that it is absolutely necessary to appeal to their senses, and that corporal punishment, with rewards in double proportion, have hitherto been the only means adopted by their legislators. But would it not be possible for ardent zeal

---

4. Jean François de Lapérouse, "A Visit to Monterey in 1786, and a Description of the Indians of California," in *California Historical Society Quarterly* 15:3 (1936) 218, in *Documentary Evidence for the Spanish Missions of Alta California (The Spanish Borderlands Sourcebook Vol. 14)*, ed. Julia G. Costello (New York: Garland, 1991), 1–8.

and extreme patience to demonstrate to a few families the advantages of society founded on the rights of the people; to establish among them the possession of property, so bewitching to all men; and by this new order of things to engage everyone to cultivate his field by emulations, or to direct his exertions to some other employment?

I admit that the progress of this new civilization would be very slow, and the attentions necessary to be paid extremely tedious; that the theater of action is very remote, and that the applause of the enlightened part of mankind would never reach the ear of him who should thus have consecrated his life to deserve them. Neither do I hesitate to affirm that human motives are insufficient for such a ministry, and that the enthusiasm of religion, with the rewards it promises, can alone compensate for the sacrifices, the boredom, the fatigue, and the dangers of this kind of life. Still I could wish that the minds of the austere, charitable, and religious individuals I have met with in these missions were a little more tinctured with the spirit of philosophy.[5]

Lapérouse, in urging that the friars patiently teach the Indians the "advantages of society founded on the rights of the people," was clearly steeped in the contemporary philosophy that all human beings had inalienable rights. In particular, his use of the word "reprehensible" buttresses his condemnation of the friars' actions.

While the French commander decried the harsh life imposed on the Indians by the friars, he was not as liberal-minded with his description of the Indians, characterizing them as "stupid." He obviously had not taken into account that depression, malnourishment, and disease had not only weakened them physically, but also instilled in them a sense of hopelessness. They could never leave Mission Carmel, were doomed to die within that suffocating compound inside fetid huts, their last sight perhaps being not the rolling hills and thick forests that they loved, but a friar leaning over them giving them last rites.

Lapérouse's observations were written in a diary that was later compiled into a report of the expedition's voyage.[6] The scientists of the Lapérouse expedition had been handpicked by French officials, each having signed

5. Jean François de Lapérouse, "A Visit to Monterey in 1786," in *A Voyage Round the World, Performed in the years 1785, 1786, 1787, and 1788, by the* Boussole *and* Astrolabe, *under the Command of J.F.G. de la Pèrouse* (London: 1799), 70–71, in *Documentary Evidence of the Spanish Missions in Alta California*, 6.

6. Tragically, both vessels were later shipwrecked in the South Pacific with no survivors. Their reports survived because they had been previously transferred to a British naval ship in Australia which sailed to Europe and returned the documents to France.

on for a voyage that would last at least four years, and each contributing notes and observations that would become part of the expedition's report. An artist with the expedition, Duché de Vancy, busily sketched his observations, providing a visual portrait of the ports and lands visited by the French. And the king's own gardener was onboard, acting as a botanist. Wherever the two ships anchored, it was his responsibility to identify and collect samples of the plant life and discover any hitherto unknown plants or trees.

The expedition stayed at the mission for several days, identifying the flora and fauna of the area while the artist sketched the mission compound, natives, and surrounding land. Early in their visit, Lapérouse and his company were invited to attend Mass in the small mission chapel. Apparently, the friars believed this would be a grand opportunity for them to display their submissive charges by lining them up outside the church doors. Whatever the intention, it certainly did not impress Lapérouse, who wrote:

> Before we had entered the church, we had passed through a square in which the Indians of both sexes were ranged in a line. They exhibited no marks of surprise in their countenance, and left us in doubt whether we should be the subject of their conversation for the rest of the day.
>
> Upon coming out of the church we passed through the same row of Indians, whom the *Te Deum* had not induced to abandon their post. Only the children had removed to a small distance and formed groups near the house of Missionaries opposite the church.[7]

In particular, Lapérouse took note of the *alcaldes*, the neophytes appointed by the friars to carry out the priests' commands:

> There are three in each Mission, chosen by the people from among those whom the Missionaries have not excluded. However, to give a proper notion of this magistracy, we must observe that these *caciques* are like the overseers of a slave plantation: passive beings, blind performers of the will of their superiors (friars). Their principal functions consist in serving as beadles[8] in the church to maintain order and the appearance of attention.[9]

---

7. Lapérouse, "A Visit to Monterey in 1786," 77–78.
8. Officials assigned to keep order during services.
9. Ibid., 88–89.

As mentioned previously, appointing enforcers of their will from within the ranks of Indians themselves gave the friars a much wider range of control. The *alcaldes* beat any Indian, no matter what age or sex, who violated mission rules or displayed reluctance to do assigned work. Nearly all the violations called for flogging, ranging from ten lashes up to fifty, which could kill a victim. While lashing was in itself a terrible ordeal, it was doubly abhorred by the Coastal Indians, whose culture considered it an ultimate punishment. Within the villages, only a truly serious crime was punishable by whipping, with the perpetrator laid out spread-eagled on the ground, tied to stakes, and then struck by branches. Afterward, he was shunned by the village and no infrequently committed suicide.[10]

Within the mission, women were not excluded from being flogged. Lapérouse described their punishment:

> Women are never whipped in public, but in an enclosed and somewhat distant place that their cries may not excite a too lively compassion, which might cause the men to revolt.[11]

In contrast, he wrote that men were lashed:

> ... exposed to the view of all their fellow citizens, that their punishment may serve as an example. They usually ask pardon for their fault, in which case the executioner diminishes the force of his lashes, but the number is always irrevocable.[12]

In his journal, the French commander also lamented that the neophytes suffered severe punishments for infractions that in other settings would have been of no consequence:

> Corporal punishment is inflicted on the Indians of both sexes who neglect the exercises of piety, and many sins, which in Europe are left to Divine justice, are here punished by irons and the stocks. And lastly, to complete the similarity between this and other religious communities, it must be observed that the moment an Indian is baptized, the effect is the same as if he had pronounced a vow for life. If he escape [*sic*] to reside with his relations in the independent villages, he is summoned three times to return; if he refuses, the Missionaries apply to the governor, who sends soldiers to seize him in the midst of his family and

---

10. Shipek, "California Indian Reactions to the Franciscans," 179.
11. Ibid., 6.
12. Ibid, 6.

conduct him to the Mission, where he is condemned to receive a certain number of lashes with the whip.[13]

An additional duty of the *alcaldes*, backed up by soldiers, was to pursue runaway mission neophytes, capture them, and force them back to the compounds. They were also charged with bringing to the missions new Indians to maintain the population. The daily regimen for the *alcaldes* consisted of roaming the mission lands and freely swinging their clubs and whips at any fellow mission Indian who violated the friars' rules. They were key factors in carrying out the policies established by Serra and Lasuén to keep the mission Indians under control through intimidation and fear of punishment.

The *alcaldes'* unrestrained and remorseless use of whips often ripped the skin from neophytes. One woman who tried repeatedly to escape was whipped so severely that bloody welts on her buttocks crawled with maggots.[14] At Mission San Gabriel, the *alcaldes* wielded an "immense scourge of rawhide, about ten feet in length, plaited to the thickness of an ordinary man's wrist! They did a great deal of chastisement, both by and without orders."[15]

It is little wonder, then, that the friars' policy of harsh punishment eventually led to acts such as the murder of Friar Andrés Quintana of Mission Santa Cruz, hated by the Indians because of his penchant for flogging them freely. In 1812, he had fashioned a horsewhip tipped with iron barbs to use against the Indians. They saw the terrible wounds the whip could inflict when the priest used it against the buttocks of a mission Indian named Donato.[16] The very Indians against whom Quintana had planned to use it killed him by strangling him and crushing his testicles.

The Indians involved in the murder were later identified and sentenced to a staggering fifty daily lashes each for nine days, and to life sentences of hard labor. The punishment was proof that even forty-three years after the

13. Ibid., 4.

14. James A. Sandos, "Junípero Serra's Canonization and the Historical Record," *American Historical Review* 93:5 1988, in *Native American Perspectives on the Hispanic Colonization of Alta California*, 464–465.

15. Susanna Bryant Dakin, *The Indians of Los Angeles County: Hugo Reid's Letters of 1852* (Berkeley: University of California Press, 1939), in *Documentary Evidence for the Spanish Missions of Alta California*, 508–509.

16. Lorenzo Asisara, "The Assassination of Padre Andrés Quintana by the Indians of Mission Santa Cruz in 1812," in *Native American Perspectives on the Hispanic Colonization of Alta California*, 3–11.

founding of the first mission, the Spanish friars were still dependent on lashing and other atrocities to make the Indians comply with their rules.

In the years prior to Lapérouse's visit, a constant challenge facing Serra and his fellow Franciscans was how to motivate the Indians into leaving their village life and joining the mission compounds. He and the friars first tried to entice them by offering beads and other gifts. The friars also let them know that if they joined the missions they would be fed three times a day, be allowed to attend Mass, enjoy the friars' European ways, use the Spaniards' tools, and wear clothing made of fabrics, something the Indians prized.

In their first encounters, the Spaniards were welcomed by Indians of all ages, who offered them nuts from their stores and fish they had caught. One of the best descriptions of the friendliness of the Indians in their initial encounters came from Friar Pedro Font, who accompanied Juan Bautista de Anza in 1775 on a trek aimed at establishing a presidio north of Monterey. Font described a visit by a number of Indians who came from a village south of San Francisco, on the west side of the bay:

> The Indians of this village were very attentive and obliging, and even troublesome, for they had so attached themselves to the camp that when it was already very late it was necessary to drive them out in order that we might get some sleep. So I think it would be easy to establish them in a mission.[17]

In a later encounter, the expedition visited another village:

> . . . we found a fair-sized village whose Indians, both men and women, were very happy to see us and very obliging. They presented us with many *cacomites*, which is a little bulb or root almost round and rather flat, the size and shape of a somewhat flattened ball, and likewise with a good string of roasted *amole*, which is another root, like a rather long onion, all well-cooked and roasted. I tried some of it and liked the taste, and the Commander gave the Indians glass beads.[18]

Font describes still another village, where an elderly Indian woman greeted them in a striking manner:

---

17. Rose Marie Beebe and Robert M. Senkewicz, *Lands of Promise and Despair: Chronicles of Early California, 1535–1846* (Berkeley, Calif.: Heyday Books, 2001), 195.
18. Ibid., 202.

... she began to dance alone, making motions very indicative of pleasure, at times stopping to talk to us, making signs with her hands as if bidding us welcome. After a short while I said to the Commander that that was enough. So he gave presents of glass beads to all the women, they regaled us with their *cacomites*, and we said good-bye to everybody in order to continue on our way. They were apparently very sad because we were leaving, and I was moved to tenderness at seeing the joy with which we were welcomed by those poor Indians.[19]

For the natives, the Spaniards and their horses were god-like, all-powerful beings that would help them fight enemies from neighboring tribes. If, as the Indians believed, the Spaniards indeed were gods, then it was logical to ally themselves with these supermen. The friars reinforced that attitude by inculcating in the Indians the belief that there was one all-powerful God who protected all human beings, including the Indians. Once a presidio and mission site was selected, the friars would give beads to the Indians who flocked to the future mission grounds. Next they would set up a crudely sheltered altar and don their robes for saying Mass. The Indians were enchanted by the priests' elaborate chasubles, which were embroidered thickly with gold thread, as well as by the gleaming chalices, gilded candelabras, and even religious paintings.

Indeed, both Visitor General Gálvez and Serra had stressed that the new churches in Alta California were to be elaborately decorated with silver and gold implements, and that the priests be clad in the gold-embroidered vestments during Mass to impress upon the Indians the importance of the Roman Catholic Church. Therefore, during the height of the mission period in California, the priests continually ordered incense, sacred implements made of silver or gold for their altars, religious paintings, statues of saints, and delicate silk and taffeta to decorate the churches and altars.

The ringing of small bells, the singing of hymns, and the aromatic clouds of burning incense during Mass added to the mystique surrounding the Spaniards. In the Indians' minds, here were powerful sacred men who could speak directly to a god each day and were willing to allow the Indians to join them. To the Indians, the priests, like the Spanish soldiers astride tall, four-legged beasts, were truly gods.

It did not take long to entice the Indians into visiting sites and helping build temporary shelters for the priests and soldiers. At each mission,

---

19. Ibid., 204.

more Indians arrived daily as word of the newcomers quickly spread to nearby villages, prompting men, women, and children to visit out of curiosity. From those visits the friars enticed small numbers to become neophytes and to join the missions.

Once the Indians had made a decision to stay, they were quickly taught just enough of Catholic doctrine to allow them to be baptized. They mouthed prayers and definitions of the Holy Trinity, the words meaningless to them since they did not understand Spanish. It was all the friars needed to pseudo–baptize them, give them Spanish names, and enslave them. Once that step was taken, as dictated by Serra, the Indians would never be allowed to leave the mission grounds without permission. Under that dictum, neither could any Indian child born within the mission compounds.[20]

After being baptized, most of the first neophytes concluded there was nothing to prevent them from returning to their villages. They were sadly mistaken. At their first attempt to say goodbye, they were told by crude sign language they could not leave. It is probable that the converts simply ignored the friars and continued their preparations to leave. If the Indians did not heed the exhortations of the friars, the missionaries then signaled the soldiers assigned to each mission to surround the neophytes and use force to keep the Indians within the mission boundaries.

The neophytes were herded into an open area adjacent to the mission and ordered to replicate their traditional huts, consisting of the simple pole framework upon which was stacked brush or branches. It was the only similarity to their former life left to them. In later years, small adobe or brick huts replaced the brush huts. No longer could they laze around their village, working only when it was necessary, as was their custom.

In particular, the lives of girls and single women were brutally stifled. Within the California missions, all single women and girls past the age of ten were crowded each night into a long building and locked inside to keep them from mingling with the boys or single men, something the friars considered an abhorrent sin. The friars called these buildings

---

20. The California mission system was an anomaly in comparison to other missions systems established in the Spanish New World. Commonly, outside of California, churches in the eighteenth century were established next to Indian settlements. While attendance at Mass was mandatory, the Indians were generally free to farm or hunt as they pleased, so long as they did not violate strict observance of Catholic rules regarding their behavior.

the *monjeria* or *convento*, Spanish for nunnery or convent, although the Indian women inside were never known to have taken vows. During his visit, Lapérouse wrote a vivid description of that policy:

> The holy fathers have constituted themselves guardians of the virtue of the women. An hour after supper, they take care to secure all the women whose husbands are absent, as well as the young girls above the age of nine years, by locking them up, and during the day they entrust them to the care of elderly women. All these precautions are still inadequate, and we have seen men in the stocks and women in irons for having eluded the vigilance of these female Arguses,[21] whose eyes are not sufficient for the complete performance of their office.[22]

The women and girls slept on narrow wooden platforms that were built lengthwise inside, along both sides of the walls, and separated by a narrow walkway running down the middle. At Mission Carmel, Lasuén described the facility as being "seventeen *varas*[23] in length, more than six *varas* in width, and the same in height. . . . The toilets are separate."[24] Sherburne F. Cook wrote: "There can be no doubt that the women were packed in tightly, and that accumulation of filth was unavoidable."[25] Further, "It is unbelievable that they (Indians) should not have resented years of being confined and locked in every night in a manner which was so alien to their tradition and nature."[26]

With unmarried women and young girls forced into those reeking rooms each night, it was inevitable that diseases like measles spread with wildfire swiftness. Those *conventos* were little more than cauldrons boiling over with bacteria, especially European diseases that resulted in terrible death tolls. The only toilet facilities inside the locked room were a bucket or two. The friars, ignorant of how disease spread, never abandoned the use of those deadly rooms throughout the mission period.

When girls reached the age of ten they were considered adults, separated from their families, and forced to sleep inside the building. Boys of

---

21. In Greek mythology, a giant having a hundred eyes ordered by Hera to watch over Io.

22. Lapérouse, "A Voyage to Monterey in 1786," 7.

23. A *vara* was a Spanish unit of measure, no longer used, equivalent to three feet.

24. Lasuén, *Writings of Fermín Francisco Lasuén*, 207.

25. Sherburne F. Cook, *The Conflict Between the California Indian and White Civilization* (Berkeley: University of California Press, 1976), 90.

26. Ibid.

that age slept with the young men. By ten years of age, mission children were considered laborers and assigned daily work.[27] The labor assigned to the children was certainly not easy for their young bodies; Lapérouse and the doctors with him noted that many of the children were suffering from hernias.

Outside the missions, other Indians became aware of the restrictions imposed on the neophytes and began shunning the compounds. And in additional to that, some of the Indians may have stayed away because of the friars' refusal to provide iron tools to them. "Missionaries' accounts," wrote David G. Sweet, in studying missions outside of California, "are quite consistent in acknowledging that iron tools for gift giving were indispensable to their work and that in the absence of an ample supply of such goods many Indian peoples would have nothing to do with the mission."[28]

Natives who wisely refused to become part of the missions were described as "*gentiles.*" Nevertheless, their lives were made miserable by the constant proselytizing and Spanish threats of force to bring them into the missions. Friars visited their villages and harangued them about the evils of their "savage" life.

Meanwhile, those Indians who had willingly joined the missions stripped their villages of the critical labor needed to sustain them. Indian group labor in a village was so delicately balanced that the loss of several men and women or teenagers could, like falling dominoes, upset the division of work and create disastrous consequences. Facing a bleak future with reduced manpower, the remaining villagers often had little choice but to join the missions.

What Indian labor couldn't supply was packed in barrels and crates aboard the Spanish ships that plied between Mexico's west coast ports and the missions, delivering equipment, chocolate, sugar, and mail for the missions and the presidios. The ships also delivered personal items for the mission friars, who asked for books, clothing, liquor, and church implements. By land, large mule trains packed with supplies set out from northwestern Mexico, driving herds of livestock amid clouds of dust that

---

27. Cook, *Population of the California Indians*, 82.
28. Weber, Sweet, *The Arts of the Missions of Northern New Spain*, 14. Also "The Ibero-American Frontier Mission in Native American History," in *The New Latin American Mission History*, ed. Erick Langer and Robert H. Jackson (Lincoln: University of Nebraska Press, 1995), 34.

could be seen for miles. The cattle, intended initially for the missions, were later provided for colonists from Mexico.

The constant delivery of supplies and the growth of the missions allowed the Franciscan friars to surround themselves with young Indian boys they called "pages," who ran small errands for the priests and kept them company. And the priests ate bountifully every day. Of note is the story of a particularly portly friar named José Viador of Mission Santa Clara, had such a wide girth he could not walk for long distances or ride a horse. To travel to nearby sites, he had mission Indian craftsmen build him a carriage to his specifications. In appearance, it looked much like the other crude carts used in Alta California at the time, except that it was built to hold only one person—the large Friar Viador. Low wheels allowed him to climb easily into the seat, which was amply padded with sheepskins. A canopy of brown cotton fabric protected him from the sun.

Viador ordered craftsmen at the mission to make a leather harness to guide a strong black mule, ridden by a small Indian boy who helped the padre control the animal. A mission *vaquero* (cowboy) rode alongside, with a lasso attached to the mule's neck to ensure that it went where it was guided. Two other *vaqueros* rode alongside the sturdy cart and attached ropes to its right and left sides. This helped pull it (and it's hefty passenger) along the road and up steep hills. Flanking the cart were three or four young Indian boys who walked alongside, ready for any instructions from Viador. Walking behind were several *alcaldes*, wielding the long poles that signified their position of authority. Attached to their hats were red and blue ribbons fluttering and snapping in the wind.[29] All this must have been a colorful and surrealistic sight. Alfred Robinson, traveling in California at that time, described Viador as a "good old man, whose heart and soul were in proportion to his immense figure."[30]

While Viador's eccentricities was part of the yearning by the friars to enhance their comforts in the isolated missions, some, like Friar Buenaventura Fortuny of Mission San José, sought intellectual inspiration. He wrote the *Colegio de San Fernando* Franciscan headquarters in

---

29. Alfred Robinson, *Life in California: A Historical Account of the Origin, Customs, and Traditions of the Indians of California* (New York: Wiley and Putnam, 1846.), 112–113. Unabridged republication of the first edition (New York: De Capo, 1969).

30. Ibid., 70.

Mexico City that he needed a set of the Sermons of Armaña. "What am I to do?" he complained. "I shall become a burro because of not having books to read." Fortuny urged the procurator in the *Colegio* to assign someone to purchase them, "and if they're simply not available, I'll be satisfied with that."[31]

Fortuny also asked that the *Colegio* send him a barrel of rum or mescal, whichever would be cheaper. If sending the rum was cheaper, he requested they "procure it at once."[32] While Fortuny may have asked for items to make his life more comfortable, he was also practical: He had earlier ordered thirty-six small scissors needed by the mission Indian women for sewing.[33]

In time, the missions became institutions that resembled the giant haciendas of Mexico, also dependent on Indians who labored as virtual slaves. One of the most successful missions was Mission San Luis Rey de Francia, the "King of the Missions," located about twenty-five miles north of San Diego. Eventually, more than 1,000 neophytes labored within its vast lands. In 1832, two years before its Indians were set free, it reported having a livestock herd of 57,330 animals, including 27,500 head of cattle and 26,100 head of sheep. It supplied most of the San Diego area with corn, beans, and wheat and was also noted for its production of soap, blankets, and shoes. In the 1830s, its final years, the mission's vineyards produced 2,500 barrels of wine annually.[34]

In the 1790s, Mission San Diego, in its annual report to the church hierarchy in Mexico City, tallied 1,200 horses, 10,000 head of cattle, and 20,000 sheep. In an area covering more than six hundred square miles above what is now called Mission Valley, it was producing wine and growing barley, corn, wheat, beans, and a variety of vegetables.[35]

---

31. Buenaventura Fortuny to Colegio de San Fernando in Mexico City, San José, 30 May, 1808. Bancroft Library, University of California, Berkeley: Banc MSS 2002/80 c, box 1, folder 1:3.

32. Ibid., box 1, folder 1:2.

33. Ibid., box 1, folder 1:1.

34. Bill Yenne, *The Missions of California* (San Diego: Thunder Bay Press, 2004), 159.

35. Ibid., 27

From 1782 to 1832, Mission San Gabriel Arcángel, located near the river of *Nuestra Señora Reyna de Los Angeles de la Porciúncula*,[36] produced 11,685 tons of agricultural products. In 1832, just two years before the Mexican government fully secularized all the missions, the friars reported having 16,500 head of cattle that were part of an overall livestock herd of 26,342. The mission's Indians also produced large quantities of wine, candles, and soap that supplied most of Alta California.[37]

At Mission San Francisco de Asís, later known as Mission Dolores, the friars reported in the early 1800s that at their peak they had 11,340 head of cattle and 11,324 sheep. From 1785 to 1832, the friars and Indians produced 120,000 bushels of wheat, plus large quantities of corn, beans, peas, lentils, and garbanzos. In 1831, the mission possessed 1,239 horses.[38]

By 1811, Mission San Juan Capistrano, about thirty-five miles north of San Diego, had bred a cattle herd of approximately 14,000 head. It also boasted 16,000 sheep grazing on its lands, where barley, beans, and wheat were grown.[39]

Although not all of the missions were as productive as these, they all became self-sustaining and were major providers of food and products for their surrounding communities. They also sustained a thriving business selling English and American merchant ships cargoes of brandy, wine, and grain—but their main focus was on selling tallow, hides, and horns, which accounted for the large herds of cattle. According to the friars' surviving records, all the profits from the sales of mission products were reinvested into maintaining the compounds, providing for the neophytes, and expanding each site's production of both agricultural and material goods.

However, according to some observers of the mission system, a certain amount of product income was hoarded by the friars. In the 1800s, Kirill Timofeevich Khlebnikov, the head of the Russian-American Company of Sitka, Alaska, which hunted fur-bearing mammals on the California

---

36. The river's name was chosen by Friar Juan Crespi on August 2, 1769, during the first land expedition of California led by Fernando Rivera Y Moncada. The word *porciúncula* stems from the gift of a small chapel given to St. Francis of Assisi by the Benedictine Order in Italy. The chapel, in Assisi, was located on what Italians called a *porziuncola*, meaning a very small parcel of land.

37. Ibid., 51–55.

38. Ibid., 67.

39. 39. Ibid., 76.

coast, described this process. He said some mission friars, claiming that they could not touch gold or money because of their Franciscan vows of poverty, would call the mission foreman, or *mayordomo*, to physically count and care for the money as property of the mission. Khlebnikov wrote: "But no sooner has the payer departed than they [the friars] accurately count the sacks with the piastres and prudently place them in their bedroom."[40]

There are no records that the mission Indians were ever paid for their labor. They were, for all practical purposes, slaves. The only difference was that the Indians were never sold, although they were occasionally loaned to nearby pueblos on condition that the friars, not the Indians, be paid for their labor.

As such, the lives of neophytes within the Franciscan compounds were marked by an unrelenting brutality. At Mission San Luis Rey, the Indians faced the twisted wrath of Friar José María Zalvidea. Previously, Zalvidea had been assigned to Mission San Gabriel, where he was described by Hugo Reid, a successful California rancher of that era, as a person who had an insatiable penchant for whipping the Indians:

> He was not only severe, but he was, in his chastisements, most cruel. So as not to make a revolting picture, I shall bury acts of barbarity known to me through good authority, by merely saying that he must assuredly have considered whipping as meat and drink to them, for they had it morning, noon, and night.[41]

Reid's sympathy for the Indians stemmed from an upbringing (he had emigrated from the East Coast to California in the early nineteenth century) that apparently instilled in him a sense of fundamental human rights. In his letters, he described Zalvidea's cruelty toward girls and women who suffered miscarriages. Instead of offering comfort and condolences, the friar did the opposite, ordering them to be lashed for fifteen consecutive days, their heads shaved, and irons bolted around their ankles for three months. Each bereaved mother also had to stand every Sunday on the steps of the church holding "a hideous painted wooden child in her arms."[42] Zalvidea's punishment stemmed from his belief that

---

40. K.T. Khlebnikov, *Memoirs of California*, tr. Anatole G. Mazour, in *The Pacific Historical Review* 9:307-336. 1940, in *Documentary Evidence for the Spanish Missions of Alta California.*

41. Reid, *The Indians of Los Angeles County*, 150.

42. Ibid., 149.

Indian women were deliberately aborting their pregnancies to prevent bringing an infant into the environment of the missions, a concern that was common among friars.

Zalvidea was cruel not only to the Indians, but to himself, practicing excessive self-punishment. This included lashing himself with a whip tipped with lacerating sharp-edged pieces of flint, and hammering nails deep into his feet. The torture was meant to drive away the devils that he imagined constantly tormented him. Eventually, he went insane and was sent to another mission, where he died. Aside from his little-known infamy, Zalvidea is also remembered for his beautiful renovations at Mission San Gabriel:

> He it was he who planted the large Vineyards intersected with fine walks, by shaded fruit trees . . . built the mill and dam . . . planted trees in the Mission square with flower garden and sun-dial in the centre— brought water from long distances.[43]

Zalvidea's actions were matched at Mission Santa Cruz by Friar Ramon Olbés. In one incident, recounted by former neophyte Lorenzo Asisara, Olbés attempted to force a childless Indian couple to have sexual intercourse in his presence to prove they had the potential to conceive. It would have proved nothing, but in Olbés's mind it would have been proof they could try, or perhaps it was merely an excuse to sate his perverted mind. The husband "refused, but they forced him to show them his penis in order to affirm that he had it in good order."

It was not the end of this shocking incident. Asisara, in his interview of 1877, describes what followed:

> The father next brought the wife and placed her in the room. The husband he sent to the guard house with a pair of shackels [sic] . . . Fr. Olbés asked her if her husband slept with her, and she answered that, yes. The Fr. repeated his question "why don't you bear children?" "Who knows!" answered the Indian woman. He had her enter another room in order to examine her private parts. She resisted him and grabbed the father's cord. There was a strong and long struggle between the two that were alone in the room. She tried to bury her teeth in his arm, but only grabbed his habit.
>
> Fr. Olbés cried out and the interpreter and the *alcalde* entered to help him. Then Olbés ordered that they take her and give her fifty lashes.

---

43. Ibid., 144.

After the fifty lashes he ordered that she be shackled and locked in the nunnery. Finishing this, Fr. Olbés ordered that a wooden doll be made like a recently born child; he took the doll to the wife and ordered her to take that doll for her child, and to carry it in front of all the people for nine days. He obligated her to present herself in front of the temple with that [doll] as if it were her child, for nine days.

With all these things the women who were sterile became very alarmed. The vicious father made the husband of that woman wear cattle horns affixed with leather. At the same time he had him shackled. In this way they brought him daily to Mass from the jail. And the other Indians jeered at him and teased him. Returning to the jail, they would take the horns off him.[44]

The Spanish crown and its bureaucracy knew little of the cruelty, daily life, or policies of the missions. Communication between the missions and Spain traveled at a snail's pace, especially since the country was busy defending itself from Napoleon Bonaparte in the Peninsular Wars, which lasted from 1799 to 1815. During that period, California was, for all practical purposes, abandoned by the Spanish crown. The vast Spanish empire was crumbling as rebellion after rebellion in Latin America forced the Iberian Peninsula to abandon its New World interests, leaving it with Cuba as its only major standard bearer.

Throughout the existence of the missions, foreign officials paid formal visits to the compounds and voiced negative opinions of how the Indians were being treated. Yet, while they may have been critical of treatment of the Indians by the friars, nearly all the Europeans shared a low opinion of the Indians.

British Navy Captain George Vancouver visited Mission San Francisco (Dolores) while exploring the California coast in 1792. What he saw within the mission was virtually unchanged since Lapérouse's visit to Mission Carmel in 1786. Regarding the behavior of the Indians, he wrote: "All the operations and functions both of body and mind appeared to be carried out with a mechanical, lifeless, careless indifference . . ."[45] Vancouver's description aptly demonstrated that the Franciscans'

---

44. *Native American Perspectives on the Hispanic Colonization of Alta California*, 426.

45. George A. Vancouver, *Voyage of Discovery to the North Pacific Ocean, and Round the World*, Vol. 2. (London: G.G. and J. Robinson, 1798), in *A Time of Little Choice: The Disintegration of Tribal Culture in the San Francisco Bay Area 1769–1810*, by Randal Milliken (Menlo Park, Calif.: Ballena, 1995), 112.

approach of freely punishing the neophytes was the most efficient method of achieving dominance and meek submission.

The stringent punishment imbued the neophytes with a terrible fear of the friars. It also traumatized the Indian children, who watched their fathers and mothers or relatives being whipped. The Franciscans, however, made one allowance to the Indians. They let them perform their native dances on holidays and Sundays.[46] Only then could the neophytes dress in their traditional ceremonial regalia, which included body paint and elaborate feather headdresses. Each year, the neophytes were also allowed to visit their native villages for a short period. If they did not return, they were hunted down and severely whipped

In 1816, twenty-four years after Vancouver's visit, another visitor also lamented the state of the neophytes. Ludovik Choris, an artist traveling with a Russian expedition, wrote that he had never seen an Indian at Mission Dolores in San Francisco laugh: "They look as though they were interested in nothing."[47] He went on to describe the plight of the Indians attending Mass:

> On Sundays and holidays they celebrate divine service. All the Indians of both sexes without regard to age, are obliged to go to church and worship (there they simply kneel down). Children brought up by the superior, fifty of whom are stationed around him, assist him during the service which they also accompany with the sound of musical instruments. These are chiefly drums, trumpets, tabors, and other instruments of the same class. It is by means of their noise that they endeavor to stir the imagination of the Indians and to make men of these savages. It is, indeed, the only means of producing an effect upon them. When the drums begin to beat they fall to the ground without making the slightest movement until the end of the service, and, even then, it is necessary to tell them several times that the mass is finished. Armed soldiers are stationed at each corner of the church. After the mass, the superior delivers a sermon in Latin to his flock.

Ten years later, in 1826, Captain Frederick William Beechey of England's Royal Navy stopped in San Francisco as part of an expedition

---

46. G.H. von Langsdorff, *Voyage and Travels in Various Parts of the World, during the years 1803, 1804, 1805, 1806, and 1807* (London: Henry Colburn, 1814), in *Documentary Evidence for the Spanish Missions of Alta California*, 108.

47. Louis Andrevitch Choris, *The Visit of the* Rurick *to San Francisco in 1816*, in *Port San Francisco and Its Inhabitants*, by August C. Mahr (Palo Alto, Calif.: Stanford University Press, 1932), in *Documentary Evidence for the Spanish Missions of Alta California*, 156.

to the Bering Strait and polar areas. By that time, California was under Mexican rule, and while newly appointed Mexican Governor José María Echeandía had ordered the Indians freed, many of the missions had not yet complied. Beechey's description of Mission San José Indians attending Mass differs little from that of Choris, with the exception of providing more detail on Indian punishment:

> Morning and evening Mass are daily performed in the Missions . . .
> at which all the converted Indians are obliged to attend . . . After the
> bell had done tolling, several *alguazils*[48] (Indian overseers) went round
> to the huts, to see if all the Indians were at church, and if they found
> any loitering within them, they exercised with tolerable freedom a long
> lash with a broad thong at the end of it; a discipline which appeared the
> more tyrannical as the church was not sufficiently capacious for all the
> attendants and several sat upon the steps . . .
>
> The congregation was arranged on both sides of the building, sepa-
> rated by a wide aisle passing along the centre, in which were stationed
> several *alguazils* with whips, canes, and goads, to preserve silence and
> maintain order, and, what seemed more difficult than either, to keep
> the congregation in their kneeling posture. The goads were better
> adapted to this purpose than the whips, as they would reach a long way,
> and inflict a sharp puncture without making any noise. The end of the
> church was occupied by a guard of soldiers under arms, with fixed bayo-
> nets; a precaution which I suppose experience had taught the necessity
> of observing. . . . The congregation was very attentive, but the gratifica-
> tion they appeared to derive from the music furnished another proof of
> the strong hold this portion of the ceremonies of the Romish[49] church
> takes upon the uninformed minds.[50]

One has to wonder how the mission Indians, or anyone, could endure kneeling without moving or shifting weight on rough stone floors for the approximate hour length of a Mass. While Spanish settlers could absent themselves from daily Mass without fear, the Indians did not have that freedom. By their required presence in those daily services, the priests apparently believed that the Indians would be graced by their devotion

---

48. Beechey used the Spanish word *alguazil*, which denotes a Spanish law enforcement official, to refer to the mission *alcaldes*.

49. Synonymous with Roman Catholic Church.

50. Frederick William Beechey, *Narrative of a Voyage to the Pacific and Bering Strait, to co-operate with The Polar Expeditions*, Vol. II (London: Colburn and Bentley, 1831), 31–32, in *Documentary Evidence for the Spanish Missions of Alta California*, 268–269.

to God, further guaranteeing that their souls would enter into heaven. To the friars, it did not matter that they could not understand one word of the Latin used in the sermon.

In 1821, when Mexico declared its independence from Spain, the Mexican government that inherited Alta California feared that without the Spanish friars running the missions, the neophytes would flee. This would collapse a productive factory system that supplied the region with food and other products. By that time, each mission had hundreds of Indians who had been taught European craftsmanship and had learned how to make rudimentary furniture, providing chairs, benches, tables, stools, cabinets, and shelves for the mission chapels and rooms used by the friars. They had also been taught adobe brick-making, blacksmithing, tanning, leather work—including the production of saddles, bridles and reins—weaving, cooking, metalwork, and soap making. Some Indians learned animal husbandry, which produced highly trained Indian *vaqueros* (cowboys), the only Indians allowed to ride horses. They learned all those skills by watching the friars or Spanish and Mexican craftsmen demonstrate the processes and the use of specific tools. The Indians then imitated them as best they could until they learned what was expected of them. Indians who lacked interest were deemed lazy, and were whipped until their attitude changed.

Despite learning those trades, the Indians were still hampered by the fact most could only speak rudimentary Spanish. In many cases, the only Spanish term that mission Indians appeared to know was *amar a Dios* (love God), taught to them by the friars as a greeting. Some neophytes, however, did manage on their own to learn how to speak Spanish. Hugo Reid was so appalled at the widespread lack of Spanish among the neophytes that he wrote: "Not one word of Spanish did they understand. They had no more idea that they were worshiping God than an unborn child has of astronomy."[51]

The policy of not teaching the Indians how to read or write Spanish was promulgated by the Spanish Visitor-General José de Gálvez. His wishes were stipulated in a letter he wrote to Serra's close friend, Friar Francisco Palóu, on June 19, 1769:

---

51. Susanna Bryant Dakin, *Hugo Reid, A Scotch Paisano: Hugo Reid's Life in California, 1832–1852: Derived from his Correspondence* (Berkeley: University of California Press, 1939), in *Documentary Evidence for the Spanish Missions in Alta California*, 500–501.

I stress my request to your most reverend person that you do not
teach the Indians how to write; for I have enough experiences that such
major instruction perverts and hastens their ruination.[52]

Palóu undoubtedly relayed Gálvez's instructions to Serra, a policy that
proved catastrophic for the Indians when they began abandoning the
missions in the 1830s. There is no way of knowing if Palóu and Serra
discussed those critical instructions from Gálvez or if Serra had, prior
to the Spanish official's directive, already decided to keep the Indians
illiterate. The friars may have realized that if neophytes were taught how
to read and write they might have sought freedom after eventually determining that Catholic doctrine and baptism did not require their captivity.

Gálvez's instruction to Palóu is a stain on the visitor-general's otherwise
enlightened reputation. While he was open to new ideas and the rights of
human beings, Native Americans were apparently not included in those
beliefs. The refusal of the friars to teach the Indians how to speak, read,
or write Spanish or do simple mathematics shattered any possibilities that
the Indians would be able to successfully exist outside the missions once
they were freed by the Mexican government. It was virtually guaranteed
they would be unable to interact with the Spanish-speaking settlers from
Mexico, who now needed laborers and craftsmen. It would have been
impossible for one of those settlers to convey instructions regarding
handicrafts or services to someone who did not fully grasp the language.
Additionally, their being treated as children and never provided the
lessons needed for the responsibilities of adulthood in a European society
further crippled any efforts at full assimilation into Alta California's
society.

This situation could have been avoided had the missions followed a
royal decree issued twenty-four years after their founding. On July 23,
1793, King Carlos IV ordered that Indians in Alta California be taught
how to read and write. A copy of that order was sent to Friar Lasuén,
who simply forwarded it to each mission on February 23, 1795 (the delay
between when the king issued the order and when it was forwarded by
Lasuén is an indication of how long it took for mail from Spain to reach
Alta California), with instructions to acknowledge, read it, and to "... take
pains to teach the Spanish language to the different converts . . . ."[53] Despite

---

52. José de Gálvez, letter to Francisco Palóu, 19 June, 1769. Santa Barbara Mission Archive
Library. Santa Barbara, Calif. Junípero Serra Collection. Folder #182.

53. Lasuén, *Writings of Fermín Francisco de Lasuén*, 329–330

this directive, neither Lasuén nor the friars took any steps to follow the King's orders. Whatever their motivation, the friars knew Charles IV was thousands of miles from Alta California and that Mexico City, the seat of the Spanish Viceroy, was likewise more than a thousand miles away. It is not beyond belief that the friars shrugged their shoulders after reading the edict, filed it away, and simply ignored it.

Those Indians who did learn how to speak Spanish learned it by listening to the friars and Spanish foremen. In some rare cases the friars taught the language to native children they considered exceptionally bright. If the Indians wanted to speak Spanish, so the friars believed, they could simply learn it on their own within the missions. At Mission San Diego, however, the friars punished the Indians for not speaking Spanish. Friars José Sánchez and Fernando Martín worked out this system for the purpose: "A suitable method to get them to speak Spanish is the one we follow, namely, we exhort and threaten them with punishment and in the case of the young we punish them from time to time. We do not know what reasons keep them from using Spanish."[54] They refused to acknowledge the obvious—Spanish classes for the neophytes were never organized.

At other missions, the friars blamed the lack of Spanish on the Indians frequent contact with "heathen" village members outside the compounds.[55] The friars at Mission San Francisco were satisfied their Indians were learning Spanish by themselves.[56] Only at Mission San Gabriel did the friars propose having the government send "male teachers in primary education for the boys and female teachers for the girls. Their utmost solicitude should be exerted so that not a single word would be uttered in school except in the Spanish tongue, not sparing any means to obtain that goal."[57] The latter part of their suggestion forecast an ominous future for what the pupils could expect in learning Spanish. No records are known to exist that teachers were ever sent or that the friars established schools within the missions to teach the Indians Spanish.

---

54. *As the Padres Saw Them: California Indian Life and Customs as Reported by the Franciscan Missionaries 1813–1815*, ed. Doyce B. Nunis, Jr. (Los Angeles: Westland Printing, 1976), 39.

55. Ibid.

56. Ibid.

57. Ibid.

With a supply of cowed labor kept ignorant of elementary reading or writing, and denied freedom and knowledge of European social customs, the mission lands were transformed from untilled soil to the economic centers of Alta California. As Mexican experts in animal husbandry arrived, attracted by the salaries paid by the missions, the friars' livestock rapidly multiplied. Ships began arriving from the eastern United States, eager to buy dried cattle hide.

Along with the livestock, the missions had demonstrated that vast irrigated acres planted with large varieties of crops could thrive in the mild coastal climate. Later, much of California, including land that was far from the coast, would be turned into a huge and profitable farming area—the legacy of the missions, albeit at a tragic cost to California's Indian. As the success of the missions became known, more and more settlers from Mexico and from the eastern United States began arriving, attracted to California's potential for farming and ranching.

However, the Spanish, and later Mexican, governors sought to break the monopoly of the missions in ranching and farming, allowing freer trade that would help the development of Alta California. The missions, rather than promoting development, were hindering it. It was difficult to compete with those compounds, which were capable of offering far more farm produce, wine, brandy, hides, tallow, and herds to buyers. Newly-arrived settlers were faced with twenty-one missions that were in actuality giant agribusinesses that controlled the best lands with a large pool of free manpower.

While the Franciscans claimed all of the profit made by the missions was spent on the Indians, the facts do not bear that out. The merchants paid the priests in gold or silver for the mission products they bought. By contrast, the friars bought little from outsiders. The neophytes wove the cloth needed to provide clothes for themselves, eventually made their own tools, and provided all the food the friars wanted. The missions were self-sustaining and needed to import only a few products they could not manufacture, such as scissors, needles, thread, looms, or iron ingots for blacksmiths. Anything else they lacked could be ordered from the *Colegio de San Fernando* in Mexico City, which kept the friars supplied with their personal needs, plus religious articles for the mission chapels.

As the missions spread up and down California and the Spanish settled into pueblos, Indian culture began to disintegrate. Despite efforts by mission Indians to keep alive their cultures by meeting secretly at night, the mission death rates were so high most of the elders who sought to maintain those traditions soon perished, their knowledge lost forever. Life for the mission Indians had become a daily struggle to escape the wrath of whip-wielding *alcaldes* and watchful Franciscan priests.

One of the most detailed descriptions of the daily regimen in the missions, albeit a somewhat biased one, was written by Pablo Tac, one of only two Coastal Indians known to have been sent to study for the priesthood in Spain and Rome in the 1830s. Tac, a member of the Luiseño Indian tribe, was one of six children born in Mission San Luis Rey in 1822 to neophytes Ladislaya Molmolix and her husband, Pedro Alcántara. Pablo's text, written sometime in the late 1830s, describes life in Mission San Luis Rey, including the punishments meted out to Indians. Tac never addresses what right or doctrine empowered the friars to enslave or punish the neophytes. That was, perhaps, to be expected from someone raised to see the mission culture only from the friars' viewpoint, thus painting a somewhat idyllic but inaccurate view of mission life.

Tac had been sent to Europe with Agapito Amamix, another Indian, after they caught the attention of the mission administrator, Friar Antonio Peyri. When Peyri returned to Mexico in 1832, he took both boys with him. Whether Peyri obtained parental permission to take the boys is not known. Tac was 10 years old and Amamix 12 when they left California. From Mexico, Peyri and the boys traveled to Barcelona, and from there they were then sent to Rome to study at the *Collegium Urbanum de Propaganda Fide*, founded in 1627 by Pope Urban VIII. Tac died in Italy at the age of 19 from an unknown disease. Amamix died earlier, also in Europe.

Tac's manuscript, *Conversión de los San Luiseños de la Alta California* (Conversion of the San Luiseños of Alta California), is preserved in the Messofanti Collection in the *Biblioteca dell'Archiginnasio di Bologna*. The manuscript includes a description of the first days of the mission, facts probably told to Tac by Friar Peyri since Tac was born twenty-four years after its founding. It was written in the present tense and begins with the encampment of Lasuén at the site.

The Fernandino[58] Father remains in our country with the little troop that he brought. A camp was made, and here he lived for many days. In the morning he said Mass, and then he planned how he would baptize them, where he would put his house, the church and as there were five thousand souls (who were all the Indians there were), how he would sustain them, and seeing how it could be done. Having the captain for his friend, he was afraid of nothing. It was a great mercy that the Indians did not kill the Spanish when they arrived, and very admirable, because they have never wanted another people to live with them, and until those days they were always fighting. But thus willed He who alone can will. They could understand him somewhat when he, as their father, ordered them to carry stone from the sea (which is not far) for the foundation, to make bricks, roof tiles, to cut beams, reeds and what was necessary. They did it with the masters who were helping them, and within a few years they finished working. They made a church with three altars for all the neophytes (the great altar is nearly all gilded), two chapels, two sacristies, two choirs, a flower garden for the church, a high tower with five bells, two small and three large, the cemetery with a crucifix in the middle for all those who die here.[59]

Tac's description of the mission spans a period of about seventeen years, after it was founded by Lasuén and then turned over to Peyri. Tac describes the contents of the compound's wine cellar as a measure of the mission's immense prosperity:

Within are 200 casks of wine, brandy, and white wine, 400 barrels, for Mass, to sell to the Spanish and English travelers who often come to the Mission to sell cloth, linen, cotton, and whatever they bring from Boston—and not for the neophytes, which is prohibited them because they easily get drunk.[60]

The Indian youth drew a layout (it has since been lost) of the mission, providing an image of its immense size. Each building and point of interest was numbered for a total of fifty-seven sites (accounting for two incorrectly numbered sites). Tac's detailed physical description of the mission captures the complexity of the compound that kept the 1,000

---

58. Tac calls the friar "Fernandino," a common title used in that period to describe the Franciscan friars in California because they were originally from the *Colegio de San Fernando* in Mexico City originally.

59. Pablo Tac, *Conversión de los San Luiseños de la Alta California*.

60. Ibid.

Indians at Mission San Luis Rey busy for six to seven hours each day, as was customary in all the Alta California missions.

Tac describes also how each day began in pre-dawn darkness, with the tolling of the mission bells calling the Indians to mass. It was a signal for the *caciques* and *alcaldes* to roust neophytes and their children from their huts, herd them to church, and assign them the day's labor, lashing out at anyone slow in getting up from the dirt floors on which they slept. The flogging continued for laggards as the neophytes shuffled toward the mission chapel. Breakfast consisted of a watery gruel of barley or corn or one or two tortillas. Initially, the neophytes were forced to partake of a meager meal that did not have sufficient calories for the labor demanded of them. Later, as the mission livestock herds grew, the Indians' meals included meat stews, and Indian couples were permitted to grow their own gardens to help supplement the mission diet.

In contrast to the neophytes' diet, friars at the well established missions enjoyed hearty daily meals that in many cases included wine, Mexican chocolate, and daily portions of beef, chicken, fish, pork, vegetables, and fruit.

From dawn to the end of the seven-hour workday, neophytes assigned to farm work were escorted by a *cacique* or *alcalde* who supervised their labor. He used a club, heavy cane, or whip against any unfortunate neophyte who was not meeting the standard of labor established at the missions.

Tac described the *alcalde's* authority, writing that all work groups were accompanied by "a Spanish majordomo and others, neophyte *alcaldes*, to see how the work is done, to hurry them if they are lazy, so they will soon finish what was ordered, and to punish the guilty or lazy one who leaves his plow and quits the field, keeping on with his laziness. They work all day, but not always."

Tac provides the following account regarding the appointment and duties of *alcaldes*:

> The Fernandino Father, as he was alone and very accustomed to the usages of the Spanish soldiers, seeing that it would be very difficult for him alone to give orders to that people, and moreover, people that had left the woods just a few years before, therefore appointed *alcaldes* from the people themselves that knew how to speak Spanish more than the others and were better than the others in their customs. There were seven of these *alcaldes*, with rods as symbol that they could judge the

others. The captain dressed like the Spanish, always remaining captain, but not ordering his people about as of old, when they were still *gentiles*. The chief of the *alcaldes* was called the general. He knew the name of each one, and when he took something he then named each person by his name. In the afternoon the *alcaldes* gather at the house of the Missionary. They bring the news of that day, and if the Missionary tells them something that all the people of country ought to know, they return to the villages shouting 'Tomorrow morning.' . . . Returning to the villages, each one of the *alcaldes*, wherever he goes, cries out what the Missionary has told them, in his language, and all the country hears it. 'Tomorrow the sowing begins,' and so the laborers go to the chicken yard and assemble there. And again he goes, saying these same words, until he reaches his own village to eat something and then to sleep. In the morning you will see the laborers appear in the chicken yard and assemble there according to what they heard last night.[61]

It is doubtful that the missions could have functioned efficiently without the *alcaldes*, who constantly harangued their Indian charges and forced each neophyte to accomplish their daily tasks. In church or outside it, the *alcaldes* ensured strict obedience to the friars' wishes. Additionally, at any moment a priest, if he perceived the slightest infraction of mission rules, could order an Indian lashed by an *alcalde*.

Tac likened the head of Mission San Luis Rey to a "king," a description that contradicts the vows of poverty taken by the Franciscans:

In the Mission of San Luis Rey de Francia, the Fernandino Father is like a king. He has his pages, *alcaldes*, majordomos, musicians, soldiers, gardens, ranchos, livestock, horses by the thousands, cows, bulls by the thousand, oxen, mules, asses, twelve thousand lambs, two hundred goats, etc. The pages are for him and for the Spanish and Mexican, English, and Anglo-American travelers. The *alcaldes* help him govern all the people of the Mission of San Luis Rey de Francia. The major-domos are in the distant districts, almost all Spaniards. The musicians of the Mission are for the holy days and all the Sundays and holidays of the year, with them the singers, all Indian neophytes. Soldiers so that nobody does injury to Spaniard or to Indian; there are 10 of them and they go on horseback. There are five gardens that are for all, very large. The Fernandino Father drinks little, and almost all the gardens produce wine, he who knows the customs of the neophytes well does not wish to give any wine to any of them, but sells it to the English or Anglo-Americans, not for money but for clothing for the neophytes, linen for

---

61. Ibid.

the church, hats, muskets, plates, coffee, tea, sugar, and other things. The products of the Mission are butter, tallow, hides, chamois leather, bearskins, wine, white wine, brandy, (olive) oil, maize, wheat, beans, and also bull horns, which the English take by the thousand to Boston.[62]

In mission life as described by Tac, the bounty produced by each compound never made life easier for the Indians. Instead, it provided additional luxuries to the friars, who lived in what apparently was great comfort for that time.

---

62. Ibid.

9

A Vision Darkened

It is evident that a nation that is barbarous, ferocious, and ignorant requires more punishment than a nation that is cultured, educated, and of gentle and moderate customs.
—Friar Fermín Francisco Lasuén, November 12, 1800, justifying the need to harshly punish California's mission Indians.

While the missions enriched themselves, the strict life imposed on the Indians by the Franciscans did not change. The mission priests did not ease the exacting toll they levied on the men and women who provided essential labor and whose souls the friars felt obligated to keep free of sin.

Lorenzo Asisara, a onetime mission Indian interviewed in the late nineteenth century, recalled how the friars were "very cruel toward the Indians. They abused them very much. They had bad food, bad clothing. And they made them work like slaves. I also was subject to that cruel life. The Fathers did not practice what they preached."[1] Each mission kept ledgers with the names of Indians who violated mission rules and the number of lashes applied, but did not provide a record of the beatings and whippings that were a daily regimen for minor infractions. Serra, his successor Lasuén, and the subsequent presidents of the missions never wavered from their belief that the Indians needed to be whipped—and often.

---

1. *Native American Perspectives on the Hispanic Colonization of Alta California (The Spanish Borderlands Sourcebook Vol. 26)*, ed. Edward D. Castillo (New York: Garland, 1991), 10.

Lasuén had no affection for the Indians. He may have even considered the Indians a nuisance, useful only as a source of labor. Nowhere in his writings does he praise the Indians, display any affection toward them, or have anything praiseworthy to say about their culture. Rather, Lasuén wrote the following in support of severe corporal punishment:

> It is evident that a nation that is barbarous, ferocious, and ignorant requires more punishment than a nation that is cultured, educated, and of gentle and moderate customs.

Additionally, Lasuén considered the Indians:

> . . . a people of vicious and ferocious customs, who know no other law than force, nor any authority other than their own free will nor reason other than mere caprice, who watched the cruelest and most barbarous practices with an indifference entirely foreign to human nature, accustomed to punish offenses against them by death. They are a people without education or government or religion or dependence. They have no reluctance whatever in throwing themselves impetuously into anything that their brutal appetites might suggest. Their inclination to lasciviousness and thievery (in the missions) is on a level with that which they show in the wild condition. It is a duty imposed on us to correct and punish men of this kind for their misdemeanors.[2]

The imposition of such a constrained life instilled a longing within the neophytes to be free. After Russian explorer Otto von Kotzebue visited Mission Dolores in San Francisco in 1816, he poignantly described the plight of neophytes who could not participate in the twice-annual outings in which mission Indians were allowed a few days visit to their ancestral lands:

> The friars called the visits a *paseo* or trip: Twice in the year they [Indians] receive permission to return to their native homes. This short time is the happiest period of their existence; and I myself have seen them going home in crowds, with loud rejoicings. The sick, who cannot undertake the journey, at least accompany their happy countrymen to the shore where they embark and there sit for days together mournfully gazing on the distant summits of the mountains which surround their homes; they often sit in this situation for several days, without taking any food, so much does the sight of their lost home affect these new Christians. Every time some of those who have permission run away,

---

2. Sherburne F. Cook, *The Conflict Between the California Indian and White Civilization* (Berkeley: University of California Press, 1976), 124.

and they would probably all do it were they not deterred by their fear
of the soldiers, who catch them, and bring them back to the mission as
criminals; this fear is so great, that seven or eight dragoons are sufficient
to overpower several hundred Indians.[3]

Depression also took its toll on the mission Indians. Some may have
simply willed themselves to die, unable to stand the terrible stress.
Disease was, however, the major killer. Newborns perished at alarming
rates in compounds that teemed with dysentery, syphilis, malnutrition, hunger, exhaustion, and respiratory illnesses. Far worse were the
pandemics of European diseases to which the Indians had no immunity. Influenza, smallpox, and measles periodically swept through the
missions, killing the neophytes and quickly spreading to the outlying
villages of the *gentiles*, the friars' term for Indians who had refused to join
the missions.

The overall result was that nearly half of the missions' populations died
each year. Randall Milliken's study of death rates among mission Indians
in the San Francisco Bay Area found: "Health conditions in the missions
were poor from the beginning. The native people were being introduced to diseases that came from everywhere in the world through the
medium of the yearly visits of the supply ships from Mexico. These new
diseases thrived not only because the population was immunologically
unprotected, but also because of the crowding and squalor that existed in
mission communities."[4]

Even vegetable gardens that Indian families grew in the later years
of the missions were not enough to keep them healthy and offset their
overall inferior diet and lack of hygiene. Human feces, and the lack of
sanitary methods to dispose of them, contributed to the contamination
of water supplies. Additionally, the denial of frequent bathing, which the
Coastal Indians had formerly practiced, enhanced the spread of illness.

Sherburne F. Cook, who made a minute examination of mission birth
and death records, states that from 1779 to 1833, the year the missions
were effectively dissolved, there were 29,100 births and a staggering
62,600 deaths. His analysis determined that of the 62,600 deaths, 40,000

---

3. Louis Andrevitch Choris, *The Visit of the* Rurick *to San Francisco in 1816* (Palo Alto,
Calif.: Stanford University Press, 1932), 145.

4. Randall Milliken, *A Time of Little Choice: The Disintegration of Tribal Culture in the San
Francisco Bay Area, 1769–1810* (Menlo Park, Calif.: Ballena, 1995), 90.

could be considered "natural mortality, leaving 22,600 to be accounted for as due to the negative effect of mission life."[5]

The situation was so appalling that in 1815, the then-president of the missions, Friar Mariano Payéras, wrote that "in many years there were three deaths to two births." From 1810 to 1820, the death rate "was 86 per cent of baptisms and 42 per cent of the total (missions') population."[6]

Kotzebue deplored the appalling death toll among the mission Indians, blaming it on the lack of proper hygiene: "The uncleanliness in these barracks baffles description, and this is perhaps the cause of great mortality: for of 1,000 Indians at St. [sic] Francisco, 300 die every year." Aside from the catastrophic death rate, Kotzebue questioned whether the Indians could even understand the Christian religion: "As the missionaries do not trouble themselves to learn the language of the Indians, I cannot conceive in what manner they have been instructed in the Christian religion; and there is probably but little light in the heads and hearts of these poor creatures, who can do nothing but imitate the external ceremonies which they observe by the eye."[7]

The missions were certainly not places where two separate cultures easily and happily melded. Still, some may contend that the descriptions of the horrors of those compounds came from visitors who were anti-Catholic or opposed the Spanish regime. But that theory is easily shattered by the proof preserved in the detailed archives and reports produced by neighboring presidios the missions themselves. Those government and mission documents recorded each birth and death, while mission documents carefully cited those punished with the name, offense, sentence, and date when the punishment was imposed. Also noted were details related to the capture of Indians who fled the missions, the deaths of Indians who resisted Spanish and Mexican rule, and, surprisingly, even protests from Spanish officials and friars who were appalled at their fellow priests' treatment of the Native Americans.

---

5. Sherburne F. Cook, *The Conflict Between the California Indian and White Civilization*, 16.

6. Hubert Howe Bancroft, *History of California, Vol. II 1801–1824* (San Francisco: The History Company, 1886), 394.

7. Otto Von Kotzebue, "From Oonashka to California." In Mahr, *The Visit of the Rurick to San Francisco in 1816*. In *Documentary Evidence for the Spanish Missions of Alta California (The Spanish Borderlands Sourcebook Vol. 14)*, ed. Julia G. Costello (New York: Garland, 1991), 147.

Among those protesting the savage regime of the missions was Friar Antonio de la Concepción Horra, who was assigned to head Mission San Miguel in 1798. Almost as soon as he arrived, Horra was shocked at the treatment of the Indians by the friars and their Indian *alcaldes*. He also criticized his fellow friars for not teaching the Indians Spanish. That same year he sent a letter to the Viceroy of Mexico, Miguel José de Azanza, expressing dismay at what he saw in Alta California:

> Your Excellency, I would like to inform you of the many abuses that are commonplace in that country. The manner in which the Indians are treated is by far more cruel than anything I have ever read about. For any reason, however insignificant it may be, they are severely and cruelly whipped, placed in shackles, or put in stocks for days on end without receiving even a drop of water.[8]

Horra also criticized the Franciscans' practice of doing business:

> With regard to the sale of cattle and other food, there is no official price except for what suits their fancy. This occurs with every purchaser. Even though there is an official price list, they do not want to follow it, and if the purchaser challenges them, they tell him to go and buy what he wants from the governor.[9]

Horra was also stunned by the selfishness of the Franciscans, despite their vows to be charitable. He cited, as a prime example, the refusal by Mission San Luis Obispo to provide a cabbage to a weaver and his family, who were traveling from San Diego to Monterey:

> They refused to give him any, even though the garden was full of them. The same thing happens every day to the soldiers of the escort. Even if they are dying of hunger and all they request is a morsel of bread.[10]

Yet, in that same letter, sent twenty-nine years after Serra founded the first missions, Horra protested against a fellow priest who had learned the Indians' language and was logically teaching them Catholic doctrine in their own tongue. It would seem that taking the time to learn the Indian language and then using it to teach the Indians would have been cause for Horra to commend the bilingual priest rather than condemn him.

---

8. Rose Marie Beebe and Robert M. Senkewicz, *Lands of Promise and Despair: Chronicles of Early California, 1535–1846* (Berkeley: Heyday Books, 2001), 272.

9. Ibid.

10. Ibid., 272–273.

Church officials answered his protests by declaring Horra insane and returning him to Spain. The viceroy declared there was no basis for his protests, despite an investigation that found the priest's accusations were justified. However, in the wake of the probe, the viceroy ordered the governor of California, Diego de Borica, to look into Horra's complaints. The governor, in turn, ordered his presidio commanders to determine if there was any truth to the priest's charges. Borica eventually wrote the viceroy:

> Generally, the treatment given the Indians is very harsh. At San Francisco, it even reached the point of cruelty.[11]

Horra's protests were not the first. Just a year earlier, in 1797, another complaint had been filed by Friar José Maria Fernández, who had been named to head Mission San Francisco after his predecessor was reassigned for mistreating Indians. When Fernández took over the mission, the two priests already there, Friar José de la Cruz Espí and Friar Martín de Landaeta, resisted his reforms and directives. Fernández, at his wit's end, could stand it no longer and wrote to Borica, saying Indians were fleeing the mission because of the abysmal treatment. In part, his letter stated:

> I also know why they have fled. It is due to the terrible suffering they experienced from punishments and work.[12]

Fernández had written the letter after the two other priests had defied specific orders not only from him, but also from Governor Borica, to let a group of mission Indians flee to the east shore of San Francisco Bay.

Even former Governor Fages had earlier written: "The unhappy treatment which they [the Franciscans] give the Indians with whose care they are charged renders the Indians' fate worse than that of slaves." The governor then continued that the friars' goal was to achieve full control "over the Indians and the Indians' wealth without recognizing any other authority than that of their religious superiors."[13]

By far one of the cruelest incidents was described in 1825 by Robert B. Forbes, the master of a New England trading ship. He visited Mission San Francisco and was shocked by the savagery of the friars. During his visit,

---

11. Ibid., 270.

12. Ibid., 262.

13. Edwin A. Beilhartz, *Felipe de Neve: First Governor of California* (San Francisco: California Historical Society, 1971), 52.

he took note of "the Christianizing Padres who . . . 'converted' the Indians by sending the *gauchos* and *rancheros* into the field to catch them with the lasso, and mark them with a cross!" He said the San Francisco friars, who he called "licentious priests," branded the Indians with an iron shaped like a cross.[14]

In the 277 years since the Spaniards had discovered the New World, little had changed in the attitudes of either the descendants of the *conquistadores*' or of the Franciscan friars toward the Indians. Still, the Spanish governors of Alta California, like Fages, made it clear that given permission, they would have gladly dissolved the missions, ridding themselves of the ongoing problem of their inhumane practices, as well as the need to support those religious institutions with troops.

The friars' disregard for the Indians' well-being was voiced chillingly in 1830 by the head of Mission San José, Rafael de Jesús Moreno. He confided in Faxon Dean Atherton, a hide-and-tallow trader, how it was difficult to convince Indians to accept European life and customs. Moreno declared, in a statement tinged with genocidal intent, the Indians, "must and will die off and disappear before the more morally educated white man." The San José priest, however, believed that if the Indians shunned their customary traits "he was certain they possessed abilities equal to the whites and would make as respectable appearances in the world if they could be made to forget the vicious habits of their fathers."[15]

During that period, California was already under Mexican rule and the missions were slowly being disbanded, although at that point the fate of the Indians had already been sealed. As the missions had grown and became wealthy, they had become like black holes in space, mercilessly sucking in all the surrounding Indians until they disappeared into what, for the natives, must have been akin to a terrible void from which they would never escape.

A detailed study by Robert H. Jackson, who focused on efforts by the mission friars in the San Francisco bay area to entice Indians into the missions, concluded in part that the bringing of non-mission Indians into those compounds led to "the destruction of the local Indian

---

14. James J. Rawls, *Indians of California: The Changing Image* (Norman: University of Oklahoma, 1984), 62.

15. Faxon D. Atherton, *The California Diary of Faxon Dean Atherton, 1836–1839*, ed. Doyce B. Nunis, Jr. (San Francisco: California Historical Society, 1964), 58.

populations."[16] The only recourse the outside natives had to escape those surprise visits on nearby villages was to flee into the interior of California. Any haphazard use of force against the missions would have been virtual suicide against Spanish soldiers armed with swords, lances, and muskets, and who were garbed in thick leather vests to protect against arrows.

Only a carefully organized attack by Indians numbering in the hundreds or thousands could have been successful. The possibility of Indians joining in a united front was a constant worry of the friars and the Spanish governors. However, organizing massive attacks to destroy the missions was unlikely because of the traditional enmity of many tribes toward each other.

As previously detailed, labor was critical to an Indian village's survival, and the loss of even a few people to the missions was intolerable. Yet disease coupled with the departure of those who willingly joined the missions destabilized many villages to the point where the remaining inhabitants were often forced to turn to the missions as a final recourse. Randal Milliken has called their overall decisions a "psychological disintegration movement."[17]

Compounding the loss of village manpower was the Spaniards' practice of taking over flat, open areas that had traditionally supported native peoples. The Indians annually burned these areas to allow edible plants to blossom and, in turn, attract the small mammals and deer that they hunted. Spanish cattle, mules, horses, and sheep gradually destroyed those sites, compacting the soil so that few plants grew. Those same domestic animals competed with wildlife for the grass that did thrive, gradually driving out the rabbits, ground squirrels, and deer.

As the Coastal Indians sought to protect their culture against the Spanish onslaught, rebellion against the invaders and the missions was inevitable. Priests were killed and mission buildings burned, but a unified rebellion did not develop.

Although violent attacks were rare, a different type of rebellion was constant at all the missions: Indians sought to flee. The Indians chafed at being ordered to work daily, being forced to attend Mass, having their personal lives tightly regimented, and being flogged by *alcaldes* for

---

16. Robert H. Jackson, "Gentile Recruitment and Population Movements in the San Francisco Bay Area Missions," in *Journal of California and Great Basin Anthropology*, vol. 6 (1984), no. 2, 235.

17. Milliken, *A Time of Little Choice*, 136.

insignificant rule violations, or at the *alcalde's* whim. Escaping became the most common form of defiance against the friars, but even those relatively few willing to risk severe punishment had little chance against Spanish soldiers on horseback.

Sherburne F. Cook estimated that at each mission, approximately 10 percent of the Indian population fled.[18] Using that number, it can be assumed that at any given time during the mission era, several hundred Indians were attempting to flee. "Fugitivism," writes Cook, "as the first active response of the neophytes to the mission environment, was of such wide scope as to constitute a mass reaction to certain elements in that environment."[19]

Statistics compiled by Cook show that by 1817, more than 1,000 neophytes had fled or attempted to escape from fifteen missions.[20] At some compounds, such as at Santa Barbara, hundreds had escaped. All too frequently, however, the soldiers and *alcaldes* caught up with the exhausted Indians and returned them to the missions.

FUGITIVES PER MISSION, 1769–1817[21]

Missions	Number of Fugitives
San Diego	316
San Juan Capistrano	254
San Gabriel	473
San Fernando	5
San Buenaventura	27
Santa Bárbara	595
La Purísima	52
San Luis Obispo	136
San Antonio	167
San Carlos	431
San Juan Bautista	174

18. Cook, *Conflict Between the California Indian and White Civilization*, 61.
19. Ibid., 64.
20. Ibid.
21. Ibid.

Santa Cruz	60
Santa Clara	310
San José	3
San Francisco	202

Preserved records from the Spanish government and archives from the missions show that in most cases escaped neophytes, when discovered either in villages of *gentiles* or in the wild, realized that it was useless to try to elude the friars and soldiers on horseback. Most accepted their fate meekly and did not resist. Yet it is difficult to believe that all of the runaways gave in so easily. Among the fugitives there were, undoubtedly, some who fought the soldiers or were successful in eluding them.

In one incident, described in a report from San José in 1794, Indians in villages surrounding Mission Santa Clara fled to the mountains for fear of being forced into the mission by its director, Friar Manuel Fernández. Commissioner Gabriel Moraga of the Pueblo de San José wrote to Lieutenant José Argüello of Presidio Monterey, explaining the reason why the Indians had fled:

> It is common knowledge among the Indians, confirmed by remarks made by the soldiers that have escorted said religious, that Indians who refused to become Christians were severely threatened. In some cases he went beyond threat to actual punishment. Confirming this was he who the Father came upon at the cornfield of soldier Ygnacio Soto, and in whose presence the Father called to one of several pagans who were gleaning corn. Because the man did not come immediately, he [Father Fernandez] asked a soldier who accompanied him for a lance, then proceeded to horsewhip the Indian with it to the utmost.
>
> Following this and other incidents, the pagans really credited the threat of the father to the effect that if those who told him (out of fear) that they would go to be baptized failed to fulfill his promise, he would have to burn their villages down.
>
> One pagan inhabitant of this pueblo, called El Mocho, came to me to complain that said Father had gone to his village and, because he would not go to the Mission and because he was accused of dissuading his relatives, ordered him tied up and given many lashes, first with a halter rope and then with a leather *riata*. The Indian was left in such bad condition

that he came in supporting himself by a cane, unable to stand upright, with waist and buttocks covered with swollen wounds.[22]

We can only surmise why Serra and his Franciscans delved into that frightful darkness. Their deceitful lures and promises to the Indians, followed by whipping and beating of the neophytes, had certainly not been a part of the priests' theological teachings. Carey McWilliams described the Franciscans' treatment of the Indians thus: "With the best theological intentions in the world, the Franciscan padres eliminated the Indians with the effectiveness of Nazis operating concentration camps."[23]

David J. Weber wrote: "Missionaries not only favored the use of force but employed it in ways that seem harsh by present day standards (and perhaps by the standards of some of their Indian clients as well). By the standards of their day, however, Missionaries' punishment of Indians fell within the range of punishments that Spaniards might inflict on one another."[24] Weber's conclusion is questionable. It is highly unlikely that a Spaniard would have been flogged for not attending Mass, attempting to escape from a religious community for which he never took vows, or whipped for laziness.

In Coahuila, Mexico, the Franciscans were known to punish any Indian who missed Mass by having them lashed four or five times "across the shoulders, in front of the cross in the cemetery."[25] The Franciscan treatment of Indians in the Southwest, however, went beyond the standards practiced in the late eighteenth century and was strongly criticized by Teodoro de Croix, the Spanish Commander in Chief of the *Comandancia General* (General Headquarters) of that region. Croix complained that an Indian becoming part of the five Franciscan missions near San Antonio, Texas, "has nothing to aspire to for the rest of his life: continuous work, nakedness, lack of liberty, and bad treatment are his fortune."[26] The Texas Franciscan missions, he said, did nothing to prepare the Indians for life outside the missions.

---

22. Milliken, *A Time of Little Choice*, 281.

23. Carey McWilliams, *Southern California Country: An Island on the Land* (New York: Duell, Sloan & Pearce, 1946), 29.

24. Weber and Sweet, *Arts of the Missions of Northern New Spain*, 14.

25. Ibid.

26. Ibid.

Perhaps the Franciscans' penchant for inflicting punishment was prompted by frustration at being far from Spain and living in an isolated environment far removed from the church quarters they had left behind. Unlike other orders, the Franciscans had vowed to spread Catholicism and did not live as monks in monasteries. In Spain, they had always received three meals a day, labored at mundane tasks necessary to maintain their order, and balanced those chores with theological studies, prayers, singing, mass, and proselytizing in the Spanish countryside. Their quarters were Spartan, but they were dry and afforded individual privacy.

The friars had ambitiously crossed the Atlantic to a New World, their thoughts brimming with how many souls they would bring to Catholicism. Most believed that the Christianization of California's indigenous people would be a simple task and had not considered the physical discomfort and loneliness that many would face, let alone the reluctance of the Indians to join the missions. Once they revealed the doctrine of an all-knowing, forgiving, and powerful God, the friars expected that their new churches would be instantly filled with parishioners just as in Spain. Tragically, no one had described the profound hardships they would initially encounter in the California wilderness. The impositions of that harsh life may have driven them to take out their frustrations on their Indian captives. Too, they were Spaniards, imbued with the attitude that Indians were beneath them, only quasi-humans who merited little consideration and were best controlled by violence, a doctrine endorsed by Serra and Lasuén.

In selecting friars to accompany him to Alta California, Serra apparently had not required that they possess a basic knowledge of construction and farming. To survive, the missions were in sore need of men who were skilled in crafts such as carpentry, or who had knowledge of how to prepare building material such as adobe bricks. Still, the friars muddled through, taking their frustrations out on their Indian charges.

Those conditions sent Serra's successor, Lasuén, into a spiraling depression. Little did he realize that California would later become one of the world's most bountiful agricultural areas, brimming with fruit, nuts, vegetables, and vineyards. To him, the land was worthless:

> The barrenness of the ground is something that is evident and
> obvious to everyone . . . unproductive, lacking in all fruit, without

humidity or irrigation: and planting is but a speculation made in the hope that the year will be one of abundant rainfall.[27]

The friar was now living in a land where most crops required irrigation systems, something of which Lasuén knew nothing. Here, rainfall was the only source of water for farming and that source of moisture was scarce in California's semi-arid coastal land.

Lasuén complained about never having enough food for the mission Indians to:

> ... satisfy the voracious way of eating which they were brought up; and none would submit to the slightest discipline if he were denied access to his hunting and fishing; to his mice, snakes, vipers, and insects; to his acorns and other loathsome and unpalatable seeds which are rendered edible only by being soaked in water and cooked over a fire. And there is none among them who knows or uses any other medium of exchange than these coarse and contemptible foodstuffs and other items of a similar nature.[28]

The only saving grace for the Indians, Lasuén apparently believed, was that they had souls that could be sent to heaven. He despised being in California despite having volunteered to join Serra. At various times, Lasuén unsuccessfully sought to be relieved of his duties and return to Mexico. Like other friars, he apparently missed the comfortable life he had known in Spain and Mexico. When a policy was contemplated that would have reduced the number of friars from two or three to only one at each mission, Lasuén wrote:

> Loneliness in this work is for me a savage and cruel enemy which has afflicted me greatly. I fled from it, thanks be to God, in the face of evident risk of dying at its hands; and now as I see it raise its ugly head, even from afar, I tremble at the inconceivable danger in return to battle.[29]

Lasuén even went so far as to threaten to resign if the plan to have only one friar at each mission was approved: "For me there is no punishment so cruel as a law like this in circumstances such as these." He described himself as "an old man and completely grey; and although it is the toll of years, the pace has been accelerated by the heavy burden of this office

27. Lasuén, *Writings of Fermín Francisco de Lasuén*, Vol II, 80.

28. Ibid., 84.

29. Ibid., 87.

which I hold, and especially by the five years which I am completing as superior at San Diego."[30]

The Franciscan priest's disenchantment with California and the Indians was not the only problem he faced in his position as padre. He also had to intercede with friars who loathed each other. In one case, Lasuén acted as a referee between two Franciscans, Friars Rubi and Garcia of Mission Soledad, who were constantly squabbling. In a letter he described the situation:

> . . . dissensions and disagreements . . . were of the most clamorous nature: so bad, in fact, that on one occasion Garcia had to have recourse to the corporal of the guard and to take him home with him to restrain Rubi, for he feared that the latter might lay violent hands on him, or even do worse. . . . Father Garcia has told me that the other carries side-arms, and that a horrible secret is attached to one of them, for he boasts that he had it with him in the college on the occasion of some disturbance unknown to me.[31]

Lasuén eventually separated both priests, with Friar Rubi staying at Soledad and Friar Garcia transferred to Mission San Antonio.[32] Time and time again, Lasuén devoted a large amount of his time writing letters seeking approval from his superior in Mexico City to allow friars who were suffering from chronic illness, serious depression, old age (and in some cases insanity) to be sent home.

On October 6, 1812, the overseas colonies' secretary, Don Ciríaco Gonzáles Carvajal of Cádiz, Spain, sent a form containing thirty-six questions seeking answers on Indian life, beliefs, and behaviors to all government and religious groups who had contact with New World Indians. The recipients were asked to complete the document and return it to Spain.

In Alta California, the questionnaire was parceled out to each mission. The friars dutifully completed the document, some doing a better job than others at answering the questions, especially those regarding Indian life and beliefs. The documents were never returned to Spain. Instead, they were gathered and remain preserved at Mission Santa Barbara.[33]

---

30. Ibid.

31. Ibid., 241.

32. Ibid.

33. The reports are part of the Santa Barbara Mission Archive Library collection. From 1810 to 1821, supply ships to California were virtually nonexistent as Spain sought to quash a rebellion in Mexico seeking independence from the European nation.

Within the stacks of completed questionnaires, the friars had written mixed descriptions of the neophytes. While they praised the Indians for being charitable, docile, respectful and obedient,[34] they simultaneously condemned them all as unchaste, lazy, prone to "fornication," and stealing.[35] "Idleness," wrote Friar Juan Amorós of Mission San Carlos, "makes them gluttons, drinkers, and gamblers and hinders graces given them as Christians from acts of love of God and holy things."[36] Friar Felipe Arroyo de la Cuesta of Mission San Juan Bautista, curiously blamed "idleness" for the Indians' propensity of fleeing the missions: "We have had sad experiences of this in the case of those who forgetful of their baptism ran away as fugitives to their pagan habitat."[37]

One question asked if the Indians were liars. The Franciscans almost unanimously painted them as such.[38] "They are inclined to tell lies especially when there is an investigation about some transgression because they dread punishment. This is at the bottom of their lies," wrote Friars José Sánchez and Fernando Martin of Mission San Diego.[39] Faced with being lashed or locked in stocks or chains, it is little wonder that the mission Indians resorted to lying to avoid such excruciating ordeals.

Some of those Indians who survived their experience in the missions were interviewed in the late nineteenth century for Hubert Howe Bancroft's *History of California*. All agreed that the friars and mission life was cruel and oppressive.

The neophyte's point of view was also recorded when a group of Saclan and Huichin Indians who had fled Mission San Francisco in 1797 were asked by Spanish officials why they had run away.[40] Twenty-three of them were recaptured by a group of soldiers led by Spanish Sergeant Pedro Amador and brought back to the mission. On July 21, 1797, California Governor Don Diego de Borica ordered Spanish soldiers to question them and determine why they had fled. Their testimony was dutifully

---

34. *As the Padres Saw Them: California Indian Life and Customs as Reported by the Franciscan Missionaries, 1813–1815*, ed. Doyce B. Nunis, Jr. (Los Angeles: Westland Printing, 1976), 43–45.

35. Ibid., 105.

36. Ibid., 106.

37. Ibid.

38. Ibid., 103.

39. Ibid.

40. Milliken, *A Time of Little Choice*, 299–303.

recorded by Lieutenant José Argüello. The names of the Indians (once baptized, all mission neophytes were given Spanish names and their original Indian names discarded) are followed by their statements:

Tiburcio: He testified that after his wife and daughter died, on five separate occasions Father Danti ordered him whipped because he was crying. For these reasons he fled.

Marciano: He offered no other reason for fleeing than that he had become sick.

Macario: He testified that he fled because his wife and one child had died, no other reason than that.

Magín: He testified that he left due to his hunger and because they had put him in the stocks when he was sick, on orders from the *alcalde*.

Tarazón: He declared that he had no motive. Having been granted license to go on *paseo* to his land, he had felt inclined to stay.

Ostano: He testified that his motive for having fled was that his wife, one child, and two brothers had died, and because he had fought with another Indian, who had been directing their work group.

Román: He testified that he left because his wife and a son had gone back to their land, because of the many whippings, and because he did not have anyone to feed him.

Claudio: He declared that he fled because he was continually fighting with his brother-in-law Casimiro and because the *alcalde* Valeriano was clubbing him every time he turned around, and when he was sick, this same Valeriano made him go to work.

José Manuel: He testified that when they went to bring wood from the mountains, Raymundo ordered them to bring him water. When the declarant wouldn't do it, this same Raymundo hit him with a heavy cane, rendering one hand useless. He showed his hand. It was a little puffed up but had movement. That was his reason for having left the mission.

Homobono: He testified that his motive for fleeing was that his brother had died on the other shore, and when he cried for him at the mission they whipped him. Also, the *alcalde* Valeriano hit him with a heavy cane for having gone to look for mussels at the beach without Raymundo's permission.

Malquíedes: He declared that he had no more reason for fleeing than that he went to visit his mother, who was on the other shore.

Liborato: He testified that he left because his mother, two brothers, and three nephews died, all of hunger. So that he would not also die of hunger, he fled.

Migilo: He declared that his motive for fleeing was that Lorenzo, who had been at the house of La Sargenta, took him along with him.

Nicolás: He says that he ran away only because his father had died. He had no other motive.

Timoteo: He declares that the *alcalde* Luis came to get him while he was feeling ill and whipped him. After that, Father Antonio hit him with a heavy cane. For those reasons he fled.

Otolón: He reports that he fled because his wife did not care for him or bring him food. The *vaquero* Salvador had sinned with her. Then Father Antonio ordered him whipped because he was not looking out for said woman, his wife.

Patabo: He says that he fled just because his wife and children died and he had no one to take care of him.

Orencio: He declared that his father had gone several times with a little niece of his to get a ration of meat. Father Danti never gave it to him and always hit him with a cudgel. Because his niece died of hunger, he ran away.

Toribio: He stated that the motive for his having fled was that he was always very hungry, and that he went away together with his uncle.

López: He explained that his reason for having run away was the following: he went one day over to the presidio to look for something to eat. Upon returning to the mission, he went to get his ration, but Father Danti did not want to give it to him, saying that he should go to the countryside to eat herbs.

Magno: He declared that he had run away because, his son being sick, he took care of him and was therefore unable to go out to work. As a result he was given no ration and his son died of hunger.

Próspero: He declared that he had gone one night to the lagoon to hunt ducks for food. For this Father Antonio Danti ordered him stretched out and beaten. Then, the following week he was whipped again for having gone out on *paseo*. For these reasons he fled.[41]

There is no reason to doubt the statements of the captured Indians. Indignant fellow friars, visitors, neophytes, and explorers who observed and wrote about mission life have corroborated accounts of the mission

---

41. A copy of the interrogation is in the *Archivos Nacional de Mexico, Ramo Californias,* Mexico City.

Indians being mistreated and experiencing hunger, daily whippings, and disease. Additionally, the testimony of the runaways may have been taken by the Spanish government in California as proof of mistreatment of the Indians by the Franciscans.

For fifty-one years, the high mortality rates within the Alta California missions continued unabated, the bodies of neophytes filling thousands of graves outside the missions with little being done to improve conditions within the compounds. The frustration of being unable to reduce those deaths finally prompted Friar Mariano Payéras, who was *padre presidente* from 1815–1819, to write to his superior in Mexico City on February 2, 1820, just one year before the country would win independence from Spain. The friar worriedly asked what answer the missions could give if, in the future, California's coastal Indian population disappeared due to the high death rate. Payéras worried blame or "undeserved reproach" would fall on the friars. "I fear that a few years hence on seeing Alta California deserted and depopulated of Indians within a century of its discovery and conquest by the Spaniards, it will be asked where is the numerous heathendom that used to populate it."[42] In reality, he said, ". . . even the most pious and kindly of us will answer: the Missionary priest baptized them, administered the sacraments to them, and buried them."[43]

He asked, in his letter, that either the head of the Franciscans or the viceroy be informed immediately of the situation, or that measures be taken "which would free us for all time from undeserved reproach . . . and censures, and would shelter us from slander and sarcasm."[44]

What if, the *padre presidente* lamented, instead of having the missions become the foundations of "a flourishing church and some beautiful towns which would be the joy of the sovereign majesties of heaven and earth, we find ourselves with missions or rather a people miserable and sick, with rapid depopulation of *rancherias*[45] which with profound horror fills the cemeteries."[46]

---

42. Sandos, *Converting California*, 105.

43. Mariano Payéras, *Writings of Mariano Payéras*, trans. ed. Donald Cutter (Santa Barbara, Calif.: Bellerophon, 1995), 227.

44. Ibid., 228.

45. *Rancherias* were sites where the mission Indians had their huts or homes. They also referred to villages that were a distance from the missions.

46. Payéras, *Writings of Mariano Payéras*, 225.

California's Indians, he said, "procreate easily and are healthy and robust (though errant) in the wilds, in spite of hunger, nakedness, and living completely outdoors like beasts," but when they "commit themselves to a sociable and Christian life, they become extremely feeble, lose weight, get sick, and die. This plague affects the women particularly, especially those who have recently become pregnant."[47]

The erosion of the Indians' health once they entered the missions is buttressed by a comparison of measurements of human bones found at mission Indian burial sites with those uncovered at pre-Hispanic graves. The latter were robust while the mission skeletal remains were considerably stunted and far smaller. It was clear proof that the diet forced on the mission Indians by the friars was inferior nutritionally when compared to the diet enjoyed by Indians prior to the establishment of the missions. Disease may have also contributed to the lack of growth.[48]

Payéras explained that the high death rate among the mission neophytes in the beginning of the conquest was due to "the change of home, climate, food, and ideas." Early friars, he said, had hoped that the deaths would lessen as the children of those first neophytes, born within the system and "having been raised in its rules and customs, would be different and would keep their normal health and constitution. However, the sad experience of 51 years has showed us all too well that we have erred in our calculation." The mission Indian, the friar wrote, "dies equally, and perhaps more so than the Indians of the Sierra, that they are consumed indiscriminately and are rapidly vanishing."[49]

In contrast to "the notable lack of people and the horrible and unusual mortality among the Indians," he wrote, the settlers from Mexico remain healthy and seldom die. For the friars, the deaths of so many Indians "is for many Father Ministers the touchstone of their greatest despair and affliction. It also makes them uneasy (although they wish to ignore it) among the Indians themselves whom they have redeemed and reared with so much sweat and labor."[50]

Payéras sought to explain that the high death rates had gone largely unnoticed because as the mission neophytes died they were replaced by Indians gathered from neighboring villages. Mission records thus showed

---

47. Ibid.

48. Lightfoot, *Indians, Missionaries and Merchants*, 79.

49. Payéras, *Writings of Mariano Payéras*, 225–226.

50. Ibid., 226.

little drop in their Indian populations. However, he said, "this decline can not be hidden in the places where the conquest has ended." As an example, he cited Mission La Purísima where, in 1819, the 228 couples of that mission gave birth to only twenty-six infants who were baptized, while, within the mission's total neophyte population of 800 to 900, sixty-six deaths had occurred. Payéras said: "This means that in one year alone it had a decrease of 40 individuals. About the same thing happens, more or less, in the greater part of the Missions . . ."[51]

The *padre presidente* placed the blame for the high death rate on the Indians themselves. He could not fathom that the filthy conditions within the missions, the cultural shock, lack of nourishment, depression, European diseases, and the severe punishments meted out to the Indians by the friars were what was actually killing the mission Indians. Instead, Payéras wrote, the neophytes die because "the natural fermentation of the gathering so many people together into one place who scarcely know innate shame." They did not, he said, "respect anything more than immediate consanguinity," nor do they "value their health as they should but rather waste it and place it secondary to vile pleasures and whims. They are a people still preserving the bad habits of barbarism and heathenism, and their beliefs and ancient customs are all destructive to their natures and constitutions."[52]

The friars had been unable to reduce the death rates, even with an ample supply of medicines, advice from surgeons of the province, and the help of *curanderos* and *curanderas*.[53] "Despite all that I have said, they die. I don't know if it can be said that they die as before, but I believe there is no human recourse to us."

The situation did not escape Spanish Governor Pablo Vicente Solá, who called a meeting of "the most serious of the religious," as Payéras's letter described them, to find a solution to the unending deaths. The truth of the situation "did not escape the sharp notice of the present Lord Governor [Solá]. From the [records of] births and deaths in a period of five years he made a frightful calculation of this rate of decline." Solá, apparently frustrated at the friars, did not mince words in telling them they had to find a solution. "His Lordship threw it in our face," wrote Payéras, with the governor exhorting the friars to "stop this evil which

---

51. Ibid.,

52. Ibid.

53. Folk medicine practitioners.

156

without any known pestilence or epidemic is rapidly sweeping away our Indians."[54]

The friar worried that "despite the great number of *gentiles* who have come from a long distance to occupy and fill the void in the original native population here, what does the next equal amount of time promise, since there are no longer any live [Indians] in many missions to fill or occupy the place of the dead? It is horrible to go through the missions now, especially those of the north, and ask after the many robust and young neophytes who lived there twenty years ago. Seldom have the Father Ministers answered me that there are one or two living whom I remember."[55]

The Franciscan's letter is of critical importance to the history of the California missions. It was an admission of a terrible failure, not by disheartened Franciscans who had criticized the treatment of the Indians, but by the head of all the missions and friars in Alta California. However, Payéras's soul-searching document came too late for the Spanish Franciscan friars to correct the great wrong. One year after Payéras wrote his letter, in 1821, Mexico won its independence from Spain. Over the next twelve years, the new nation ended the existence of the twenty-one missions but imposed its own tragic hardships on the Indians.

When Mexico became an independent nation, the missions, far from Mexico City, remained unchanged initially. The new government, fearful that immediate closure would create an economic collapse in Alta California, ordered that they operate as before. The Indians would be denied freedom and continue as forced labor within the missions. The only difference was that the missions would be administered by Mexican officials.

Those officials, instead of making life easier for the neophytes, maintained the same restrictions that the Spanish friars had imposed on them. Julio César, a Luiseño Indian who was born in the early 1820s in Mission San Luis Rey, was interviewed for historian Hubert Howe Bancroft's *History of California* on May 25, 1878. He recalled never being paid for his mission work, nor did the misery of life in that compound improve

---

54. Ibid.
55. Ibid., 227.

even under Pío Pico,[56] an administrator appointed by the Mexican government:

> When I was a boy, the way the Indians were treated was not good at all. They didn't pay us anything. They only gave us food, a loincloth, and a blanket which they replaced each year. They did, however, give us plenty of whippings for any wrongdoing, however slight. We were at the mercy of the administrator, who ordered that we be whipped as many times and whenever he felt like it. Pío Pico, as well as those who followed him, were despots. Señor Pico required us to carry our hat in our hand as long as we were within his range of vision, even if we were at a distance from him.[57]

César also said the Indians were never taught how to read or write, even under Mexican authority: "We were only taught to pray and sing Mass from memory. They did not teach me how to read church music. There were singers and musicians, but everything was done from memory. I never saw a sheet of music placed in front of anyone."[58]

Not until Mexican Governor José María de Echeandia arrived in Alta California in 1825 were the Indians freed. He decreed that they could not be used as forced labor. That order denied the Franciscan priests and the newly appointed Mexican administrators the engine needed to drive the compounds. Within a few years after Echeandia's arrival, the Indian population in the missions plummeted. Only a handful of neophytes, mostly elderly ones who could not have survived outside the missions, remaining at each compound. Unable to continue operating without forced labor, the missions collapsed by 1833. California's settlers cheered their demise, knowing that much of the vast mission lands would thus become available to them.

Eventually, Mexican Franciscan friars from the state of Zacatecas were sent to California to replace the Spanish Franciscans who were ordered to leave Mexico as part of a nationwide order banning Spaniards from the country or its territories. In California, only the oldest or infirm of the

---

56. Pío Pico, who later became the governor of California, was the son of one of the guards at Mission San Luis Rey.

57. Beebe and Senkewicz, *Lands of Promise and Despair*, 470–471.

58. Julio César, *Recollections of my Youth at San Luis Rey Mission: The memories of a full-blooded Indian, of affairs and events witnessed at one of California's most famous "cathedrals of the sun,"* ed. trans. Nellie Van de Grift Sanchez, *Touring Topics* 22:42-43. 1878, in *Native American Perspectives on the Hispanic Colonization of Alta California*, 13–15.

Spanish priests were allowed to stay. Most of the missions were abandoned, although some closer to towns were turned into simple parish churches.

The Franciscans stubbornly clung to policies that ground away the neophytes' lives during the nearly sixty years that the missions existed, but many Indians did not passively accept the mission life forced on them. They seethed with anger at the gray-robed priests—and their fury eventually exploded into violent rebellion, as they sought to restore their previous life and freedom, and regain their ancestral lands.

10

Rebellion

*I hate the padres and all of you for living here on my native soil, for trespassing
upon the land of my forefathers and despoiling our tribal domains.*
—Toypurina, an Indian sorceress, at her trial for rebellion against the missions
(January 3, 1786).

In 1785, as the newly-created United States prepared to organize its
historic Constitutional Convention in Philadelphia, another revolution was fomenting in the Spanish-controlled territory of Alta California,
3,000 miles west. A handful of Spaniards controlled a vast swath of coastal
land ranging from San Francisco Bay to what is now the California-
Mexico border. The area had been home to its indigenous people, but
only sixteen years after the first missions were established the number
of coastal Indians had been already appallingly reduced by their contact
with the Spanish intruders. Within the missions, thousands of Indians
worked and lived under brutal conditions, spawning resentment toward
the Franciscan friars and the soldiers who guarded them. Since the incep-
tion of the missions in 1769, any violence toward the friars or the soldiers
was promptly and harshly suppressed. Still, Junípero Serra had already
warned that a combined attack from united tribelets could wipe out all
the missions.[1]

In a native society controlled by men, it was an Indian medicine
woman of the Gabrieleño tribe named Toypurina who, in 1785, organized
warriors to attack the missions and kill those who had invaded and now
controlled her people's land. Hers would be the only known Indian rebel-

---

1. Junípero Serra, *Writings of Junípero Serra*, Vol. II, 295.

lion in North America to have a woman at its helm. A full description of what occurred can be gleaned by an analysis of the rebellion done by Thomas Workman Temple II.[2]

Toypurina was a Tongva Indian living in a village called Japchivit and was probably 9 or 10 years old when the Spanish expeditions arrived in the spring and summer of 1769 to found the first mission in San Diego. As a girl, she lived virtually free of worry. Food was bountiful along the coast and whether it was winter or summer, the coastal weather was always mild.

Two years later, the Franciscan friars founded Mission San Gabriel just east of Los Angeles, in the area where Toypurina's Tongva tribe lived. Its members rejected being baptized, apparently aware of the unhappy fate of those Indians who had already joined the mission. By shunning the mission, Toypurina escaped the dreary routine of performing chores during the day and being locked up each night in the *convento*. From outside the mission compound, she watched the daily floggings of Indians who had transgressed Serra's strict regulations. Like other non-baptized *gentiles*, Toypurina despised the friars and the Spanish soldiers who had destroyed her community's easy life and doomed thousands of her people.

In the early fall of 1785, Toypurina, who had gained a reputation among the mission Indians as a sorceress, was approached by Nicolas José, a neophyte and a tribal member whose animosity toward the friars had increased after they restricted native dances at the mission. Although baptized, José was apparently able to leave the mission on several occasions, either surreptitiously or with permission. Together the two began organizing a complex conspiracy calling for an uprising involving warriors from six surrounding Indian villages.

Under the leadership of Toypurina, an attractive, green-eyed young woman of 24, the Gabrieleño Indians would launch a surprise attack on the night of October 25, 1785, the date of the new moon in the skies over Mission San Gabriel, north of San Diego. They planned to kill the hated friars and Spanish soldiers, sack the mission buildings, and burn them. Indians at other missions would then also join the uprising with the

2. Thomas Workman Temple II, "Toypurina The Witch and the Indian Uprising at San Gabriel" and James A. Sandos, "Levantamiento: The 1824 Chumash Uprising Reconsidered." In *Native American Perspectives on the Hispanic Colonization of Alta California (The Spanish Borderlands Sourcebook Vol. 26)*, ed. Edward D. Castillo (New York: Garland, 1991), 301–342.

goal to destroy every last remnant of the missions and presidios in Alta California.

Word spread quickly and quietly among the Indians. Secret meetings were held nightly to plan details of the attack, while Toypurina and other tribal members went from village to village enlisting help. Once the strategy was completed and an alliance formed, they waited patiently for the October new moon.

It is ironic that, given the friars' general refusal to learn Indian languages, the entire plan was discovered by a Spanish soldier named José Maria Pico who had taught himself the Tongva language. Undetected and hidden behind a tree, he overheard two Indians discussing the plan in its entirety. Pico raced back to the mission and reported what he had overheard to Corporal José Maria Verdugo. This vital intelligence gave the San Gabriel friars and the handful of soldiers assigned to protect the mission enough time to call for reinforcements.

The success of the Spaniards in thwarting the attack would hinge on one critical detail that Pico had overheard: Toypurina had convinced the Indians that her magic was so powerful that when they attacked the mission, they would find the friars already dead in their bedrooms. Verdugo quickly developed a plan that he hoped would use Toypurina's claim of sorcery against her Indian followers. The plan called for the friars to retreat to the safety of the chapel and remain there while two soldiers, Juan José Dominguez and Manuel Nieto, would feign death in the friars' room. Clad in the priests' habits and with the hoods pulled over their faces, the soldiers would be stretched out on the floor of their chamber as if dead, their arms crossed over their chest and candles burning at their feet, head, and middle.

On the night of October 25, Dominguez and Nieto assumed their death-like poses on the stone floor. Outside, Toypurina and Nicolas José ran toward the mission, followed by dozens of heavily-armed Indians. Reaching the mission, Toypurina's men effortlessly vaulted over the wall and entered the main compound. Within seconds the band of Gabrieleños, their faces covered with war paint and armed with bows, arrows, and spears, were running to the friars' chambers.

At the entrance to the friars' room they quietly pushed the door open. The sight made them gasp. Toypurina's magic was indeed powerful. The friars were dead, just as she had predicted, the funerary candles casting a soft yellow glow in the room. The Indians crept closer to get a better look. Suddenly, a shout of "Santiago!"[3] rang through the building, signalling waiting soldiers to attack. The seemingly dead friars jumped to their feet. From dark corners and nooks, soldiers, clad in full leather armor and armed with rifles and fixed bayonets, sprang out, yelling at the top of their voices. Terrified, the Indians dropped their weapons in panic and bolted. Most made it outside the mission walls. Others, including Toypurina and José, were surrounded at bayonet point and captured.

Within minutes, the prisoners were being marched to a holding cell in the mission to await trial and punishment. It would take over two months after the unsuccessful attack before Governor Don Pedro Fages was able to travel from Monterey to Mission San Gabriel for the conspirators' trial. When he arrived in January 1786, he determined that the four ringleaders—José, Toypurina, and two Indian chiefs—would face trial. Seven other Indians were strapped to a tree and lashed fifteen to twenty times each, then freed after being warned never again to challenge Spanish authority. As they left they swore a terrible vengeance against Toypurina, whom they blamed for inducing them to join the failed attack.

On January 3, 1786, the trial opened in the mission compound. For the proceedings, Pico, the Spanish soldier who had learned of the attack, was appointed interpreter. Corporal Manuel de Vargas of Monterey was assigned as notary, while Sergeant José Ygnacio Olivera of Santa Barbara would oversee the entire hearing. Fages, as the region's highest official, would witness the trial.

Chief Tomassajaquichi of the Juyuvit village was brought in by three soldiers, who held him tightly as he struggled against the ropes that bound him. The chief finally quieted down after he was threatened with flogging. Surprisingly, he placed the entire blame on Toypurina. He called her a "witch" with a "serpent's tongue" who had enticed him into joining the conspiracy, even though he had no grudge against the Spaniards. Flying into a rage, he threatened to catch Toypurina and strangle her with his own hands.

Tomassajaquichi was followed by Aliyvit, the elderly chief of the village Jajamovit, about eight miles from the mission. The small-statured chief said he had joined the raiding party only by coincidence, when he came across the warriors in their war paint and weapons as they raced to

---

3. "Santiago" was the battle cry used by Spaniards, in honor of Saint James, the patron saint of Spain.

the mission. He tagged along just to see what they would do. His story amused the officials.

Toypurina's co-conspirator, Nicolas José, was next. Surprisingly, the mission Indian had always displayed what seemed a devotion to Catholicism, so much so that he was used by the friars to witness Indian weddings and serve as godfather to Indian children. Yet he bragged that it was he who had enticed Toypurina into organizing the attack. The sorceress, he said, was a woman of great power and courage who could kill a victim by simply thinking about it. It was she, he said, who had convinced the villagers that her magic was strong enough to kill the padres. With the hated friars out of the way, the warriors could have then easily overcome and cut down the unprepared Spanish soldiers. Just before he was led away, José boldly said he had no regrets about what he and Toypurina had done.

José's hatred toward the missions and the friars had apparently developed because of the deaths of his first wife and first son. His second wife also perished eight months after they wed. At the time of the uprising he had remarried.[4] Also simmering within José's mind was Governor Fages's order to the friars to prohibit mission Indians from gathering and performing dances they considered sacred for the season. Why Fages issued the order is not well understood, but he may have thought that by prohibiting such dances, the Indians would eventually forget them and assimilate faster into the Spanish life of Alta California.

José received the harshest punishment of the four. He was exiled to the mission most distant from San Gabriel and sentenced to six years of hard labor in shackles. The Indian chiefs Tomassajaquichi and Aliyivit would be imprisoned in the San Gabriel presidio jail for two years. At the end of their term they would be free to return to their villages.

Finally, Toypurina was brought in, her green eyes blazing with anger and hatred. She seethed at being in the presence of the Spaniards, and when one of the soldiers offered her a stool, she angrily kicked it across the room. She stood tall and unbowed before her inquisitors. The officials were awed by her beauty and courage. When asked why she had conspired against the padres and soldiers, she said, angrily:

---

4. Steven W. Hackel, *Children of Coyote, Missionaries of Saint Francis: Indian-Spanish Relations in Colonial California, 1769–1850* (Chapel Hill: University of North Carolina Press, 2005), 264–265.

> I hate the padres and all of you for living here on my native soil, for trespassing upon the land of my forefathers and despoiling our tribal domains.[5]

Pico asked why she had joined the attack party. Glaring at Fages, she hissed:

> I came to inspire the dirty cowards to fight, and not to quail at the sight of Spanish sticks that spit fire and death, nor retch at the evil smell of gun smoke—and be done with you invaders.

Yet, as the questioning continued her countenance softened. When the trial ended, she surprisingly asked to become a Christian and promised to mend her ways. Toypurina may have done this out of a real concern that her followers had turned against her and would have literally torn her apart if she were ever set free. Realizing, too, that her only hope of escaping possible execution was to repent, she reversed her initial claims and placed the blame on José for talking her into joining the uprising by giving her some beads. The once fiery defendant also said it was José who did all the planning and who had brought the chiefs of six villages together to join the attack.

Toypurina spent the next year in the mission presidio's jail (her repentance apparently had softened her sentence) and was later baptized with a Christianized name, Regina Joséfa Toypurina, on March 8, 1788. Officiating was Friar Miguel Sanchez, the same padre she had vowed to kill in 1786.

Under the governor's orders, the onetime rebel leader was exiled to Mission San Carlos de Borromeo de Carmelo. There she eventually married a Spanish soldier. At her wedding, a sponsor was Governor Fages himself, beaming proudly at the way in which Toypurina had changed her ways. The couple eventually moved to Mission San Luis Obispo, where they had four children and were welcomed by the Spanish families of that settlement.

Toypurina lived only fourteen years past her attempted rebellion, dying in 1789 at age 38 at Mission San Juan Bautista. In the end, the only Indian woman in North America to ever challenge the Spanish kingdom with ouright rebellion died quietly, and was accorded all the sacraments of her adopted church. She lies buried in the San Juan Bautista mission cemetery.

---

5. Ibid., 338.

Toypurina was not the first nor the only native to rise up against the Spaniards and the missions. From the beginning, the Indians fought back. Within weeks of the onset of the Mission era, in San Diego in July 1769, Indians attacked the encampment where Serra and his friars were ministering to sick soldiers in their party The attack was small, involving perhaps twenty natives angry that the Spaniards had not been forthcoming with the gifts that would traditionally have been presented by another Indian party upon arriving on their lands. The San Diego Indians surmised that they could walk away with anything they desired because the horses of the Spaniards had trampled their sown fields and were also eating the grain they depended on for their winter stores of food.

The Indians had initially been allowed to roam through the camp freely, visiting daily, but they were carefully watched to prevent them from stripping it of supplies. The visitors prized fabric of any kind, using it to drape themselves. On one occasion, they turned their attention to the Spanish ship *San Carlos*, rowing out in their boats made of rushes. Once aboard they began nonchalantly cutting a large piece of canvas from one of the sails. Sailors on board shouted at the Indians and quickly stopped the attempt, then forced them from the ship. Guards for the vessel were subsequently reinforced and the Indians were forbidden to come aboard.

When pleas to stop the Indians from pilfering their camp proved ineffective, the Spaniards took matters into their hands and use force to put a halt to the thefts. This caused the Indians to retreat; but the trouble would not end there.

It took the natives only a day to regroup and return, this time armed, their faces covered in war paint. On August 14, they strode into the camp and again began taking supplies, even ripping sheets off the beds in the makeshift hospital where the scurvy-stricken soldiers and sailors were being tended. The Indians shoved aside the Spaniards and brandished war clubs in the faces of anyone trying to stop them. Realizing they were under attack, the soldiers shouted an alarm and rushed to their armory, where they donned their thick leather vests and grabbed their weapons. As the soldiers, now ready for combat, approached the Indians, the natives unleashed a hail of arrows that initially fell harmlessly into the camp. One of the first to arm himself against the Indians was the expedition's blacksmith, who, as he assumed a firing stance, shouted, "Long live the faith of Jesus Christ, and may these dogs, enemies of that faith, die!" With that, his musket boomed, spewing out a cloud of smoke and sending a musket ball spinning into the startled Indians.[6] He and four soldiers, plus a carpenter, aimed their muskets again and fired a volley at the Indians. They counterattacked, at a distance, with their spears and arrows.

With arrows, musket balls, and gun smoke filling the air, Serra and Friar Vizcaíno rushed into one of the camp's huts for safety. Serra, clasping his hands, began loudly praying, "commending all to God, asking that all be delivered from death, the pagans so that their souls would not be lost without baptism." From inside the hut, both priests could only hear the sound of the muskets firing and the war whoops of the Indians. Vizcaíno, curious about the attack, approached the doorway and carefully lifted the fabric curtain. Almost immediately an arrow pierced his hand. He dropped the curtain and flew back from the doorway, loudly commending himself to God. The priests' faithful servant, Joséph María, stumbled into the hut and dropped at Serra's feet, shouting, "Father, absolve me, for the Indians have killed me!" An arrow was embedded in his throat and blood was streaming from the fatal wound. He died just as Serra hurriedly gave him absolution.

Outside, the defenders fired volley after volley at the attacking Indians, killing some and wounding others, who were then dragged away by their companions. The Indians, realizing that they were being overwhelmed by the superior firepower of the soldiers and that their arrows were having little effect, retreated.

A few days later, the Indians timidly returned to the camp, seeking peace and carrying their wounded. For the first time in their lives they had experienced the devastating effect of gunpowder and musket ball on human flesh, which created terrible and strange wounds the Indians could not treat. The Spaniards readily accepted the entreaties, and the expedition's surgeon began treating the wounds. Under the doctor's care, all recovered.[7]

Another factor that severely upset the Indians in the early years was the behavior of the Spanish soldiers. The friars justly complained to the military commanders and governors of California that the actions of Spanish

---

6. Francisco Palóu, *Relacion Historica de la Vida y Apostólicas Tareas del Venerable Padre Fray Junípero Serra, y de las Misiones que Fundó en la California Septentrional, y nuevos establecimientos de Monterey* (Mexico City: Zuñiga y Ontiveros, 1787), in *La Vida de Junípero Serra*, March of America Facsimile Series, no. 49 (Ann Arbor: University Microfilms Inc., 1966) 76–77.

7. Ibid., 77.

soldiers, among them the rape of Indian women, were causing serious unrest among the Indians. In one case, an Indian chief whose wife had been raped by a Spanish soldier was killed. The sexual assault occurred in late summer of 1771 at what would eventually become Mission San Gabriel. The chief, furious at the Spanish and vowing revenge, gathered men from neighboring villages and set out to find the soldier. They discovered him and another soldier grazing the mission's horses at a meadow too far from the mission compound to call for help. As the soldiers saw the Indians approaching, they raced to don their protective leather jackets and load their weapons. Once the attackers were within range, they unleashed a cloud of arrows aimed only at the soldier they sought. The same soldier fired one shot at the Indian who, he assumed, was the chief, killing him almost instantly. The arrows meanwhile bounced harmlessly off the soldier's thick jacket of layered deerhide.

The Indians, stunned at the unfamiliar burst of flame and smoke, saw one of their leaders suddenly collapse, bleed profusely, and die. They stopped momentarily, then broke and ran. Like the attack at San Diego, it was the first time they had ever seen, heard, and experienced the deadly power of a musket, against which they were absolutely defenseless.

Although the Indians were now hesitant to attack, the commandant nevertheless halted the planned founding of Mission San Buenaventura and rushed sixteen soldiers to guard Mission San Gabriel, including the two friars and all the supplies that had been destined for the new mission. Once it was determined there would not be another attack, the commander and a group of soldiers headed toward Monterey. Unknowingly, they took the soldier-rapist and got him out of the Indians' sight. Two years after the founding of Mission San Gabriel, seventy-three Indians, including the widow of the chief who was killed, had become neophytes.[8]

Within six years after coming to California, Serra faced a crushing blow that brought into doubt whether the mission system could survive. On November 4, 1775, a massive Indian attack was launched against Mission San Diego, far larger than the skirmish that had occurred in 1769. In the battle, Friar Luis Jayme was stripped and beaten to death and all the compound's buildings burned to the ground by a force estimated at 600 to 1,000 Indians.

---

8. Ibid., 120.

The Indian attackers had been recruited by two native chiefs, Francisco and Cárlos, who had been neophytes at the mission.[9] The two journeyed separately to surrounding villages, pleading with chiefs and their warriors to unite and launch a surprise attack to kill the Spaniards and burn the mission and nearby presidio. Only then could they reclaim their lands and village members that the foreigners had taken. Probably just as important was their concern that the friars' proselytizing was stripping many Indians away from the villages near the missions, endangering the survival of those who remained free. Fifteen villages out of twenty-five within thirty-one miles of the mission agreed to provide warriors for the attack.[10]

The now-united villages entered into a state of war as men and women prepared for combat. On the evening of November 4, the attackers massed at a prearranged point, then strode toward Mission San Diego and the unsuspecting Spaniards. They split their force into two parts, the first group targeting the mission while the second headed for the presidio. The plan called for the first group to the mission afire, thereby signaling the waiting second force to attack the presidio and prevent its soldiers from rushing to the mission. However, as the second group approached the presidio they saw the mission already in flames. Not being in position for their assault on the presidio and fearing that the soldiers would now ride to defend the mission, the second group raced to the compound to reinforce the Indian force already there.[11] Inside the burning compound were friars Luis Jayme[12] and Vicente Fuster; three soldiers, Alejo Antonio Gonzalez, Juan Alvarez, and Joaquin Armenta, and their corporal, Juan Estévan Rocha; a blacksmith; and two carpenters, José Urselino and Felipe Romero. Two boys, the son and nephew of the military commander at the presidio,[13] were with the friars.[14] No sentries were posted and all had been asleep when the attack started.

9. Hubert Howe Bancroft, *History of California, Vol. I, 1542–1800* (San Francisco: A.L. Bancroft, 1884), 253.

10. James A. Sandos, *Converting California: Indians and Franciscans in the Missions* (New Haven: Yale University Press, 2004), 59

11. Ibid., 59, 61.

12. Friar Jayme's name is spelled "Jaume" in Bancroft's *History of California*, but in Geiger's translation of Palóu's Serra biography the name is spelled "Jayme," the proper Spanish spelling of the name. I have chosen to use the latter on the basis that it is accurate and Bancroft's spelling may be a typographical error.

13. The two boys were probably staying at the mission and being schooled by the friars.

14. Ibid., 250.

The Indian force rushed the mission just after midnight, smashing through the chapel doors, taking everything they could lay their hands on, then tossing flaming torches into the chapel and the rest of the compound. Their first targets were the roofs made of rushes which covered the mission's crude adobe and wooden structures. The torches arced through the air, creating a hellish sight as they dropped into the tinder-dry roofs that exploded into rapidly spreading flames.

Inside, soldiers, craftsmen, and the friars heard the loud crackle of the flames and were showered with glowing embers. With the mission ablaze and lighting up the night sky with a brilliant yellow glow, hundreds of attacking and screaming warriors quickly slipped arrows from their quivers, pulled back their bows, and aimed volley after volley toward the buildings.

Awakened by the screaming Indians, the friars were the first to be roused. Friars Jayme and Fuster and the two boys raced from their burning rooms to escape the falling embers. Jayme suddenly halted as they sought shelter and, believing he could placate the Indians, greeted them with "*Amar a Dios, hijos*" (love God, my sons).[15] With Jayme distracting the Indians, Fuster ran to get the boys to a safe hideaway. Jayme's valiant act may have saved the other three from being killed.

Meanwhile, inside the blacksmith's shop, the blacksmith bolted from his bed, grabbed a sword and raced outside, only to be struck by two arrows. He stumbled back into the room, the arrows jutting out of his body. He turned and gasped to Romero, "*Compañero, me han matado*" ("My friend, they have killed me"), collapsed, and died. Romero, despite being stunned by his friend's death, grabbed a musket and flung himself behind the bellows of the blacksmith's furnace for cover. As one of the attackers rushed inside, he fired, killing the Indian. Romero then dashed to another building, where the soldiers were setting up a defensive position. Urselino, the other carpenter, was already there but had been unable to shield himself—two arrows had pierced his body. Fatally wounded, he died a few days later.

Inside the barracks, where the survivors had taken shelter, flames from the roof drove the men into one of the rooms set aside for the friars. At that point Fuster, realizing that Jayme was missing, raced through the buildings and even outside, trying to find the friar. He was unsuccessful, and as he rejoined the others, the group dashed to a three-walled roofless

15. "*Amar a Dios*" was the greeting neophytes had been ordered to use toward the friars.

adobe structure where they could escape the burning roofs and make a stand. The group, joined by two soldiers who had been struck by arrows, then scrambled to build a barricade across the open front of the structure.

The structure was shielded by a tree's thick branches and the attackers, unable to force the Spaniards outside by setting the roof afire, resorted to hurling clubs and torches and firing arrows into the small enclosure. Huddled inside, Rocha, the corporal, made a quick decision: the carpenter and one of the soldiers would reload the muskets, and he alone would fire at the Indians. This tactic provided him with an extremely rapid rate of fire.

For hours, Rocha, maintained his fire, cutting down any attacker made visible by the bright flames of the burning buildings. With fifty pounds of gunpowder and a plentiful supply of musket balls, the group did not lack ammunition. Fuster, meanwhile, flung his habit over the barrels of gunpowder to shield them from the Indians' torches. Finally, as dawn began breaking, the Indians broke off the attack, realizing they were suffering far too many casualties from Rocha's circulating musket supply. Taking their dead and wounded, they left behind a scene of devastation. All of the mission buildings had been destroyed; the blackened ruins of some still burning, the flames leaping into the air and casting a thick pall of black smoke over the entire area. Spent arrows littered the ground, along with smoldering torches that had missed the buildings.

Rocha, slightly wounded and now exhausted, waited for another onslaught. Instead, the mission's neophytes began arriving, saying that when the attack began they had been told by the invaders to stay inside their hutches. As the survivors assembled, a search was quickly launched to find Friar Jayme. Neophytes soon located him, stripped of clothing, with eighteen arrows jutting from his body. His bloodied face had been so crushed by blows that he was unrecognizable.[16] The neophytes gently lifted his corpse and carried it to the mission compound. Two messengers raced to the presidio where the guard had slept through the entire attack. Only four of the ten soldiers there were able to help. Four were sick and two others in jail. All were under the command of Corporal Mariano Verdugo, who immediately marched to the mission with his small force

---

16. Bancroft, *History of California Vol. I*, 252.

and began organizing a retreat to the presidio. All the wounded eventually recovered, enduring painful arrowhead removal.[17]

Ortega, the commander of the San Diego Presidio, began scouring the countryside with his troops, looking for suspects. When Indians who had participated in the attack were found, they were asked why they had burned the mission. Their answer was simple: "They wanted to kill the fathers and soldiers in order to live as they did before."[18]

Serra received news of the attack by letter delivered to him on December 13, more than a month later. He is said to have exclaimed: "Thank God that that ground has now been watered (with blood): Now, certainly we will achieve the conversion of the Diegueños."[19] It is puzzling why Serra would believe that the spilling of blood would result in converting the San Diego Indians.

---

17. Removal of Indian arrowheads was a traumatic and bloody process. A surgical instrument, if available, had to be slipped carefully into the path cut by the arrowhead, then maneuvered to cover the arrowhead's back edges, which pointed backwards. The end of the arrowhead was wider at the bottom than at the top; covering the back edges kept them from ripping and tearing more tissue as the arrow was removed.

18. Sherburne F. Cook, *The Conflict Between the California Indian and White Civilization* (Berkeley: University of California Press, 1976), 66.

19. Palóu, *Relacion Historica de la Vida y Apostólicas Tareas del Venerable Padre Fray Junípero Serra*, March of America Facsimile Series, p. 184. This publication of Palóu's *Life of Junípero Serra*, printed directly from a microfilm copy of the original 1787 book, differs from Maynard Geiger's translation of the same passage, which is found on page 167 in his *Palóu's Life of Fray Junípero Serra* (Richmond, Va.: Byrd, 1955). Geiger translates Serra's statement as "Thanks be to God, now indeed that the land has been watered [with blood]; certainly now the conversion of the San Diego Indians will be achieved." In the original 1787 work, as published by the March of America Facsimile Series, Serra's statement, as recorded by Palóu for Serra's biography, in Spanish is: *"Gracias á Dios ya se regó aquella tierra: ahora sí se conseguirá la reduccion de los Dieguinos."* The term *reduccion*, (reduction) was used in the Spanish New World to refer to a process in which Indians would be converted to Catholicism and assimilated into Spanish life. In English, it means to subjugate, reduce in numbers or conquer. It is the English translation of the word that was used by Hubert Howe Bancroft in his *History of California, Vol. I, 1542–1800*, in which Bancroft translated *reduccion* as "reduction." Likewise, C. Scott William's translation of Palóu's biography, *Life and Apostolic Labors of the Venerable Father Junípero Serra Founder of the Franciscan Missions of California* (Pasadena, Calif.: Wharton James, 1913), p. 179, has Serra saying "Thanks be to God that that soil has now been watered with blood. We shall now soon see the complete subjugation of the Indians of San Diego". The differences in translation is probably because of Bancroft and William not knowing how the term *reduccion* was used in Colonial Spain.

A year later, Indians at Mission San Luis Obispo burned the thatched roofs of that site, while in 1777, Ipai Indians of the Pamó village in Southern California organized another attempt to rid their lands of the Spaniards. In a major blunder by the Indians, a message was sent to the soldiers challenging them to fight. Warned of the challenge, a military force was organized and a preemptive attack was made on the village. Two Indians were killed and several others burned to death; the rest surrendered. The chiefs of four villages were captured and without legal authority executed on March 11, 1778. Friar Lasuén, Serra's successor, agreed to the unauthorized executions.[20]

The most successful Indian uprising occurred on July 17, 1781, when the Quechan Indians wiped out a mission and two settlements founded by the Spaniards on the California side of the Colorado River, just south of its intersection with the Gila River. The Quechans organized the attack after the Franciscan friars and settlers began whipping the Indians. The new settlers had also brought in livestock that began eating the Quechan crops, denying the Indians an already-scarce food source.[21]

In a ferocious battle that stretched over two days, the Indians killed 110 Spaniards, including four Franciscan friars and thirty-one soldiers, and took seventy-two prisoners.[22] All the settlements were burned to the ground. Three military expeditions sent into the area were unsuccessful and had to retreat in the face of numerous skilled Quechan fighters who used guerilla tactics to harass and inflict heavy casualties on the soldiers. The Indians were also the first in the region to attack on horseback and use firearms taken from the Spanish.[23] The Spanish forces later began talks with the Indians, resulting in the release of the Spanish prisoners. Spanish officials ultimately abandoned plans to re-establish the settlements in that hostile country.

Resistance against the friars was not limited to mass uprisings. Individual efforts by Indian men to rid California of the Franciscan priests also

20. Bancroft, *History of California, Vol. I,* 315–316

21. Edward D. Castillo, "The Native Response to the Colonization of Alta California," in *Columbian Consequences Vol. 1: Archaeological and Historical Perspectives on the Spanish Borderlands West,* ed. David Hurst Thomas (Washington, D.C.: Smithsonian Institution Press, 1989); *Native American Perspectives on the Hispanic Colonization of Alta California,* 432.

22. Ibid.

23. Ibid., 433.

occurred. Many Indians were highly skilled in using medicinal herbs and potions. They also knew about poisonous plants and used that knowledge against the priests. In 1801, three neophytes at Mission San Miguel are believed to have poisoned both of the mission priests. It did not end there. When a third friar arrived to help, he also became ill and died thirty days later.[24] However, it was never determined with certainty that poison had actually been used against the friars.

Three years later, poison was used against Mission San Diego Friar José Pedro Panto. His personal cook, Nazario, was accused of mixing it into his food. Panto suspected he had been poisoned when he detected a bitter taste and a white residue in one of the dishes prepared for him. He suffered severe vomiting after his meal, but recovered the next day. The neophyte later admitted that before making his decision to poison the sadistic priest, he had endured whippings of fifty, twenty-five, twenty-four, and twenty-five lashes in succession.[25] He was severely punished.

In 1805, an enraged neophyte used a stone to try to beat a friar at Mission San Miguel. The Indian received a horrific punishment: twenty-five lashes on each of nine successive feast days, and thirty-five to forty lashes on nine successive Sundays, each time before the mission's assembled neophytes.[26] Three years later, neophytes at Mission San Diego killed a brutal *alcalde*, Pedro Miguel Alvarez.[27] Other acts of individual rebellion included the murder of Friar Andrés Quintana at Mission Santa Cruz in 1812 for fashioning a whip tipped with iron barbs. Neophytes could endure only so much punishment before they retaliated.

Throughout the sporadic uprisings and all through the mission era, neophytes never gave up in their efforts to escape the stifling and deadly life within the missions. In one of the most dramatic instances of Indians turning into fugitives, more than 200 neophytes successfully fled Mission San Francisco in 1795 to escape the cruelties of Friar Antonio Danti.[28]

Eighteen years later, Indians turned against a Spanish force that included Indian auxiliaries. This group was attempting to capture runaways from Mission San José. In late October 1813, twelve Spanish soldiers and 100 Indian auxiliaries, enlisted by the Spaniards, set out

---

24. Bancroft, *History of California, Vol. II*, 147–150.

25. Ibid., 345.

26. Ibid., 163–164.

27. Cook, *Conflict Between the California Indian and White Civilization*, 129.

28. Bancroft, *History of California, Vol. I*, 709

to capture the fugitives. The soldiers, ten from Mission San Francisco under José Argüello and two from Mission San José under Master Sergeant Francisco Soto, joined forces.[29] Five days later, they attacked the village where the runaways were supposed to be hiding. Instead of fleeing, the Indians, armed and prepared, counterattacked fiercely, nearly surrounding the Spaniards. As they fought they taunted the soldiers, shouting that the Spaniards were useless fighters when they were off their horses.

Using their knowledge of the terrain to maintain cover, the Indians, estimated by Argüello at 1,000 or more, unleashed hails of arrows on a military force that answered with gunfire volleys. In a battle that lasted for three hours and filled the air with clouds of white smoke and arrows, the Indians disappeared into the thick brush and swampy ground, beaten back by Spanish gunfire. Argüello and Soto, declaring a moral victory and confident they had inflicted heavy casualties, decided to return to Mission San José. They never recaptured the runaways.

In cases where runaways were recaptured, the result could be horrific. In 1815, Vassili Petrovitch Tarakanoff, a Russian, was taken prisoner by the soldiers and friars of Mission San Fernando near the central California coast. He and several Aleut Indians had been sent ashore from a Russian vessel to hunt for fresh meat. The Russians and Aleuts were in the area hunting sea otters and seals when they were suddenly surrounded by Spanish soldiers and forced to march for two days to the mission. A high-ranking Spanish official who visited the mission said he wanted to have Tarakanoff and the Aleutians released. The friars, Tarakanoff recalled years later, shouted, "*No, Indios, Indios*" ("No, they're Indians! Indians!"). Tarakanoff was eventually released years later.

During his stay at the mission, Tarakanoff was shocked at the savagery of the friars and soldiers, who had just recaptured a group of Indians who had fled the mission:

> The Indios had been away several days when a great number of
> soldiers came to the Mission, and they and some of the priests went
> out and stayed away many, many days, and when they came back they
> brought most of the natives. They were bound with rawhide ropes, and

---

29. Sherburne F. Cook, "Colonial Expeditions to the Interior of California, Central Valley, 1800–1820," *Anthropological Records* 16, no. 6 (Berkeley: University of California Press, 1961), in *Native American Perspectives on the Hispanic Colonization of Alta California*, 359.

some were bleeding from wounds, and some children were tied to their mothers.

The next day we saw some terrible things.

Some of the runaway men were tied on sticks and beaten with straps. One chief was taken out to the open field, and a young calf which had just died was skinned, and the chief was sewn into the skin while it was yet warm. He was kept tied to a stake all day, but he died soon, and they kept his corpse tied up. The Spaniards must have put some poison on the calfskin that killed the man.

After that time the Spaniards treated us all much worse . . .[30]

Time and time again, neophytes fled from the compounds or refused to return after they were given permission to go on a *paseo* to spend time on their ancestral lands. There were few places they could hide and most runaways could not survive in the wild. As their native villages gradually eroded into empty sites of crumbling brush huts and cold, black fire pits, the wilderness skills that had served the Indians for thousands of years also withered. In some areas, runaway neophytes were shunned by the *gentiles*, who steadfastly refused to have anything to do with the missions or their inhabitants. In many cases, the *gentiles* threatened the runaways with death if they did not leave. The *gentiles*, or at least those living some distance from the missions, had seen what happened to villages nearest the compounds. They did not want their homes to also disappear, or suffer the wrath of friars or soldiers because they had helped a runaway. Despite those fears, some villages did offer shelter and helped mission Indians escape. A dangerous cycle of escape, punishment, resentment, and flight pushed the Indians to flee the missions time and time again. Some neophytes simply accepted mission life and did not rebel. Many were elderly or very young and could not imagine life outside the mission.

Mexican reports indicate the whipping of a young neophyte man by a soldier triggered the Great Chumash Uprising of February 21, 1824, which involved three entire missions—Santa Inés, La Purísima, and Santa

---

30. Rose Marie Beebe and Robert M. Senkewicz, *Lands of Promise and Despair: Chronicles of Early California, 1535–1846* (Berkeley: Heyday Books, 2001), 296–7.

Barbara.[31] California was now under Mexican rule following that nation's independence from Spain in 1821, but the new Mexican commanders had done little to ease life for the neophytes.[32]

Discontent, coupled with frustration that the new rulers had not liberated the mission Indians, seethed within the compounds. In the uprising, the young victim had walked from Mission La Purísima to visit a relative jailed at neighboring Mission Santa Inés. When he arrived, he asked Corporal of the Guard Valentin Cota if he could see his relative. His request was denied, and the neophyte reacted in a manner that Cota considered insolent. The corporal ordered him whipped. When news of the youth's flogging spread to Mission La Purísima, Indians at both compounds were outraged. Men from La Purísima suddenly left their compound and marched to join those at Santa Inés.

Once the Indian forces were combined, they attacked the soldiers with volleys of arrows. The soldiers fired in return, killing two Indians. A building was set afire as the Indians continued attacking the soldiers and the friar who had taken shelter with the guards. Not until reinforcements were spotted en route to the mission did they break off the attack and retreat to La Purísima. Men, women, and children from Santa Inés then joined the uprising and crowded the path to La Purísima.

Nearly all the Indians who joined forces at Mission La Purísima were linked to either Mission Santa Inés or Mission Santa Barbara. Earlier, the friars had transferred a number of neophytes from those two missions to Mission La Purísima after having had little success in replacing neophytes who had perished. The result was that Indians at all three missions were closely intertwined and all were members of the Chumash tribe, considered by the Spaniards to be the most advanced of California's coastal Indian tribes.

At Mission La Purísima, warriors surrounded and attacked the soldiers and the two mission priests. Running out of ammunition, the soldiers hurriedly asked the padres to negotiate a safe passage for them to Santa

31. Two Indian sources, Luisa Ygnacio and Maria Solares, interviewed by ethnographer John P. Harrington in 1914, describe a different reason for the uprising. In their account, the rebellion was caused by a Spanish sacristan at Mission Santa Inés who told the priests the mission Indians were going to attack them, then told the Indians that the priests were going to punish them the following Sunday. (*Native American Perspectives on the Hispanic Colonization of Alta California*, 59–68.)

32. By 1821, three years before the Chumash uprising, Spanish soldiers in Alta California—unpaid for years and demoralized—were replaced by Mexican troops.

Inés. The Indians granted their request but one of the padres, Antonio Rodriguez, remained with the Indians, pleading with them to give up their rebellion. His pleas were ignored and the Indians began preparing for a forthcoming siege. By this time they had assembled a substantial arsenal that included rifles, lances, bows and arrows, and even two small ceremonial cannons used by the friars to signal the celebration of religious holidays.

The Indians were not haphazard in designing their defensive positions and fields of fire. A force of 180 neophytes received military training at Mission Santa Barbara under the auspices of Friar Antonio Ripoll, who was concerned about the mission's vulnerability to attack from menaces such as French sea captain Hipólito Bouchard, who had attacked six years earlier in 1818. The Indian battle group was drilled in basic military formations and strategy, and formed into 100 archers reinforced by fifty men carrying large "chopping knives" (machetes) and thirty cavalry lancers. Ripoll named the force *Compañia de Urbanos Realistas de Santa Bárbara*[33] (Royal Civil Company of Santa Barbara).

Similarly, at Mission La Purísima, Friar Mariano Payeras of Mission La Purísima had trained a force of neophytes to either to defend the compound or, if needed, rush to the aid of Mission Santa Barbara. Payeras was so brimming with pride over how well the Indians had taken to the highly disciplined military training that he wrote Governor Pablo Vicente Solá: "It would cause me joy if you could see the preparation and enthusiasm of these Indians."[34]

James Sandos states that the military training had additional results that the friars had not expected:

> Military organization superimposed upon Mission organization provided new networks for preserving the old social structure and taught a new sense of power and the awareness of large group collective action. Formal military training, added to the learning that could be obtained from watching the padres fire their Mission cannons on significant feast days, all permitted the Chumash to learn effective ways of resisting Spanish power militarily.

---

33. James A. Sandos, *Levantamiento!: The 1824 Chumash Uprising Reconsidered*, in *Native American Perspectives on the Hispanic Colonization of Alta California*, 301.

34. Ibid., 312.

With military training, the Indians were capable of meeting a frontal attack by the Mexican soldiers who had replaced the Spanish forces. The neophytes were confident that their superior numbers could defeat the small mission and presidio forces of five or six soldiers, or even troops of up to 100 men. What they lacked were sufficient rifles and ammunition. At Mission La Purísima, the Chumash hunkered down behind their fortifications, honed their military skills, and prepared for the attack that would surely come.

Using heavy tools, the mission defenders began knocking out narrow firing slits in the walls of the mission buildings, and erecting high defensive walls made of dirt and anything found in the mission storerooms. The small cannons were wheeled in front of the mission church and aimed to cover the area from where the soldiers were expected to arrive.

Meanwhile, at Santa Barbara, neophytes were already in the midst of an uprising. When Santa Inés rebelled, Indian couriers raced to Mission Santa Barbara and Mission San Buenaventura, seeking support from the neophyte populations at those locations. At San Buenaventura, the messenger was betrayed by the *alcalde* and jailed.

When told of this situation, Andrés, Santa Barbara's *alcalde*, immediately joined the rebels—but used guile before tipping his hand. He hurried to Friar Ripoll and said, worriedly, said that the Indians from Missions Santa Inés and La Purísima had threatened to kill him unless he joined them. His only hope of surviving was to have Ripoll remove the soldiers from the mission grounds. Ripoll raced to the Presidio and asked the commander to recall the Mission guards.

It was all that Andrés needed to muster the mission's neophyte militia. When the friar returned, he found the Indians armed with the weapons used in their training. While Ripoll had raced to the presidio, Andrés had led the Indian paramilitary group to the mission storerooms where they smashed the doors and distributed the weapons among themselves. Surrounding Ripoll upon his return, they verified that the padre had indeed obtained the order from the presidio commander to withdraw the guard. The Indians demanded that the soldiers leave their firearms behind. When they balked, two were slightly wounded by Indians wielding machetes. Ripoll, stunned by the Indians' defiance and fearing for his life, decided to join the soldiers heading to the presidio. There, the commander, hearing of the rebellion, immediately mustered his soldiers to attack the mission.

Holding the advantage of high ground, the Indians were able to spot the approaching soldiers and attacked first. Surprised at the unbelievable sight of a large number of armed Indians charging against them in a tight, disciplined, line-abreast formation, the Mexican soldiers began retreating—a wise strategy considering they were seriously outnumbered. Their retreat, however, was not fast enough. In the ensuing clash, the Indians managed to wound four soldiers while suffering three dead and two wounded. With Mission Santa Barbara in their hands, they stripped it of all they could carry, including the fabrics they valued; a substantial treasury of gold coins, with gold and silver accouterments used in the large church; plus its tools, grain, seed, and food. Virtually nothing was left behind.

The neophytes then abandoned the mission. They formed a column numbering in the hundreds and began retreating up the nearby steep coastal mountains. The hurried trek eventually took them thirty miles from the mission. Meanwhile, the soldiers regrouped and launched a second attack. Instead of an armed line of Indians, they discovered an abandoned mission stripped of all its valuables and goods. All that remained were elderly Indians who had been left behind. Five of the remaining, defenseless Indians were killed by the soldiers, who then began looting the Indians' quarters and Ripoll's room in the mistaken belief that he had led the soldiers into a trap. Ripoll said nothing and instead sent a courier to contact Andrés, urging him to lead the neophytes back to the mission. Andrés, in an effort to buy time, responded that the only reason the Indians had fled was that they feared the soldiers would kill them if they returned. To add veracity to that notion and ensure that none of the Indians returned to the mission, Andrés quickly passed the word that the soldiers intended to kill them all. The ruse worked. Andrés, once over the mountains, moved the group deep into the southern part of the San Joaquin Valley.

Ripoll, in a later description of the uprising, stated that when he sought to persuade the Indians to return, Andres replied dramatically:

> We shall maintain ourselves with what God will provide us in the open country. Moreover, we are soldiers, stonemasons, carpenters, etc., and we will provide for ourselves by our work.

With Andrés skillfully evading detection and Mission Santa Barbara empty of Indians, Mexican reinforcements, numbering 109 soldiers, focused their attention on retaking Mission La Purísima. With them was a heavy, four-pound cannon that they hauled over the coastal mountains. The mission had been converted into a fort. Defending it were 400 neophytes and neighboring *gentiles*, persuaded by the mission Indians to join them in their fight for independence.

From behind their parapets, the Indians watched the column approaching: the soldiers, polished bayonets glistening in the sun, and a large Mexican flag curling and snapping in the wind at their head. The sight did not faze the neophytes. Outnumbering their enemy four to one, they expected to win. At a safe distance from the mission, the Mexican commander halted his troops and split the force, sending units to the rear to block any attempt to escape. Once that was done, the soldiers assembled into a frontal attack formation, line abreast, and began marching head-on toward the mission, bristling with waiting Indian riflemen. With a deafening roar, the Indians unleashed a volley of musket fire, filled the air with arrows, and fired their cannon. However, they were unskilled in both firing and aiming the muskets and the cannon. Although they could reload and fire the two cannons, they had no knowledge of artillery ballistics that would have allowed them to elevate or depress the barrels to increase or decrease their range respectively, and loading the proper amount of gunpowder to increase or decrease their range. Thus, the cannons were essentially useless as defensive weapons.

By contrast, the Mexican force used their four-pounder with deadly accuracy, shattering a mission wall and showering the Indians with shrapnel and rocks.[35] The air filled with gun smoke and the blast of rifle volleys, thunderous cannon fire, and the screams of the wounded and dying from both sides. Amid the deafening din of the battle, the Indian rebels realized that if they outnumbered the attacker, they were still being expertly outgunned. After suffering sixteen fatalities and a large number of wounded, they decided to retreat but found their way blocked. At that point, they abruptly called on Friar Rodriguez to negotiate the Indians' surrender. Defeated, they laid down their weapons and awaited the dreaded punishment that would befall them.

In the wake of the rebellion, the Mexican authorities tried seven Indians, found them guilty of murder, and executed them. Four leaders of the uprising were sentenced to ten years of labor at the presidio, along

---

35. Ibid., 315.

with perpetual exile; eight other participants each received eight years of labor at the presidio.

In a hearing held on June 1, Mexican officials launched an investigation into the uprising. They discovered that the Mission Santa Barbara Indians, once they left the mission, gleefully engaged in gambling and love making. The attempt to change the Indians into devout Catholics had failed dismally. Once free of the constraints of the mission and the friars, they had reverted to their free and independent spirit, casting aside the strict Roman Catholic beliefs and behavior the friars thought they had instilled in them. The Indians had never forgotten the free and easy lives they had enjoyed before the friars arrived.

While Mexican forces accompanied by friars did succeed in bringing back some neophytes to Mission Santa Barbara, the others disappeared into the San Joaquin Valley. In 1834, the Bonneville Expedition, seeking a passage through the Sierra Nevada to California, stumbled upon those Indians. They had settled near busy Walker Pass, about fifty-three miles northeast of modern Bakersfield.

Zenas Leonard, a member of that expedition, wrote that the Indians told him they had "rebelled against the authority of the country, robbed the Church of all its golden images and candlesticks, and one of the priests of several thousand dollars in gold and silver."[36] They numbered 700 to 800 and had well-tended fields of corn, pumpkins, melons, and other produce, along with herds of horses that they rode and bartered. Then, they mysteriously disappeared. There is no record or accounting of them in the 1850 population census of California despite their location near the pass, one of the main routes that led to the gold fields of the 1849 Gold Rush. Sadly, the community may have died in an outbreak of malaria that wiped out much of California's Indian population between 1833 and 1846.[37]

The Chumash Rebellion meant freedom for hundreds of tribe members, who fled as far as they could from the missions and reestablished their tribal life while adopting the farming techniques and craftsmanship they had learned at the mission. Perhaps, had Serra and his successors not defied the Spanish crown's orders to educate the Indians for ten years and then release them, California would have been dotted with thriving Indian communities such as the one discovered by the

36. Ibid., 319.
37. Ibid.

Bonneville Expedition. Andrés, the *alcalde* from Santa Barbara, was a superb leader whose only goal was to return to a life free from the dangers of Franciscan missions.

Another noted Indian rebel was Estanislao, also a former *alcalde*. Unlike Andrés, he gathered a large following and proceeded to lead and organize a rebellion against the missions and the Mexican soldiers. Estanislao is described in Jack Holterman's fine account of his rebellion as "about six feet tall, a bit more fair in complexion than usual, a man of athletic physique with a face well bearded and an air of gallantry on horseback." He was born at the mission "with some Spanish ancestry" and became a *vaquero* (cowboy) who then rose to become an *alcalde*.[38]

Estanislao outwardly appeared to have become a trustworthy fixture of the mission's administration. Inwardly, he yearned to be free of mission life. In 1828 he and members of his tribe called Lacquisamnes[39] left the mission for the annual autumn *paseo* to their tribal home along what is now called the Stanislaus River (commemorating Estanislao). During the *paseo*, he and his group decided not to return to the mission, defiantly sending word of their decision back to Friar Narciso Duran:

> We are rising in revolt. . . . We have no fear of the soldiers, for even now they are very few, mere boys, and not even sharpshooters.

Furious at the neophytes' insolence, Friar Duran called on the Mexican commander to send a troop of soldiers to capture Estanislao and the others. Duran wanted them all back so "that a sample punishment of sound throttlings be given to those who deserve it." He added: "By the way, I recall that our gunpowder here is worthless—pure carbon. The troops should bring their own cartridges."[40] There was no kindness or understanding in Duran's Franciscan mind for anyone who dared defy him or Roman Catholicism.

Meanwhile, word spread to Missions Santa Clara, Santa Cruz, and San Juan Bautista of Estanislao's bold move. Within days, numbers of neophytes began fleeing from the three missions to join the rebels taking horses with them. Estanislao's chief ally was another Indian named

---

38. Jack Holterman, *The Revolt of Estanislao*, in *Native American Perspectives on the Hispanic Colonization of Alta California*, 287.

39. Ibid., 287. (Holterman spells the name of the tribe as Lacquisamne, but it is also spelled "Lakisamne" on p. 366 of *Lands of Promise and Despair*.)

40. Ibid., 288.

Cipriano, who had escaped from Mission Santa Clara. Day by Day, Estanislao's group was growing larger and more powerful.

Soon after Duran's request to return the runaways, fifteen Mexican soldiers under Corporal Antonio Soto arrived at the mission to pick up supplies and set out for what they thought would be a simple task. The soldiers plodded and sloshed headlong into treacherous swamps, called *atascaderos*, where then found their way blocked by walls of thick swamp grass and tules. With the soldiers trapped in the mud and rushes, Estanislao and his men easily surrounded them. Hiding behind rushes, they hooted at the soldiers, fired volley after volley of arrows that arced into the sky, and then came down on Soto and his men. This sudden, ferocious attack killed two soldiers outright and wounded four others. One arrow plunged into Soto's face, burying itself deeply below his right eye and inflicting a fatal wound. Still in command, the dying corporal gasped to his second-in-command and ordered a retreat to the mission.

Not until the following spring was another effort launched to recapture Estanislao and his followers. During the winter, the rebel group raided ranches, driving off cattle and horses throughout the region. Hiding deep in the woods and hills along the Stanislaus River, the Indian leader and his band also began fortifying their large campsite, adopting European military defense strategies. Across the only path leading to their hide-away, they dug wide and deep trenches to keep cavalry from passing. The trenches were deep enough to allow Indian defenders to stand upright, behind log walls added for their protection. Any effort to dislodge them would be costly for the soldiers.

During this period, Estanislao's band surprised two neophytes from Mission San José on a fishing trip to San Joaquin and stripped one of them, Macario, of his horse, saddle, clothing, and equipment. The second neophyte, Benigno, unhesitatingly joined the rebels. Macario was sent back to the mission with a bold message from Estanislao to Duran:

> You will tell our good Father that from now on our real exploits begin. Soon we shall fall upon the very ranches and cornfields. . . . And for the troops, now as always, we have nothing but contempt and defiance![41]

The message, received in early March, threw Friar Duran into a rage. He demanded another attempt to capture Estanislao, this time with forty

---

41. Ibid., 289.

soldiers. Their commander was Corporal Pablo Pacheco, who set out in April to capture the Indian leader. This effort was as unsuccessful as the first. The soldiers realized they could not penetrate the trenches and stockades built by the Indians and returned empty-handed.

Estanislao was now running rampant throughout the area, raiding more ranches and making off with cattle and horses. A third attempt to capture him involved between thirty and forty soldiers and a small cannon from the San Francisco presidio, plus 100 Indian auxiliaries and a group of militiamen from Mission San José. They reached the Stanislaus River on May 7, 1828 and tried to flush the Indians out by setting the woods on fire; but the trees, filled with springtime sap, did not catch fire. Although the smoky fire did not drive the Indians out into the open, it did arouse their curiosity. Several showed themselves, albeit briefly. The troops' commander, Ensign José Sanchez, instantly ordered his men to fire the cannon with a resounding blast that shook the woods.

Its only effect, however, was to prompt the small Indian band to fire a hail of arrows and then slip away. The next morning, two soldiers who had strayed from the main group were found seriously wounded; another two disappeared and were later found dead. Ensign Sanchez, the commander, had a total of eight wounded, while the Indian auxiliaries suffered one fatality and eleven wounded. Again, the Mexican force retreated and returned to the mission.

Undaunted, still another force, this time just over 100 soldiers equipped with two cannons, fifty Indian auxiliaries, and a number of militiamen, set out from Mission San José under the command of Ensign Mariano Guadalupe Vallejo, the acting military commander at Monterey, and his subordinate, Ensign Sanchez. They arrived at the site where the other troops had been forced to retreat in late May. Within a short time, the Indians unleashed a storm of arrows, prompting the soldiers to set fire to the woods and roll up their cannon. The fire was a reckless maneuver that backfired against Vallejo's force.

At about 4:00 P.M., under a glaringly hot sun, the soldiers advanced in battle formation toward the first stockade trench and were met by more arrows from Indians hiding in the brush and trying to surround the troops. Once again the deadly volley of arrows forced the soldiers to retreat. Reaching a safe distance from the stockade, Vallejo ordered the cannons fired. The defensive position was instantly blown away, showering the area with deadly splinters and dirt. The Indians, realizing their stockades were useless against the cannon, hastily retreated to their second line of defense—the trenches they had dug to stop any cavalry charge and from which they could fire under cover. Sanchez, however, realizing his men were exhausted from fighting in the heat and with the flames of the forest threatening to engulf them, wisely retreated.

Next morning, the force returned to the previous day's battle site. They found it abandoned and quiet. Sanchez, after earlier capturing a Tuolomne Indian carrying a load of seed who had apparently strayed into the area, decided mistakenly that the Tuolomne Indians were involved and made plans to attack a nearby village of that tribe. The attack occurred at dawn. A cannon was rolled up (the other was left behind after its wheels collapsed) and shrapnel fired toward where the main body of Indians was believed to be located. The Indians responded by shouting insults to the soldiers and firing volleys of arrows. Trees and thick brush were set ablaze and, combined with the fires previously set, again threatened the soldiers, who had now run out of ammunition.

The stubbornness and fighting skills of the Indians stunned Vallejo, who had never imagined they were capable of a well-planned strategic defense. As his men began to retreat, he shouted for a squad to guard the nearby Tuolomne River and keep it from being used as an escape route. Several Indians, trying to reach the river, were ambushed by the soldiers and killed. That same day, an Indian named Matias had surrendered to the troops and told them the Tuolomne Indian, who had been captured the previous day and who had agreed to try to convince the attacking Indians to surrender, had actually warned Estanislao's men to go deeper into the woods. That Indian was promptly shot, and Matias replaced him as a go-between between Estanislao's forces and the soldiers.

At one point, Matias's entreaties to the rebels that they should surrender were answered by defiant shouts from the Indian defenders that they "would prefer to die on the spot." The troops answered with musket fire and cannon blasts, which only prompted more hoots and derision from the Indians crouched in the thick underbrush. Later, when the soldiers reached a series of trenches, they pulled out three elderly women cowering under a bush and shot them. During the battle, an Indian was captured who admitted to burning the bodies of the two soldiers killed in the third attempt to capture Estanislao:

He was immediately surrounded by the Indian auxiliaries who pleaded to kill the prisoner with their own hands. They were given permission. So the Indian auxiliaries formed a semicircle, placed him in the middle, and four of them began to shoot arrows at him. But no matter how hard they tried, they could not kill him. Finally seeing that he did not die, a cavalry soldier shot him in the head with his carbine, and only then did he die. Seventy-three arrows were counted in his body. From there they took him to an oak tree and hung him up.

Matias, the Indian who had surrendered, was shot and killed by one of the civilians for no apparent reason. The Indian auxiliaries hanged him from a large oak tree. Four other men and four women captured in the fight were also hanged from the same tree. Vallejo and his men, angry and frustrated at Estanislao, were viciously lashing out at any Indian they found. Those acts evoked an outcry from Friar Duran at Mission San José. Grief-stricken, he realized that in his lust to capture Estanislao he had unleashed a series of terrible atrocities against innocent Indians.

Despite all the fighting, Estanislao was nowhere to be found. In actuality, he was galloping back to Mission San José to seek forgiveness and sanctuary from Friar Duran. When he slipped into the mission, Friar Duran not only forgave him, but also provided him sanctuary, safeguarding him from the military. Efforts by Vallejo to arrest Estanislao were countered by Duran with the charges of brutality and atrocities committed during the recent attacks. Eventually, it was decided that Estanislao could remain in the mission so long as he did not cause trouble. It was the most efficient way to keep track of him.

Meanwhile, a remorseful Duran angrily called for an investigation of Vallejo and his men, accusing them of criminal acts in their search for Estanislao. In a subsequent hearing ordered by Mexican Governor José María de Echeandia, charges were brought against a Monterey soldier, Joaquin Alvarado, in the killing of a woman. A military court recommended that he be sentenced to "five years of penal servitude on the frontiers of Baja California."[42]

As for Estanislao and his followers, all were granted immunity from prosecution. Ultimately, the former runaway disappeared from Mission San José. In 1830 he was sighted, reportedly rustling cattle and horses again, this time in California's Central Valley. Estanislao later died at Mission San José during the 1839 malaria epidemic.

---

42. Holterman, *Revolt of Estanislao*, 296.

Another neophyte who rebelled against the missions was Pomponio, who escaped from either Mission San Francisco or Mission San Rafael. For three years he staged hit-and-run raids in the Francisco Bay area. He was hunted down by Spanish soldiers, tried, and executed at Monterey in the fall of 1824.[43] At one point, his trusted accomplice, Gonzalo, was also jailed. He attempted to escape by cutting off his heels, allowing him to slip restraining iron rings off his ankles and feet. The next day, Spanish guards were enraged when they discovered all that remained of Gonzalo was a large, coagulating pool of blood, with the chunks of flesh from his heels on the jail cell floor.

One of America's most famous frontiersmen, Kit Carson, also figured briefly in the history of mission revolts by helping recapture a group of neophytes who escaped from Mission San Rafael in 1830. The mission priest, on learning of the escape, organized a party of fifteen Indians to seize the runaways, but it was driven back by the escapees and members of the village where they had taken refuge. The pursuers then sought help from Carson's group, which was camping along the Sacramento River nearby, waiting for the trapping season to begin. Ewing Young, the leader of the beaver trappers, ordered Carson and eleven other men to help the Indians recapture the escapees. An attack was launched and a ferocious struggle ensued lasting "one entire day." Eventually, Carson recalled, "The Indians were routed, lost a great number of men. We entered the village in triumph, set fire to it and burned it to the ground."

Next morning, Carson and his group "demanded the runaways and informed them that if not immediately given up we would not leave one of them alive. They complied with our demands. We turned over our Indians to those from whom they had deserted and we returned to camp."[44] Whether Carson was aware of the treatment of the Indians within the missions, or whether he even considered it, is not known.

During the mission period, many neophytes—starved, beaten, and separated from their traditional way of life—were forced into surrendering their rights as human beings. Despite the threat of harsh

---

43. Auguste Bernard, Duhaut-Cilly, *Voyage autour du Monde, principalement á la Californie et aux Iles Sandwich, pendant les annés 1826, 1827, 1828, et 1829*, tr. Charles Franklin Carter (Paris: 1834-1835), in *Native American Perspectives on the Hispanic Colonization of Alta California*, 406.

44. Charles L. Camp, "Kit Carson In California With Extracts from His Own Story," in *Quarterly of the California Historical Society*, Oct. 1922, 4–5.

punishment and even death, Indian leaders did arise who led escapes, insurrections, and fought trained Spanish solders in pitched battles, demonstrating the depth of Indian opposition to the missions and their way of life. That the rebellions could not bring about the end of the missions is understandable, but it stands as evidence that individuals were willing to sacrifice their lives to try to halt an inhumane system.

11

After the Missions

Your Honor must also understand that I need servants—for example, one or two youths and one or two cooks.
—Friar José Antonio Anzar, January 29, 1835, seeking money from the Mexican governor to maintain his lifestyle as a mission priest at Mission San Juan Bautista.

In 1832, as the Indians fled the missions[1], members of the Mexican territorial assembly, seeking liberal reforms such as the establishment of schools, called for an end to "the detestable system of the missions."[2] Those compounds, the decree stated, had "oppressed" the Indians. What the assembly sought was to convert California into "a place of liberal institutions and commerce."[3]

By 1835, neophytes had abandoned the missions in droves. Under a Mexican law passed in August of 1833, the priests could no longer keep them against their will. Without the forced labor of the Indians, the missions plunged into ruin and many of the Franciscan friars, with no one to do their bidding, likewise walked away.

At Mission San Juan Bautista, where his Indian servants had abandoned him, Friar José Antonio Anzar submitted a plea for money to maintain his previous lifestyle, in which he had been surrounded by neophyte servants. His request was scoffed at by the Mexican administrator of the mission, José Tiburcio Castro, who had been appointed

---

1. Between 1834 and 1843, the population of mission neophytes plunged from 30,000 to 5,000.

2. Rose Marie Beebe and Robert M. Senkewicz, *Lands of Promise and Despair: Chronicles of Early California, 1535–1846* (Berkeley: Heyday Books, 2001), 345.

3. Ibid.

by the Mexican governor as part of the plan to turn the missions into simple parish churches. The vast mission lands were to be distributed equally between the Indians and the government and, under the 1833 law, Indians were meant to become productive members of California society. It didn't work out that way.

The Indians who had left the missions were ill-equipped for life outside the tightly-structured system. Nearly all were illiterate and lacked the experience to deal with a secular society. That naiveté allowed *Californios*—who had been born in California or were among the early immigrants from Mexico—with ranches and communities established during the mission period to take advantage of the former neophytes, cheating them out of their property with liquor and a few pesos. Many of the mission lands were also seized by corrupt government officials.

Under Mexican rule, the monopoly the Alta California missions had held on the territory's best farmland and pastures came to an end. Most Indians, now free to leave, hurriedly abandoned the missions, leaving behind only those who were too old and had nowhere to go. Little remained of the pre-Hispanic ancestral life the Indians had enjoyed. The culture the Indians had developed over thousands of years, which had allowed them to thrive in the coastal areas of California, had disappeared by 1837. The villages that once teemed with life no longer existed. Over the sixty-five years of the missions' existence, most of the traditions, customs, beliefs, and skills of the various tribes had been forgotten. There were virtually no elders, and too few traditional Indian craftsmen survived to successfully pass along their knowledge to a younger generation. Some tribelets simply disappeared without a trace, their members dying within the missions,

Without the cohesion of traditional tribal customs to moderate their behavior, the Indians celebrated their freedom with a joyous romp of liberation—something that further contributed to their ruination. Most never realized they now had full control of themselves, and so could not function efficiently in the give-and-take of normal life. Their rigid life in the missions had failed to instill in them any concept of how to survive in a unfamiliar society. Drinking brandy and wine, which had been forbidden by the friars, became a favorite pastime for many. Some Indian were even hired by ranchers and paid in alcohol instead of wages. Others lapsed into gambling and stealing horses and cattle, not only to resell but simply to provide food. In some cases, they herded horses across Nevada and sold them to Midwestern Indian tribes. Ranchers fumed at the near-constant raids and swore vengeance. They considered the Indians vermin that needed to be exterminated. The murder of Indians by ranchers and Mexican soldiers, and later by settlers moving into the area, was so horrific that it can only be described as a genocidal campaign.

California's Spanish friars were dumbfounded when they learned of the new Mexican nation's 1827 decree ordering all Spaniards under the age of 60 to leave Mexico. Some, especially those who were elderly or sick, were allowed to stay at the missions, where they would quietly sun themselves on mission benches, waiting to die, watching their once sprawling empire literally crumble around them. When Mexican troops first arrived in California, shortly after Mexico's 1821 independence from Spain, the Mexican commandants of the California presidios barred the friars from leaving, knowing that without them the missions would be pillaged and looted by their former Indian slaves. Most of the Spanish friars were eventually replaced by Mexican Franciscan friars charged with converting the missions into parish churches. In one case, the Mexican administrator of Mission San Luis Rey complained that the Indians, now aware that they were free, ignored his demands that they stay at the missions, shouting instead: "We are free! We do not want to obey! We do not want to work!"[4]

A few friars at some of the missions secretly stole away before the 1827 deportation decree, taking with them bags of money. At Santa Barbara mission, Friars Antonio Ripoll and Friar José Altimira managed to board an American brig, the *Harbinger*, which was sailing east to United States' territory. Ripoll took with him an undetermined amount of gold and at least 7,000 francs,[5] claiming the amount was accumulated from the $400 annual stipend the Spanish government paid each mission friar. Ripoll's claim, however, was in direct violation of the Franciscan's vows to forever live in poverty and never accumulate personal wealth. Under the Franciscans' strict regulations, the stipend was never sent to the friars in cash; instead, the friars listed what they needed and their requests were

---

4. Zephyrin Engelhardt, *San Luis Rey Mission* (San Francisco: Barry, 1921), 96–97.

5. Auguste Bernard, Duhaut-Cilly, *Voyage autour du Monde*, tr. Charles Franklin Carter (Paris: 1834–1835), in *Native American Perspectives on the Hispanic Colonization of Alta California*, 406.

sent to Mexico City, where the items were purchased and then delivered.[6] Neither Ripoll nor Altamira were ever heard of again.

What became of most of the Spanish friars who abandoned the missions is unclear. Some apparently managed to reach the Spanish-ruled Philippines. Others sailed to the east coast of the United States and presumably returned to Europe. Other Spanish friars simply disappeared, boarding whatever foreign merchant ship was available to take them away. What is certain is that there is no full accounting of the wealth amassed by the missions during their peak period, from the end of the eighteenth century through the early 1800s.

Six years after the expulsion of the Spaniards, the Mexican Congress of the Union issued another decree on August 17, 1833: *Decreto de la Secularización de las Misiones de California* (An Act for the Secularization of the Missions of California). This secularized the missions and all their lands, making them property of the Mexican government. The Roman Catholic Church and the Franciscans were stripped of any authority over the missions. Although their mission chapels could still be used for Mass, the lands and buildings were administered by government appointees.

At Mission San Gabriel, Spanish Friar Tomás Estenaga, when notified of the edict, flew into a rage and angrily ordered the neophytes remaining at the compound to destroy the mission. Outbuildings were ripped apart, roof tiles torn off and smashed, and ceiling timbers burned. All of the mission's implements were distributed to the neophytes and the thousands of remaining cattle were slaughtered and the meat given to the Indians before it spoiled. Tens of thousands of carcasses of cattle, sheep, and goats littered the fields as vultures filled the skies, feasting on the rotting flesh. However, when Friar Estenaga ordered the Indians to also destroy the mission's vineyards, the neophytes defied him and refused to carry out the act.[7]

Soon after the Spanish priests left, exiled from Mexican land, and the Indians abandoned the missions, the adobe and brick structures, without the constant maintenance they needed, quickly fell apart. They were for all practical purposes abandoned. Outside of populated areas, the roofs quickly collapsed. Within cities, church goers sought to save them, but

6. Lasuén, *Writings of Fermín Francisco de Lasuén*, Vol. I., 231; Serra, *Writings of Junípero Serra*, Vol. II, 474n79.

7. Susanna Bryant Dakin, Hugo Reid, *A Scotch Paisano: Hugo Reid's Life in California, 1832–1852* (Berkeley: University of California Press, 1939), 516.

the repair work was too much for parishoners and many were closed until restoration began in the late nineteenth century.

On the California coast, a French captain described Mission Santa Cruz as a dismal sight of decay: *"Un spectacle de misere et d'abandon s'offrit à mes regards."*[8] In 1837, British Commander (later, Admiral) Sir Edward Belcher described California as a place where "everything was decaying. . . . The missions, the only respectable establishments in this country, are annihilated; they have been plundered by all parties."[9] A few missions provided shelter for some settlers, but in most places on windy days, the mournful sound of doors banging against crumbling adobe walls echoed through rooms and corridors that had been long vacant.

One American traveler, Edwin Bryant, on a journey with a companion through California in 1846, poignantly described Mission San José:

> We soon entered through a narrow street the Mission of San José, or St. Joseph. Passing the squares of one-story adobe buildings, once inhabited by thousands of busy Indians, but now deserted, roofless, and crumbling into ruins, we reached the plaza in front of the church and the massive two-story edifices of the padres during the epoch of the establishment. These were in good repair, but the doors and windows with the exception of one were closed, and nothing of moving life was visible except a donkey or two. . . . we entered the open door and here we found two Frenchmen dressed in sailor costume, with a quantity of coarse shirts, pantaloons, stockings and other small articles, together with *aguardiente* (liquor) which they designed retailing to such of the natives in the vicinity as chose to become their customers. They were itinerant merchants. . . . I passed through extensive warehouses and immense rooms, once occupied for the manufacture of woolen blankets and other articles with the rude machinery still standing in them, but

---

8. Cyrille Pierre Théodore Laplace, *Campagne de Circumnavigation de la frégate l'Artémise pendant les années 1837, 1838, 1839, et 1840 sous le commandement de M. Laplace, capitaine de vaisseau . . .* (Paris, 1841–54), in Bancroft, *History of California Vol. IV, 1801–1824* (San Francisco: Bancroft, 1886), 154.

9. Sir Edward Belcher, *Narrative of a Voyage Round the World, Performed in Her Majesty's Ship* Sulphur, *During the Years 1836–1842* (London: Henry Colburn, 1843), in Bancroft, History of California. Vol. I, 143.

unemployed. Filth and desolation have taken the place of cleanliness and busy life. . . .[10]

As Bryant and his friend explored the abandoned mission, they came upon its jail. He described it as a "miserable dark room of two apartments, one with a small loophole in the wall, the other a dungeon without light or ventilation." The instruments used for punishing the neophytes, "the stocks, and several other inventions," were scattered inside the "calaboose."

Continuing his journey, Bryant next visited Mission Santa Clara and marveled at the broad *alameda*, shaded by elms and willows that had been planted during the mission era and now swayed gently in the wind. The entire road formed a "most beautiful drive or walk." It had been built by Indian labor to allow the residents of the nearby pueblo of Santa Clara, to stroll comfortably under the shade of the trees to attend mass at the mission. While the chapel appeared to be still in use:

> . . . the rich lands surrounding the Mission are entirely neglected. . . .
> The picture of decay and ruin presented by this once flourishing establishment, surrounded by a country so fertile and scenery so enchanting, is a most melancholy spectacle to the passing traveler, and speaks a language of loud condemnation against the government.[11]

Traveling north, the pair visited Mission San Francisco (Dolores):

> The church of the Mission and main buildings are in tolerable repair. In the latter, several Mormon families, which arrived in the ship *Brooklyn* from New York, are quartered. As in the other Missions I have passed through, the Indian quarters are crumbling into shapeless heaps of mud.[12]

Another visitor to the abandoned missions during the same period was William D. Phelps, the captain of the American merchant ship *Alert*. In Santa Barbara, Phelps sought to obtain an Indian skull at the mission and was told by the friar there that just six weeks before, the skulls of 2,000 Indians had been buried after previously being placed in a charnel house.

---

10. Edwin Bryant, *What I Saw in California: Being the Journal of a Tour by the Emigrant Route and South Pass of the Rockey Mountains, Across the Continent of North America, the Great Desert Basin, and Through California, in the Years 1846, 1847* (New York: Appleton, 1848), 309–311.

11. Ibid., 317–318.

12. Ibid., 320–321.

The priest indicated that only skulls were buried. Phelps does not describe what happened to the rest of the bones, and portrayed the mission as "poor and going to decay."[13]

The sea captain likewise described Mission Carmel, near Monterey, as being in a state of ruin only six years after being secularized. Phelps noted that "the Indians in their wild state are more healthy than those which have been subject to the Missions, and it may be said with equal truth of the Indians here as of those in our Western States that 'civilization is death to the Indian.' Unaccustomed to restraint, their free spirits sicken and die in the presence of a master."[14]

Phelps—his thoughts echoing those of the early French visitor Lapérouse—was highly critical of the California Franciscans and their methods, asking: "[What] have the natives of California gained by their labours; what service have those Friars rendered to the Spanish nation, or to the world in general?" Although he described the friars as "honest men . . . who . . . pursued with assiduity what they believed to be their duty . . . we must entirely condemn their system and lament its results."[15]

While free of the oppression of mission life, the Indians now faced a new round of shameful treatment from arriving settlers and the Mexican government. They were pejoratively labeled "digger" Indians for their custom of using sticks to dig for edible roots. "It was a term of denigration . . . a handy rubric to suggest all the qualities of extreme primitiveness that European travelers had for decades attributed to California Indians."[16]

The American writer Washington Irving lamented the treatment of the Indians by Mexicans, whom he described as committing "infamous barbarities" against them. The Mexicans, he wrote, hunted the "poor Root Diggers . . . like wild beasts killing them without mercy" by lassoing them around the neck then dragging them until they were dead.[17]

During the 1850s, the treatment of Indians in California, now part of the United States, reached its lowest point—they were being kidnapped

---

13. William Dane Phelps, *Alta California 1840–1842: The Journal and Observations of William Dane Phelps, Master of the Ship* Alert, ed. Briton Cooper Busch (Glendale, Calif.: Arthur Clark, 1983), 77.

14. Ibid., 144.

15. Ibid., 129.

16. Rawls, *History of California*, 49.

17. Ibid., 59.

and sold as slaves, similar to the African slaves of America's Southern plantations. J. D. Borthwick, who visited California during that period, haughtily declared there was no place for the Indians in the state. They were, he stated, "not compatible with . . . a civilised community, and, as the country becomes more thickly settled, there will be no longer room for them. Their country can be made subservient to man, but as they themselves cannot be turned to account, they must move off, and make way for their betters."[18]

By 1861, in the midst of the American Civil War that was being fought to ban slavery in America, bands of armed men were raiding Indian villages in northern California and kidnapping Indian children for sale. George M. Hanson, the superintendent of Indian Affairs in California, described these raids "as a crime against humanity." He called for an end to the kidnappings, which had been started by American settlers who had flocked to California beginning in the late 1830s. Children as young as three and four years were being bought for $50 apiece, and "near Yuba City a boy between eight and ten years old was sold for eighty dollars as a hog driver, and a younger boy for fifty-five dollars. Prices for Indians in Mendocino County at the same time were said to range from thirty to a hundred and fifty dollars 'according to quality.'"[19]

On October 5, 1862, the *San Francisco Alta California* newspaper published a story stating:

> Mr. August Hess, who has returned to this city from a prospecting tour through the lower part of Lake county, informs us that he saw a number of men driving Indian children before them to sell in Napa, Solano, Yolo and other counties of the Sacramento basin. In one instance, he saw two men driving nine children; in another, two men with four children; in another, one man with two girls, one of them about fourteen years of age apparently. The age of these children varies from six to fifteen years. Rumor says that about a hundred children have been taken through Lake County this summer, for sale. They do not follow the main roads, but usually take by-paths. Rumor says further, the hunters catch them in Mendocino and Humboldt counties after killing their parents.

---

18. J.D. Borthwick, *Three Years in California* (Edinburgh: William Blackwood and Sons, 1857), 289.

19. Ibid., 97.

The practice prompted the *Sacramento Union* to speak out in a July 31, 1860, editorial:

> ... [It] was an outrage in which the most disgusting phase of this species of slavery is the concubinage of creatures calling themselves white men with squaws throughout various portions of the State. The details of this portion of the 'apprenticeship' system are unfit to commit to paper.

The children were sold to serve as farm workers or servants in the homes of those who bought them. Younger Indian children were assigned to be household servants. One resident of Humboldt County described the Indian children serving in the houses as "frequently the brightest and cunningest little chaps you ever saw. They are very cheerful, laugh at jokes and seem fond of playing practical ones occasionally on their white playfellows." The same man had an Indian bootblack whom he described as "always jolly, and always whistling."[20]

The kidnapping of Indian children was being committed under a legal loophole of a California law—the Act for Government and Protection of Indians—which had been passed in 1850 and amended in 1860. It allowed children to be taken from their Indian parents for training as "apprentices" so long as the parents consented. It was, in reality, a license for kidnappers to first kill the parents, seize their children, and then claim to have obtained parental consent. No one questioned them.[21]

California's Indian Apprenticeship Law was repealed in 1863. Yet the practice of Indian slavery continued into the early 1870s. After that, law enforcement ended it, prompted by a public outraged at the practice, especially in the wake of the Civil War.

For California's Indians, ravaged first by the Spanish and Franciscan friars, then by Mexican and American settlers, life was a never-ending nightmare. Even into the early twentieth century, the coastal Indians were denigrated and considered subhuman. The suffering they endured for more than 100 years was a legacy of the religious fanaticism, cruelty, and arrogance that began in 1769, directed by Franciscan friar Junípero Serra.

Sherburne Cook writes that California's Indians suffered from three major calamities after the Spaniards' arrival: "The first was the food supply ... The second factor was disease ... A third factor, which

---

20. Rawls, *Indians of California*, 101.
21. Ibid., 101.

strongly intensified the effect of the other two, was the social and physical disruption visited upon the Indian. He was driven from his home by the thousands, starved, beaten, raped, and murdered with impunity. He was not only given no assistance in the struggle against foreign diseases, but was prevented from adopting even the most elementary measures to secure food, clothing and shelter. The utter devastation caused by the white man was literally incredible, and not until the population figures are examined does the extend of the havoc become evident."[22] From an estimated 300,000[23] coastal Indians in 1769, their number dwindled to 16,624 in 1890.[24]

The missions, where thousands of Indians remain buried in unmarked mass graves, were resurrected in the 1890s and early 1900s and rebuilt as monuments to a concocted past that featured a loving, cooperative relationship between the friars and the Indians. Many California leaders, either ignorant of the truth or choosing to ignore what had happened, joined in this duplicity.

The publication in 1884 of the novel *Ramona*, written by Helen Hunt Jackson, a writer who had worked tirelessly to improve life for California's Indians, described the pathos of Indian life in the state. However, the book also glorified the missions and helped further the myth of the idyllic relationship between the friars and their Indian charges.

The inaccurate rewriting of history led to the 1927 commissioning of Santa Barbara sculptor Ettore Cadorin to create a dramatic statue of Junípero Serra for placement in the National Statuary Hall in the United States' Capitol (installed in 1931). Each state is allowed to place two statues to represent important people in its history. At the beginning of the twenty-first century, California's two statues were of Serra and U.S. President Ronald W. Reagan, a former California governor. In one hand, Serra's image cradles a model of a mission, while in the other his he grips a large cross. Other monuments to Serra are on the grounds of the

---

22. Sherburne F. Cook, *The Population of the California Indians, 1769–1970* (Berkeley: University of California Press, 1976), 200.

23. Other figures place the population from 133,000 to more than 700,000. I have chosen Sherburne Cook's estimate.

24. Robert F. Heizer and M.A. Whipple, "Number and Condition of California Indians Today," in *The California Indians: A Source Book*, 2nd ed. (Berkeley: University of California Press, 1971), 576.

California capitol and at the entrance to San Francisco's Golden Gate Park. The many monuments to him scattered across the state reinforce his being called the "Apostle of California" for his work in establishing the first nine of twenty-one missions that span the state, from San Diego to San Francisco Bay.

The veneration of Serra extends to the Vatican where, on September 25, 1988, Pope John Paul II conferred beatification on him, a major step toward declaring him a saint. The latter has not been implemented. Native American groups have protested the process, declaring Serra unworthy of sainthood because of his policy of harsh physical punishment of the Indians and for facilitating the destruction of their culture.

Despite the carefully preserved documents providing proof of a nightmarish life for the Indians, Friar Mariano Payéras's damning letter, and the statements of the Indians themselves, the missions are still widely perceived as sites where kindness and goodness prevailed.

In 1966, Father Florian F. Guest, a Franciscan scholar, decried Serra's and Lasuén's lack of enlightenment in the eighteenth century: "Distant thousands of leagues from libraries, salons, and cultured centers of Europe, uninfluenced by the more advanced writers of the age, the padres trod blindly and unthinkingly in the footsteps of the past. What they needed most was not a conference on charity. It was a lecture on criminology."[25]

Guest then criticizes the Indians' "tenacious hankering" for an "easy, irresponsible life of laziness." It was the natives' indolence which stood in their way of embracing "a civilized life."[26] Yet that pathway, he wrote, was also blocked by the friars' harsh use of the "lash, the shackles, and the stocks," adding that such punishment "easily disillusioned Indians in the blessings of the new European way of life. Finally, the restrictions of Christian morality were not easily endured."[27]

Guest apparently did not consider the Indian way of life worth preserving, nor did he provide a valid contemporary explanation of why and by what right Serra and his Franciscans established, in the Century

---

25. Florian F. Guest, "The Indian Policy Under Fermín Francisco de Lasuén, California's Second Father President," *California Historical Society Quarterly* 45, no. 3, September 1966, 207.

26. Ibid., 208.

27. Ibid., 209.

of Light, a movement that had a goal of crushing the civilization of California's coastal Indians. Imprisoned within the missions, where they died by the tens of thousands, the Indians saw their lands lost and their culture all but extinguished.

Epilogue

Never tell anyone you're Indian. Tell them you are Mexican.
—Indian mothers' advice to their California children to shield them from being kidnapped in the nineteenth century and being scorned in the twentieth century.

For nearly 200 years, California's Coastal Indians have struggled to piece together what remains of their culture, languages, and traditional lands, which were essentially destroyed, silenced, and seized during the mission period. This decimation of Indian people and their cultures by the twenty-one missions between 1769 to 1834 has made it extremely difficult for descendants today to recover those facets that once made them distinct tribes, each with one language and one history tied to a specific area of land.

In 1851, hope of reclaiming some of their own land glimmered, then quickly faded. That year, federal Indian commissioners were ordered to negotiate treaties with California Indian tribes and distribute 8.5 million acres of land among them. A total of eighteen agreements were reached and turned into treaties pending ratification.

However, California's legislators, arguing that the land (where gold had been discovered in 1849) was far too valuable to turn over to Indians, sought to have the U.S. Congress reject the treaties. They were successful. In secret session, the U.S. Senate killed any further consideration of the treaties and ordered them sealed by the president for fifty years. California tribes who had signed the treaties, and who were never told of the Congressional double cross, waited for more than half a century before bluntly being told that the treaties they had signed were worthless.

The genocidal juggernaut launched by the missions and the Franciscan friars who ran them was compounded disastrously by California Governor Peter H. Burnett's genocidal proclamation in 1851, as described in the previous chapter.

Forty years later, after the brutal deaths of thousands of California Native Americans, the federal government launched an effort to provide the Indians their rightful place in the sun. It was a bill called "An Act for the Relief of Mission Indians in the State of California" and its goal was to provide a "just and satisfactory settlement" for those victims of the Franciscans. Signed into law in 1891 by President Benjamin Harrison, the measure recognized the brutal hardships suffered by the state's Indians, first at the hands of Franciscan friars in the missions and later by settlers from the Eastern United States.

Under the federal act, commissioners were appointed and directed to provide a reservation for the tribal band or villages linked to each mission. However, the measure considered the Indians at each of the twenty-one missions as being members of only one tribe, albeit a different nation at each compound. That description was absolutely flawed. In reality, each compound contained a blend of many different Indian nations, each with different cultures and often different languages. The missions initially had scoured all Indians from adjacent lands, but many of those first mission Indians—especially the very young and the very old—quickly died from the dreadful conditions within the compounds. The Franciscans then moved further afield, penetrating the boundaries of small nations distinct from those they had first encountered. The missions thus became a deadly, spreading ground fog, slowly moving outwards to envelope all Indians in a dark embrace.

Instead of identifying the different tribes captured for each compound, the Franciscans cavalierly identified all Indians within their areas as belonging to one tribe. For example, Indians surrounding Mission San Diego became the *Diegueños*. Those from Mission San Gabriel were called *Gabrieleños*, while in Mission San Luis Rey de Francis the Indians became the *Luiseños*. Some friars simply identified all the Indians by the name of the dominant tribe.

The federal act had minimal effect in correcting the injustice suffered by California's Indian nations. The appointed commissioners were assigned to determine how to allocate land to the Indian nations affected by the missions, but ultimately only a handful of tribes, most of them in San Diego County, were rewarded.

Little more was done to provide land to the mission Indians until 1927, when Indian Field Service Superintendent L.A. Dorrington provided a report outlining the land needs of California's 220 landless Indian groups. It was a worthless study. On its face, the twenty-seven-page study appears to have been an exhaustive effort requiring a tremendous amount of field work. Yet, Indian critics maintain Dorrington merely referred to a 1906 Indian census and simply made up descriptions of the tribes. The Indian Affairs official never described his methodology nor explained why Indians who had jobs or homes were denied land.

Nor did the study identify the Native Americans by their tribe, but only by the town or site where they resided. In Placer County, Dorrington wrote: "No land is required for the Todd's Valley band, nor is any land required for the Clifford Gap band"[1] (the report identified Indians only by the name of the geographical area where they lived, not by their tribal affiliation).

In Sonoma County, Dorrington wrote that, "Little is known of the Bodega Bay Indians. However, it is understood that they live along the coast of the Bay as squatters on property belonging to the various persons, making their living primarily as fishermen. The writer is not in position to make definitive recommendation concerning this band at the present time, but from information at hand it would seem that no land will be required."[2] In reference to a group of Indians living in the vicinity of Chico, California, he wrote: "There are approximately eighty-six Indians; these do not comprise any one band but are members of other bands that have gone to Chico to procure work and have established their homes there. They are living the same as white citizens, are of the laboring class, and consequently no land is required."[3] Dorrington also decided that twenty Indians near Wespoint in Calaveras County " . . . are somewhat scattered and it will not be necessary to purchase any land for them."[4]

---

1. L.A. Dorrington, Sacramento Indian Agency, Indian Field Service, *Report on Indian land needs to the Commissioner of Indian Affairs of the United States Department of the Interior* (Sacramento, June 23, 1927), 20.

2. Ibid.

3. Ibid., 5.

4. Ibid.

Dorrington, in a few instances, does report that either land or homes have been purchased for Indians. Those descriptions are far outweighed by the number of times the Indian Affairs official rejects purchase of land. One of the most egregious descriptions states that, "In San Benito County we find the San Juan Baptista [sic] band, which reside in the vicinity of the Mission San Juan Baptista [sic] which is located near the town of Hollister. These Indians have been well cared for by Catholic priests and no land is required."[5]

In 2004, Valentin J. Lopez, chairperson of the Amah Mutsun Tribal Band of Ohlone/Costanoan Indians, one of the tribal bands seeking government recognition, formally asked to have San Juan Bautista Mission review its records to determine if Dorrington's statement regarding Indians being cared by priests from the mission in 1927 was true. The following reply was dated September 3, 2004, and signed by Father Edward Fitz-Henry, then the pastor of the mission:

> I made a thorough search of the records we have at the Old Mission San Juan Bautista. I found nothing that mentions Mr. Dorrington or the Indian Field Service.

Had Dorrington or one of his agents investigated the situation regarding the mission caring for the Indians, the federal query would have been noted in the mission records. Additionally, the mission would have also kept a detailed record of the supposed Indians under its care during that year. No such records were found. As a consequence of Dorrington's report, no Indian land or reservations exist between San Francisco and San Luis Obispo.

"More than one hundred of California tribal bands suddenly disappeared," Lopez observed. In one stroke of Dorrington's pen, as far as the federal government was concerned, they ceased to exist as Indian groups. The action was in direct violation of United States law, which granted federal recognition to all Native Americans and granted them land or funds to maintain their way of life. Only an act of Congress can deny them that right.

For decades, few tribes or bands sought to obtain federal recognition. The Depression, World War II, the Cold War and an indifferent Bureau of Indian Affairs pushed any Indian requests to the back rooms where they

---

5. Ibid., 16.

piled up, ignored, abandoned, and forgotten. Few Indian groups could afford appeals requiring expensive attorneys.

Beginning in the last half of the twentieth century, indigenous tribes and bands, not only in California but across the nation, gradually began requesting federal recognition to make their members eligible for the same federal benefits enjoyed by recognized bands. An exacting and painstaking procedure for submitting these requests was established by the government in 1978. Preparing those requests required tribal members to sit for weeks, sometimes years, in government offices, archives and libraries and in the missions themselves, leafing through ancient documents and scrolling through microfilm viewers to obtain the needed information.

Despite their efforts, most would never succeed. The Bureau of Indian Affairs would take years before even turning the first page. In most cases, the BIA rejected the requests and it was not uncommon for the government agency to take twenty years before passing any judgment.

Since 1978, only one California tribe has been recognized by the BIA. The Timbasha Shasone Tribe in Death Valley achieved that goal in 1983 after submitting a fifty-two-page petition. Other tribes or bands have waited for twenty-five years, and California Indian leader Valentin Lopez has asked in frustration: "What do we have to do, sell our souls?"[6]

In 1992, in testimony before a Congressional hearing, Bud Shepard, former assistant secretary of the BIA, called the 1978 regulations "fatally flawed." Not even tribes that have already been granted federal recognition, he said, could possibly meet those standards. Lopez added that even a revision of those requirements made by the BIA in 2013 "does nothing to change the regulations in a substantial or meaningful way."[7]

In a nine-page letter sent on September 24, 2013, to Elizabeth Appel, acting director of the Office of Regulatory Affairs and Collaborative Action within the U.S. Department of the Interior, Lopez outlined needed changes to streamline the recognition procedure and make it a fair and logical process. The letter was the result of input from fifteen different California Indian bands and tribes. Those groups were the Chalon Indian Nation, Winnemem Winto Tribe, Fernandeño Tataviam Band of Mission

---

6. Series of interviews with Valentin Lopez, 2013–2014.

7. Valentin Lopez, letter to Elizabeth Appel, Office of Regulatory Affairs and Collaborative Action, U.S. Department of the Interior. Washington, D.C., September 24, 2013, p. 5. The full text of Lopez's letter can be found in the Appendix.

Indians, Muwekma Tribe of Ohlone Indians, Ohlone Costanoan Esselen Nation, Chowchilla Yokuts Tribe, Dunlap Band of Mono Indians, Santa Barbara Chumash Tribe, Susanville Indian Rancheria Maidu, Juaneno Band of Mission Indians, Konkow Valley Band of Maidu, North Fork Mono, Amah Mutsun Tribal Band of Costanoan/Oholone Indians, and the South Valley Yokuts.

Uppermost in the tribes' and bands' minds was that the Office of Federal Recognition be removed from the Bureau of Indian Affairs and be placed in the Civil Rights Division of the Department of Justice. Lopez said the Division, created in 1957 by the enactment of the Civil Rights Act of 1957, is aimed at upholding the "Constitutional rights of all Americans, particularly some of the most vulnerable members of our society. . . ."[8]

Additionally, he criticized what he called a clear "conflict of interest" in that the Bureau of Indian Affairs "has a responsibility to act in the best interest of federally *recognized* tribes." A historical review of the BIA clearly shows the agency therefore virtually ignores the "best interests" of non-recognized tribes. Lopez states: "[It is] not in the best interest of recognized tribes for additional tribes to be recognized." Doing so would dilute the resources for health care, education, and economic development, which recognized tribes would have to share with an even larger number of tribes.

While an overhaul of the BIA requirements for tribal recognition was being studied in 2014, including adopting a policy to consider the unique history of California Indians, Lopez said the unrecognized California groups face extreme difficulty in detailing their history because of the devastation the Native Americans suffered within the Franciscan missions. He wrote:

> The federal government cannot expect tribes to have maintained their tribal continuity when they were forced into slavery or near slavery conditions. It is extremely difficult for tribes to pass down their indigenous knowledge regarding culture, traditions, ceremonies, etc., when they're struggling just to survive.

Lopez's appeal that the BIA establish a policy of fairness in reviewing petitions from California's unrecognized tribes is a profound document that clearly analyzes the need to steer the federal agency toward proce-

---

8. Ibid.

dures that helps all Native Americans in the United States—not just those it has already recognized.

In an era of computers, and with many of the affected Indians living in or near the world's center of high technology in Silicon Valley, it is nothing short of an embarrassment that the Bureau of Indian affairs takes twenty years or more to rule on tribal recognition requests. The age when federal offices were filled with the noisy clickety-clack of typewriters, and desks piled high with papers and manila folders in cavernous rooms, has long passed.

The Bureau of Indian Affairs is playing Russian roulette with the heritage of the United States. Each year that passes as the agency, perhaps deliberately, moves at a ponderous snail's pace on petitions for recognition, Indian elders die and along with them the history, language, knowledge, and traditions of the first Americans. These are facets of the priceless cultural diamond that is the United States. Without passing on the knowledge that these elders keep in their heads to a younger generation, the sparkle of that jewel will dim, leaving thousands of Native Americans not knowing where they came from, their traditions, or their language—only that they are Indians.

Appendix

CALIFORNIA MISSIONS, FOUNDING DATES AND CURRENT ADDRESSES

1769
Mission San Diego de Alcalá
10818 San Diego Mission Road
San Diego, CA 92108

1770
Mission San Carlos Borromeo de Carmelo
3080 Rio Road
Carmel, CA 93923

1771
Mission San Antonio de Padua
P.O. Box 803
Jolon, CA 93928

1771
Mission San Gabriel Arcángel
428 South Mission Drive
San Gabriel, CA 91776

1772
Mission San Luis Obispo de Tolosa
751 Palm Street
San Luis Obispo, CA 93401

1776
Mission Francisco de Asís (Dolores)
3321 Sixteenth Street
San Francisco, CA 94114

1776
Mission San Juan Capistrano
31414 El Camino Reál
San Juan Capistrano, CA 92675

1777
Mission Santa Clara de Asís
500 El Camino Reál
Santa Clara, CA 95053

1782
Mission San Buenaventura
211 East Main Street
Ventura, CA 93001

1786
Mission Santa Bárbara
2201 Laguna Street
Santa Barbara, CA 93105

1787
Mission La Purísima Concepción
2295 Purísima Road
Lompoc, CA 93436

1791
Mission Santa Cruz
State Historic Park
144 School Street
Santa Cruz, CA 95060

1791
Mission Nuestra Señora de la Soledad
36641 Fort Romie Road
Soledad, CA 93960

1797

Mission San José de Guadalupe
43300 Mission Boulevard
Fremont, CA 94539

1797

Mission San Juan Bautista
Second and Mariposa Streets
San Juan Bautista, CA 95045

1797

Mission San Miguel Arcángel
775 Mission Street
San Miguel, CA 93451

1797

Mission San Fernando Rey de España
15151 San Fernando Mission Boulevard
Mission Hills, CA 93145

1798

Mission San Luis Rey de Francia
4050 Mission Avenue
Oceanside, CA 92057

1804

Mission Santa Inés
1760 Mission Drive
Solvang, CA 93464

1817

Mission San Rafael Arcángel
1104 Fifth Avenue
San Rafael, CA 94901

1823

Mission San Francisco de Solano
114 East Spain Street
Sonoma, CA 95476

SPANISH GOVERNORS

1769–1770 Gaspar de Portolá (military commander of colonizing expedition)

1770–1774 Pedro Fages (Alta California military commander)

1774–1777 Fernando Rivera y Moncada (Alta California military commander)

1777–1782 Felipe de Neve (Governor of the Californias)

1782–1791 Pedro Fages (Governor of the Californias)

1791–1792 José Antonio Roméu (Governor of the Californias)

1792–1794 José Joaquin de Arrillaga (Interim governor Californias)

1794–1800 Diego de Borica (Governor of the Californias)

1800 Pedro de Alberni (acting governor)

1800–1814 José Joaquin de Arrillaga (Interim governor Californias and Governor)

1814–1815 José Dario Argüello (Interim governor Alta Califowrnia)

1815–1822 Pablo Vicente de Solá (Alta California Governor)

Mexican Governors

1822 Pablo Vicente de Solá (holdover from Spain)

1822–1825 Luis Antonio Argüello

1825–1831 José María de Echeandía

1831 Jan. 6 to December, Manuel Victoria

1831–1833 José María de Echeandía (south Alta California)

1831–1832 (20 days) Pío de Jesus Pico

1832–1833 Augustin V. Zamorano (Northern Alta California)

1832–1833 José Maria de Echeandía (Southern Alta California)

1833–1835 José Figueroa

1835 September to 1836 January José Castro

1836 August to November Nicolás Gutiérrez (interim)

1836, May to July Mariano Chico

1836 August to November Nicolas Guitérrez

1836 November to December José Castro

1836–1842 Juan Bautista Alvarado

1836 José Castro (contra government)

1842–1845 Manuel Micheltorena

1845–1846 Pío de Jesus Pico

1846 to 1847 José María Flores

1847 January Andrés Pico

California Indian Tribes Most Commonly Identified by Spaniards by the Mission Nearest the Indians

Luiseños	Mission San Luis Rey de Francia
Juaneño	Mission San Juan Capistrano
Gabrieliño	Mission San Gabriel Arcángel
Fernandeño	Mission San Fernando Rey de España
Diegueño	Mission San Diego de Alcalá
Ventureño	Mission San Buenaventura
Barbareño	Mission Santa Bárbara
Ynezeño	Mission Santa Inés
Purismeño	Mission La Purísima Concepción
Obispeño	Mission San Luis Obispo de Tolosa
Migueleño	Mission San Miguel Arcángel
Antoniano	Mission San Antonio de Padua

REQUERIMIENTO

[The full text of the Requerimiento is provided]:

I (name of the Spanish official), messenger, servant and captain of the most powerful and highest kings of Castile and Leon, who conquered barbaric nations, herby notify you and declare as clearly as I can, that our Lord God, who is one and eternal, created the heavens and earth and also man and woman, from whom all of us are descended.

Now understand that during the past five thousand years all men and women spread to different parts of the world dividing themselves into separate kingdoms and provinces because clearly they could not all live only in one country since they would have been unable to feed themselves.

Given those conditions, our Lord God named one man, Saint Peter, to be in charge of the human race. This allowed all men to yield obedience to him no matter where they were born or in whatever faith or place they were educated.

God has thus subjected the entire world to Saint Peter's jurisdiction and commanded him to establish his residence in Rome as the most proper place for the government of the world. He also promised and empowered him to establish his authority in every part of the world, and to judge and govern all Christians, Moors, Jews, Gentiles, and all other people no matter of what sect or faith they may be. He is named Pope, signifying great father and guardian since he is the father and governor of all men. Those who lived in the time of this holy father, Saint Peter, obeyed and acknowledged him as their Lord and King, and the superior of the universe. All those who have been chosen to pontificate since the time of Saint Peter have been recognized similarly. Thus it now continues, and will continue until the end of the world.

One of those Pontiffs, as lord of the world, has granted these islands, and also the Terra Firme of the oceans and seas and all they contain to the glorious Catholic Kings of Castile, our sovereigns, Don Fernando and Doña Isabela, and their successors. All this is expressed in the documents that were passed on that occasion, which are available for you to study.

Under the stipulation of those deeds, His Majesty is King and Lord of these islands, and of the continent. Most of the islands which were read in this document have already, voluntarily and without resistance, recognized His Majesty, the aforesaid King and Lord, and now yield obedience and subjection to him as their lord. Also, without hesitation, as soon as they received this information, they obeyed the religious men sent by the King to preach to them, and to instruct them of our holy faith; thus all the men and women, of their own free will, and without any recompense or gratuity, became Christians and continue to be so. His Majesty having received them graciously under his protection, has commanded that they should be treated in the same manner as his other subjects and vassals. You are bound and obliged to act in the same manner.

Therefore, I now entreat and require you to carefully consider what I have declared to you so that you may fully understand it. Take reasonable time to make your decision allowing you to acknowledge the Church as the superior and guide of the universe along with the holy father called the Pope, and His Majesty, by his appointment, as King and sovereign lord of these Islands and of the Terra Firme; and that you consent that the aforesaid holy fathers shall declare and preach to you the doctrines previously described.

But, if you do not do this, and maliciously make delay in it, I certify to you that, with the help of God, we shall powerfully enter into your country, and shall make war against you in all ways and manners that we can, and shall subject you to the yoke and obedience of the Church and of their Highnesses; we shall take you and your wives and your children, and shall make slaves of them, and as such shall sell and dispose of them as their Highnesses may command; and we shall take away your goods, and shall do you all the mischief and damage that we can, as to vassals who do not obey, and refuse to receive their lord, and resist and contradict him; and we protest that the deaths and losses which shall accrue from this are your fault, and not that of their Highnesses, or ours, nor of these cavaliers who come with us. And that we have said this to you and made this Requisition, we request the notary here present to give us his testimony in writing, and we ask the rest who are present that they should be witnesses of this Requisition.

Declaration of the Spanish Monarchy 1513

Letter from Valentin Lopez, Chairman of the Amah Mutsen Tribal Band, to Elizabeth Appel, U.S. Department of the Interior

September 24, 2013

Ms. Elizabeth Appel
Office of Regulatory Affairs and Collaborative Action
U.S. Department of the Interior
1849 C Street, N.W. MS 4141-MIB
Washington, D.C. 20240

RE: 1076-AF18

Dear Ms. Appel,

The Amah Mutsun Tribal Band submits the following comments regarding the draft revision to the criteria for federal recognition. These comments contain input from the unrecognized tribes who attend meetings on July 6 and July 25.

It is widely accepted by the legal community, ethnohistorians, academicians, recognized tribes and unrecognized tribes of California that the history of California Indians is unique. Any revision to the recognition criteria must take into account a tribes history. Therefore, recognition criteria must be customized depending on regional, state, geographic, or historical considerations. This letter presents; (1) the unique history of California Tribes; (2) Important Consideration Regarding Federal Recognition Standards; and (3) provides recommendation for revision to the federal recognition process.

1. Mission and Early Rancho Period: 1769 –1834:

- The mission and early rancho period was devastating for those tribes and Indigenous Peoples that were forcefully taken to the missions, including Indigenous Peoples who remained behind in villages after exploitation;

- It is estimated that approximately 40% of all Indigenous Peoples within the newly formed California boundaries died during the mission period;

- There are many documented examples of disease, massacres, physical and psychological brutality, and genocide, this history is seldom reported in history books, museums, etc.;

- The rape and violence of indigenous women and children by Spanish soldiers, landowners, and priests was rampant during mission times.

- The Missions were unequaled in their brutality and led to the extermination of tribes and the social order of indigenous peoples.

- As many as 80 tribes were taken to any one particular mission and forced to live and work together. During this time many tribes that went the missions became extinct.

- At the closing of the Missions, there was no single Tribe which could have continued openly intact, maintaining indigenous culture, knowledge and traditional ways. However individual families, clans and small tribes maintained their autonomy and passed on their culture.

- At the closing of the Missions, there was no single mission tribe which could have continued openly intact and maintained its culture, indigenous knowledge and traditional ways.

- The Spaniards and Franciscans are on record as stating their intent was to return the land to the Indians. Land rights and resources which was never ceded by indigenous peoples.

- Impact of Mission and Early Rancharia Period on federal recognition:

- Many natives that survived the missions remained together to form a native community of different tribes or attempted to return to their traditional tribal territory. The seven criteria for federal recognition do not acknowledge the unique history of the Indigenous Peoples.

2. Mexican Period:1833–1848

- During the Mexican Period huge swaths of land (ranchos) were granted to powerful citizens of Mexico. It is estimated that the total

Indigenous Peoples population was reduced through extermination, migration, or forced assimilation by *** peoples.

- During the Mexican period the land owners needed a work force to manage the land. The Indigenous Peoples were used as a slave labor force by most land owners;

- Many land owners did not allow Indigenous Peoples or tribes to live on their property/ranchos which had been their traditional Indigenous Peoples territories for tens of thousands of years;

- Huge herds of horses, cattle, sheep, required that the landscape be changed to grazing grasses as did the planting of non-indigenous crops. This resulted in the flora and fauna be eliminated or drastically reduced. The loss of these cultural resources had a adverse impact on the ecology of California and traditional cultural ways. This resulted in many indigenous peoples and tribes being unable to continue their traditional ways on their traditional territory.

- The Mexican government through the secularization act acknowledged their intent to return half of mission land to the indigenous people living at each mission.

Impact of Mission Period on Indigenous Tribes and individuals: This resulted in the impoverishment, disenfranchisement, and enslavement of the indigenous tribe and peoples.

3. Early American Period: 1848–1900

- The discovery of gold in the foothills of California in 1848 brought an enormous emigrant invasion from all over the globe. This resulted in a second wave of ongoing genocide of California indigenous peoples.

- From 1851–1852 the U.S. Indian commissioners, acting on behalf of the United States, negotiated 18 treaties with California Indian Tribes. These 18 treaties provided 8,500,000 acres of land for the Indians. The California legislature recognized the value of the land and voted to submit resolutions to oppose the ratification of the treaties. The U.S. Senate, in a secret session, rejected the ratification of these treaties. These treaties were ordered to be sealed for fifty years by the president of the US. All California tribes and all indigenous peoples were identified for relocation to these reservations.

- In 1849 "An Act for the Government and protection of Indians, Chapter 133, legalized genocidal crime against California Indians.

- On January 7, 1851 Governor Peter H. Burnett of California signed an Executive order to exterminate all Indians in California. As a result of this order bounties were paid for the heads of dead Indians. In addition, the State of California, through its own and federal funding, paid over $1,500,000 on military, militia, and volunteer expeditions to exterminate Indians.

- These military expeditions are often referred to as the "Indian Wars" and were often for the protection of gold miners and kidnappers of Indians and in particular Indian children.

- From 1850 to 1866 the kidnapping of Indians was rampant and in many cases legal in California. Indigenous Peoples were sold for $30.00 to $150.00.

- In 1858 California passed a law to legalize "indentured servitude" which is legalized slavery. It is reported that some Indigenous Peoples were indentured into the 1930s.

- 1872 the US ceased to engage in treaties with any indigenous tribe. This severely impacted a tribe's ability to stay together as they had no land base.

- In 1891 An Act for the Relief of Mission Indians in the State of California was passed and signed by the President of the United States. This act provided for a" just and satisfactory settlement" to Mission Indians residing in the State of California. Appointed commissioners were to select a reservation for each band or village of the twenty one Mission Indian tribes residing within said State. Several Mission Indian Tribes in San Diego County received land, but no other Mission Tribe received land.

It is our understanding that the Twenty Nine Palms Band of Mission Indians received their reservation under the Act of 1891. What's interesting about this is that the Twenty Nine Palms Band of Mission Indians was not a mission tribe as it had never been missionized.

The American government is on record as stating their goal was to give Indians land for them to live. Indigenous Peoples not approved to be placed under federal recognition regulations within California continue to wait for this goal to be fulfilled.

4. American Period : 1900 to Present

- In 1900 the U.S. Census identified the number of Native Americans living in California.

- In 1906 there was a special Indian census that identified the Native American population living in California.

- In 1910 the U.S. Census identified the number of Native Americans living in California.

- 1906–937 – landless Indians received allotment land. These allotments were granted to individuals and not to tribes.

- In 1927, L.A. Dorrington, Superintendent, Indian Field Service, Sacramento Indian Agency, submitted his report regarding the land needs of California's landless tribes. In all, the report covers approximately 220 tribes. Of that number, approximately 180 tribes receive no land. It's important to understand that most of these tribes were federally recognized tribes at this time based on the BIA determination that the Muwekma Tribe was a previously recognized tribe based largely on this report. Therefore we can only conclude that the Dorrington report illegally terminated up to 180 tribes. By law only an Act of Congress can terminate a Tribe and no such Act ever occurred. Dorrington's report only provided a 2–3 sentences justification for not providing land to each tribe. In no case did Dorrington provide evidence or documentation to support his conclusions. It's important to note that a review of the 18 boxes of his archive materials at the National Archives in San Bruno, California, provides no evidence of any research for this report. For example, no known record exists evidencing Dorrington ever visiting or corresponding with the tribes, churches or governments between San Francisco and San Luis Obispo.

Some of the reasons Dorrington provided for not giving land to the tribe included:

— "No land is required for this band at this time."

— "No land will be needed for this band."

— "These Indians have been well cared for by Catholic priests and no land is required."

- In 1928 Indians not living on reservations were given the full rights of citizenship including the right to own land without relinquishing their tribal affiliation.

- When Yosemite became a National Park the Indians were removed; this was true for all National Parks. Today the Yosemite Tribe is a non-federally recognized tribe.

- When the Santa Inez Chumash Tribe, a federally recognized tribe, received tribal land the report also recommended that the Esselen Tribe receive tribal land. The recommendation that the Esselen Tribe receive land was ignored, consequently today they are a federally unrecognized tribe.

- The Indian reorganized act of 1934 allowed for Tribes to reorganize and a lot of tribal reorganizations occurred at this time. Because the unrecognized tribes were not included in this reorganization act their recognition status was administratively terminated.

- Indigenous Peoples not approved to be placed under federal recognition regulations are very seldom included in any legislation, regulations, policies, etc. that apply to federally recognized tribes. For example, in November or 2012 four departmental Secretaries and the Chair of the Advisory Council on Historic Preservation signed a Memorandum of Understanding regarding the protection of Sacred Sites. This legislation does nothing to protect the Sacred Sites of Indigenous Peoples not under federal recognition regulations. Also, on June 26, 2013 President Obama issued an Executive Order to Establish the White House Council on Native American Affairs. This Executive Order established a government to government relationship with federally recognized tribes. There are hundreds, if not thousands, of examples like these regarding every facet of our culture and our life that make it impossible for non-federally recognized Indigenous tribes and Peoples to fulfill their obligations as a tribal government.

- In 1978 the BIA developed a process to acknowledge the federally non recognized tribes. In 1992 the former Assistant Secretary of the BIA, Bud Shepard, the person who approved the regulations regarding recognition, testified before congress that the regulations were "fatally flawed" and that no recognized tribe of today could meet these standards. To the unrecognized tribe's complete detriment, these regulations have never been substantially changed. The current revision that was recently sent out for review also does nothing to change the regulations in a substantial or meaningful way.

- The recognition regulations had a "previous, unambiguous recognition" designation. Tribe considered this to be a very important distinction which should lead to an expedited path of reaffirmation or restoration. We believed that this designation put the burden of proof on the BIA to show how the previous recognition status was terminated. In the Muwekma court case the BIA answered this question by saying the Muwekma's federal recognition status "withered away." Another reason cited in the Muwekma court case for their previous unambiguous recognition being terminated was that the "statute of limitations" for the Tribe to appeal the decision to terminate the tribe had passed.

- Annually the President meets with federally recognized tribes. Non-federally recognized tribes are not included at these meetings. Our absence at this meeting give us the clear message that we are not considered part of the indigenous community in the United States.

Important Consideration Regarding Federal Recognition Standards

1. The federal government should remove the Office of Federal Recognition out of the Bureau of Indian Affairs (BIA) as there is a clear conflict of interest. The BIA has a responsibility to act in the best interest of federally recognized Tribes. It is clearly not in the best interest of recognized tribes for additional tribes to be recognized. The resources for health care, education, economic development, etc. would have to be shared with an even larger number of tribes. Furthermore, the BIA has a history of not acting in the best interest of non-recognized tribes.

It is our recommendation that the Office of Federal Recognition be placed in the Civil Rights Division of the Department of Justice. This Division was created in 1957 by the enactment of the Civil Rights Act of 1957 and works to uphold the civil and constitutional rights of all Americans, par-

ticularly some of the most vulnerable members   of our society. Furthermore, this Division enforces federal statutes prohibiting   discrimination
on the basis of race, color, sex, disability, religion, familial status and
national origin.

2. It is widely believed that the current process is designed to "weed out"
tribes. The federal recognition process should be designed to affirm tribes
by assisting them to understand the criteria and to actively work with
them providing professional assistance (at no cost) to help them meet the
standard.

3. Since 1978 only one California tribe has successfully made it through
the BIA's federal recognition process. In 1983 the Death Valley Timba
Sha Shoshone were federally recognized. The petition of the Death Valley
Timba Sha Shoshone was 52 pages long. Three other California tribes
have been administratively restored by the BIA; the three tribes are Ione,
Lower Lake, and Tejon.

The Samish Tribe of Washington was denied federal recognition by the
BIA only to have their federal recognition reaffirmed by a Court. Today
OFA takes credit for affirming the Samish Tribe, this is a misrepresenta-
tion of OFA's actions. If a court can see the evidence related to the Samash
tribe and conclude that they should have their recognition reaffirmed
how can tribes have confidence in the OFA process?

The Duwamish Tribe of Washington State and the Eastern Pequot Tribe
of Connecticut were acknowledged under the OFA process during the
Clinton administration. However, the federal recognition of both these
tribes was reversed under the Bush administration.
The facts presented under number 3 clearly show that there is no objec-
tivity in the federal recognition process. When only one California tribe
is federally recognized in 35 years, when a court reverses a BIA decision,
when three California tribes are administratively restored, and when a
new presidential administration is able to reverse a BIA decision affect-
ing two tribes one must question the issues of fairness and validity in the
federal recognition process of OFA.

4. Initially the burden of proof was on the BIA to prove that an unrec-

ognized Tribe shouldn't be recognized. Somewhere along the line the burden of proof shifted and now the burden of proof lies with the unrecognized tribes to prove they do meet the criteria. We believe the burden of proof should be on the BIA.

5. The time it takes to be federally recognized takes too long. Many tribes have been in the recognition process for over 30 years and they are still waiting for their federal recognition status to be determined.

6. It is unfair to have a federal recognition requirement that the majority of current day federally recognized tribes could not meet at the time they received their federal recognition status.

7. The unique history of California tribes, as discussed above, needs to be considered. The federal government cannot expect tribes to have maintained their tribal continuity when they were forced into slavery or near slavery conditions. It is extremely difficult for tribes to pass down their indigenous knowledge regarding culture, traditions, ceremonies, etc. when they're struggling just to survive. These are important factors to consider when one looks for fairness within the federal recognition process.

8. The historic trauma of Indigenous Peoples and Indigenous Tribes must be considered in the development of federal recognition criteria. Historic trauma paralyzed our ancestor and forced many of them into isolation in their attempt to survive. The current criteria punishes tribes and lineages for our survival.

9. The U.S. Supreme Court Carcieri decision has eliminated investor interest in funding federal recognition efforts of unrecognized tribes. The investor's interest was the economic development on Indian trust land. The Carcieri decision greatly raised the risk that trust lands may not be available for economic development and therefore investors are no longer talking to unrecognized tribes. As a consequence very few, if any, tribes have the resources to fund a federal recognition petition or to go through the federal recognition process. By doing nothing the OFA could be out of business in a very short while.

10. Indigenous Peoples not approved to be placed under federal recogni-

tion regulations receive no financial assistance from the federal, state, tribal, or any governmental body. It is very difficult to keep a tribe together without tribal offices, land or financial sustainability for travel, phone, internet, etc. It is vitally important for the Bureau of Indian Affairs act quickly to determine which non-federally regulated Indigenous tribes are to receive federal funding to ensure those tribes survival into the future.

11. Many of our tribal elders who would have provided critical information for meeting the federal recognition standard have died during the long delays of the recognition process. With the passing of each elder it becomes more difficult for tribes to document their tribal history and continuity during the critical years, for example the 1920s–1950s.

12. The current criteria require the submittal of historic documents that don't exist in many cases. It is not unusual for generations to not know how to read or write. Some of our ancestors lived in tents along rivers and streams into the 1950s and 60s. Additionally many of our elders did not have the financial resources to document the historic shifts in the Indigenous communities. It is unreasonable for these members to be expected to have stayed in touch with the BIA or to voice their tribal concerns in public forums etc. that would have provided the documentation trail that the BIA now requires?

13. Due to economic pressures many tribal members had to move from their traditional tribal territories. In some locations starter homes were selling for $350,000 or more. Tribal members earning wages that are close to the minimum wage had to move from their homelands just to survive. Moving from their homelands was not a choice or conscious rejection of their tribe. How were these tribes supposed to hold their members together under these conditions?

14. The standards for federal recognition gets more difficult with the review of each petition. It seems like the OFA/BIA looks at the evidence provided for each tribe as a tribe's effort to find a loophole in the recognition process. After such loopholes are found the OFA/BIA is quick to shut these loopholes. Two good examples of this was the designation of "previously recognized" tribal status. This designation was significant for non-federally regulated tribes because if a tribe was previously recog-

nized then only an Act of Congress could have terminated that tribe. Because no such Act of Congress ever occurred the tribe should have been immediately restored. Rather than restoring the tribe(s) the OFA/BIA stopped assigning this designation. A second example is when the Assistant Secretary of the BIA administratively restored the recognition of the Tejon Tribe. This administrative process should have been used to restore the tribes that were determined to be previously recognized. It is our understanding that the BIA will no longer recognize Tribes by having the Assistant Secretary administratively restore tribes.

15. Many California Tribes that are non-federally recognized tribes today were referred to as landless tribes. It's interesting to note that these Indians were prevented from legally owning property prior to 1928. Furthermore, these Indians did not become citizens or have the right to vote until 1924. It's very difficult to hold tribes together without a tribal land base.
1
6. In 1925 Alfred Louis Kroeber, an anthropologist from U.C. Berkeley, published a book titled, "Handbook of the Indians of California." This book, recognized as the definitive book on California Indians, erroneously reported that Indians from various regions were "extinct." We believe it is very possible that this book greatly influenced the BIA's decision to discontinue any effort to support or assist many California tribes. Some of these extinct tribes are the unrecognized tribes of today.
1
7. We believe that the basic precept of the federal regulation standards is erroneous. Rather that asking tribes to prove they deserve to be recognized under the BIA's criteria, we believe the BIA should be asking why aren't you recognized and then the federal government should conduct research to answer this question?

Proposals for Revised Federal Recognition Standards

1. BIA should change their philosophy on the recognition process. Rather that have a process that is designed to deny the recognition process they should work to identify Tribes that are truly historical and have the capacity to substantially restore their Tribe.

2. The BIA should recognized that the indigenous knowledge of these

tribes is of great value and is important to solving a lot of problems that exist today. This is particularly true regarding environmental issues. Traditional tribal foods, land stewardship, water management, knowledge of wildlife, coastal protection and many other concerns are currently considering the use of indigenous knowledge to solving these problems. Indigenous Peoples tribes can contribute to solving environmental problems and the federal government should ensure the survival of non-federally regulated indigenous tribes into the future for the benefit all mankind. It's important to note that a number of non-federally regulated tribes are currently working on research projects regarding their indigenous knowledge with major universities, California state departments, federal agencies, and many others solely for that purpose.

3. The BIA should reinstate the "previously recognized" designation and administratively restore the previously recognized tribes.

4. Tribes that are currently known and recognized as being historical and continuous by the Hearst Museum of UCB, the Fowler Museum of UCLA, the California State Assembly, the State of California, and more than one congressional leader, federal governmental agencies such as the BLM or the NPS should be administratively recognized. It's important to note that a number of current day non-recognized tribes meet all of the above criteria.

5. Tribes that have signed MOU or MOA with federal governmental agencies should be federally recognized.

6. The federal recognition process should not be available to non-historic tribes. Tribe who are new formulated, who have members from various tribes who only came together in recent times, who have submitted fraudulent documents to the BIA in an attempt to appear legitimate, or Tribes whose leadership is non-Native should not be federally recognized.

7. Accept as evidence documentation of early anthropologist and ethnohistorians from the Smithsonian Institute or other approved institutions who documented tribes and tribal members prior to 1950. This oral history needs to be respected.

8. We request that the federal recognition criteria be validated by a professional industrial organization psychologist firm and that any recommendation of this firm be implemented into the process. We request that all recommendations be shared with the public.

9. The federal guidelines must be revised to recognize the special conditions and considerations of the non-federally recognized tribes and Indigenous Peoples of California.

Sincerely,

Valentin Lopez, Chairman
Amah Mutsun Tribal Band

Bibliography

Alley, B.F. "A History of San Mateo County Vol. II." *California Historical Society Quarterly*. (Nov. 1924).

Almquist, Alan J. and Robert F. Heizer. *The Other Californians: Prejudice and Discrimination under Spain, Mexico, and the United States to 1920*. Berkeley: University of California, 1972.

Archibald, Robert. "Indian Labor at the California Missions Slavery or Salvation" in *The Journal of San Diego History*. Spring 1978. Vol. 24, No.2. http://www.sandiegohistory.org/journal/78spring/labor.htm

The Arts of the Missions of Northern New Spain: 1600-1821. Exhibition. Curators: Clara Bargellini and Michael K. Komanecky. Mexico City: Mandato Antiguo Colegio de San Idelfonso, 2009.

As The Padres Saw Them: California Indian Life and Customs as Reported by The Franciscan Missionaries 1813–1815. Edited by Doyce B. Nunis, Jr. Los Angeles: Westland, 1976.

Asisara, Lorenzo. "The Assassination of Padre Andrés Quintana by the Indians of Mission Santa Cruz in 1812: The Narrative of Lorenzo Asisara." In *Native American Perspectives on the Hispanic Colonization of Alta California (The Spanish Borderlands Sourcebook Vol. 26)*, Edited by Edward D. Castillo New York: Garland, 1991.

The Ashley-Smith Exploration and Discovery of a Central Route to the Pacific 1822–1829. Harrison C. Dale, editor. Norman, Okla.: Arthur H. Clark, 1941.

Atherton, Faxon Dean. *The California Diary of Faxon Dean Atherton 1836–1839*. Edited by Doyce B. Nunis, Jr. San Francisco: California Historical Society, 1964

Bancroft, Hubert Howe. *The Works of Hubert Bancroft Vol. XIX History of California Vol. II 1801–1824*. San Francisco: The History Co.,1886.

————. *The Works of Hubert Bancroft Vol. XIX History of California Vol. IV 1801–1824.* San Francisco: The History Co., 1886.

Bannon, John Francis. *Indian Labor in the Spanish Indies; was there another solution?* Boston: Heath, 1966.

Bay of San Francisco: The Metropolis of the Pacific Coast and its Suburban Cities, A History Vol. I, Chicago: Lewis, 1892.

Bean, Walton, Rawls, James J. *California, an Interpretive History.* New York: McGraw-Hill, 1968.

Beck, Warren A., *The California Experience: A Literary Odyssey,* Santa Barbara, Calif.: Peregrine Smith Inc., 1976.

Beechey, Frederick William. "Selection from a Narrative of a Voyage to the Pacific and Bering's Strait (1831)." In *Documentary Evidence for the Spanish Missions of Alta California (The Spanish Borderlands Sourcebook Vol. 14).* Edited by Julia G. Costello. New York: Garland, 1991.

de Benavides, Alonso. *Benavides Memorial of 1630.* Translated by Peter P. Forrestal. Washington, DC: Arrow Service, 1954.

Berger, Thomas R. *A Long and Terrible Shadow: White Values, Native Rights in the Amerias 1492–1992.* Vancouver, B.C.: Douglas & McIntyre, 1991.

Borthwick, J.D. *Three Years in California.* Edinburgh: William Blackwood and Sons, 1857.

Boscana, Gerónimo. "Selections from Chinigchinich : Historical Account of the Belief, Usages, Customs and Extravagances of the Indians of this Mission of San Juan Capistrano Called the Acagchemem Tribe." Translated by Alfred Robinson. Banning, Calif.: Malki Museum, 1978. In *Documentary Evidence for the Spanish Missions of Alta California (The Spanish Borderlands Sourcebook Vol. 14).* Edited by Julia G. Costello. New York: Garland, 1991.

Bouvier, Virginia M. *Women and the Conquest of California, 1542–1840: Codes of Silence.* Tucson: University of Arizona, 2004.

Bowman, J.N. "The Neophytes (Existentes) of the California Missions 1769–1834." In *Historical Society of Southern California Quarterly.* 4:2. 1958. In *Native American Perspectives on the Hispanic Colonization of Alta California (The Spanish Borderlands Sourcebook Vol. 26),* Edited by Edward D. Castillo New York: Garland, 1991.

Brace, Charles L. *The New West: or California in 1867–1868.* New York: G. P. Putnam & Son, 1869.

Brewer, William H. *Up and Down California in 1860–1864: The Journal of William H. Brewer, Professor of Agriculture in the Sheffield Scientific School from 1864 to 1903.* Edited by Francis P. Farquhar.ss New Haven: Yale University Press, 1930.

Brown, Alan K. "Pomponio's World. San Francisco Corral of Westerners." Argonaut. 6:1. 1975. In *Native American Perspectives on the Hispanic Colonization of Alta California (The Spanish Borderlands Sourcebook Vol. 26)*, Edited by Edward D. Castillo New York: Garland, 1991.

Bryant, Edwin. *What I Saw in California: Being the Journal of a Tour by the Emigrant Route and South Pass of the Rockey Mountains, Across the Continent of North America, the Great Desert Basin, and Through California, in the Years 1846, 1847.* New York: Appleton, 1848.

The California Indians, A Source Book. Compiled and edited by R. Heizer and M.A. Whipple. Second and First editions. Berkeley: University of California Press, 1971 and 1962.

Camp, Charles L. *Kit Carson In California. In the Quarterly of the California Historical Society.* San Francisco: October, 1922.

del Castillo, Bernal Diaz. *The True History of the Conquest of Mexico.* New York: Robert M. McBride & Co., 1927.

Castillo, Edward D. "The Native Response to Colonization of Alta California." In Columbian Consequences. Vol. 1: *Archaeological and Historical Perspectives on the Spanish Borderlands West.* Edited by David Hurst Thomas. Washington, D.C.: Smithsonian, 1989. In *Native American Perspectives on the Hispanic Colonization of Alta California (The Spanish Borderlands Sourcebook Vol. 26)*, Edited by Edward D. Castillo New York: Garland, 1991.

Castillo, Edward, Jackson, Robert H. *Indians, Franciscans, and Spanish Colonization: The Impact of the Mission System on California Indians.* Albuquerque, New Mexico: University of New Mexico, 1995.

César, Julio Sanchez. "Recollection of My Youth at San Luis Rey Mission: The memories of a full-blooded Indian, of affairs and events witnessed at one of California's most famous 'Cathedrals of the sun." Translated and edited by Nellie Van de Grift Sanchez. Touring Topics. 22:42. 1878. In *Native American Perspectives on the Hispanic Colonization of Alta California (The Spanish Borderlands Sourcebook Vol. 26)*, Edited by Edward D. Castillo New York: Garland, 1991.

Chamisso, Adelbert Von. *Voyage Around the World with Romanzoff's Expedition of Exploration in the years 1815-1818 on the brig* Rurik, *Master Otto Von Kotzebue. Diary of Adelbert Von Chamisso in The Visit of the* Rurik *to San Francisco in 1816.* Translated by August C. Mahr. Stanford: Stanford University, 1932.

Chapman, Charles E., *The Founding of Spanish California: The Northwestward Expansion of New Spain, 1687–1783.* New York: Macmillan, 1916

———. *A History of California: The Spanish Period.* New York: Macmillan, 1939.

Choris, Andrevitch. "Port San Francisco and its Inhabitants." *In The Visit of the Rurick to San Francisco in 1816.* Translated by August C. Mahr. Palo Alto: Stanford University Press, 1932. In *Documentary Evidence for the Spanish Missions of Alta California (The Spanish Borderlands Sourcebook Vol. 14).* Edited by Julia G. Costello. New York: Garland, 1991.

"The Chumash Revolt of 1824: A Native Account." Edited by Thomas Blackburn Thomas. *Journal of California Anthropology.* 2:2. 1975. In *Native American Perspectives on the Hispanic Colonization of Alta California (The Spanish Borderlands Sourcebook Vol. 26),* Edited by Edward D. Castillo New York: Garland, 1991.

Constanso, Miguel. *The Portolá Expedition of 1769–1770: Diary of Miguel Constanso.* Frederick J. Teggart, editor. Berkeley: University of California Press, 1911.

Cooke, Sherburne F. *The Conflict Between the California Indian and the White Civilization.* Berkeley: University of California Press, 1976.

———. "Expeditions to the Interior of California Central Valley 1820–1840 Uprising at Mission San Buenaventura, 1819." In University of California Anthropological Records. 20.5. Berkeley: University of California Press, 1962.

———. "José Arguello's Attack on an Indian Village, 1813." In *Colonial Expeditions to the Interior of California, Central Valley, 1800–1820.* University of California Anthropological Records. 16:6. 1960b. In *Native American Perspectives on the Hispanic Colonization of Alta California (The Spanish Borderlands Sourcebook Vol. 26),* Edited by Edward D. Castillo New York: Garland, 1991.

———. "José Dolores Pico's Diary." In *Colonial Expeditions to the Interior of California, Central Valley, 1800–1820.* University of California Anthropological Records. 16:6. 1960a. In *Native American Perspectives on the Hispanic Colonization of Alta California (The Spanish Borderlands Sourcebook Vol. 26),* Edited by Edward D. Castillo New York: Garland, 1991.

———. *The Population of the California Indians 1769–1970,* Berkeley, University of California Press, 1976.

The Conquistadors. Edited and translated by Patricia de Fuentes. New York: Orion Press. 1963.

Cook, David Noble. *Born to Die: Disease and New World Conquest 1492–1650.* Cambridge: Cambridge University Press, 1998.

Coulter, Thomas. "Notes on Upper California." *Journal of the Royal Geographical Society of London.* Vol. 5. 1835.

Dale, Harrison C. *The Ashley-Smith Exploration and Discovery of a Central Route to the Pacific, 1822–1829.* Glendale, Calif.: Arthur H. Clark, 1941.

Davis, William Heath. *Sixty Years in California: A History of Events and Life in California; Personal, Political and Military, Under the Mexican Regime; During the Quasi-Military Government of the Territory by the United States and After the Admission of the State Into The Union, Being a Compilation by a Witness of the Events Described*. San Francisco: Leary, 1889.

Denis, Alberta Johnson. *Spanish Alta California*. New York: Macmillan, 1927.

The Destruction of California Indians: A collection of documents from the period 1847 to 1865 in which are described some of the things that happened to some of the Indians of California. Edited by Robert F. Heizer. Santa Barbara, Calif.: Peregrine Smith, 1974.

Dillehay, Tom D., Pino, M., Ramirez, C., Collins, M.B., Rossen, J., Pino-Navarro, J.D. "Monte Verde: Seaweed, Food, Medicine, and the Peopling of South America." *Science*. 320:5877 (2008).

Duhaut-Cilly, Auguste Bernard. "Duhaut-Cilly's Account of California in the years 1827-1828". Translated by Charles Franklin Carter. In *California Historical Society Quarterly*. 8:130. 1929. In *Documentary Evidence for the Spanish Missions of Alta California (The Spanish Borderlands Sourcebook Vol. 14)*. Edited by Julia G. Costello. New York: Garland, 1991.

Engelhardt, Zephyrin. *San Antonio de Padua, the Mission in the Sierras*. Ramona, Calif.: Ballena Press, 1972.

European Treaties bearing on the History of the United States and its Dependencies to 1648. Edited by Francis Gardiner Davenport. Washington, D.C.: Carnegie Institution of Washington, 1917.

Fagan, Brian, *Before California, An Archaeologist Looks at Our Earliest Inhabitants*, Walnut Creek, Calif.: Rowman & Littlefield/AltaMira Press, 2003.

Fages, Pedro. *A Historical, Political, and Natural Description of California by Pedro Fages, Soldier of Spain, Dutifully Made for the Viceroy in the Year 1775*. Translated by Herbert Ingram Priestly. First published, Berkeley, Calif.: University of California, 1937. Republished Ramona, Calif.: Ballena Press, 1972.

Farnsworth, Paul. "The Economics of Acculturation in the Spanish Missions of Alta California." In *Research in Economic Anthropology* Vol. 11, 1989.

Fehrenbach, T.R. *Fire and Blood: A History of Mexico*. New York: Macmillan, 1973.

Fogel, Daniel. *Junípero Serra, the Vatican and Enslavement Theology*. San Francisco: Ism Press, 1988.

Forbes, Alexander. "State of Agriculture in Upper California. Its Produce in Grain and Live Stock." *California: A History of Upper and Lower California (1937)."* San Francisco: John Henry Nash, 1937. Reprinted in 1972 by Kraus Reprint, New York. In *Documentary Evidence for the Spanish Missions of Alta California (The Spanish Borderlands Sourcebook Vol. 14).* Edited by Julia G. Costello. New York: Garland, 1991.

de Gálvez, José. Letter to Francisco Palóu, dated June 19, 1769. Santa Barbara, Calif.: Santa Barbara Mission Archive Library, Junipero Serra Collection, Folder #182.

Gamble, Lynn H. *The Chumash World at European Contact: Power, Trade, and Feasting among Complex Hunter-Gatherers.* Berkeley, Calif.: University of California, 2008.

Garnett, Porter. *San Francisco One Hundred Years Ago.* San Francisco: Robertson, 1913.

Geiger, Maynard J. *The Life and Times of Fray Junípero Serra, OFM, or The Man who Never Turned Back (1713–1784).* Richmond, Va.: William Byrd, 1959.

Guest, Florian. F. "The Indian Policy under Fermín Francisco de Lasuén, California's Second Father President." *California Historical Quarterly.* 1966, September. pp 195-224.

Hackel, Steven W. *Children of Coyote, Missionaries of Saint Francis: Indian Spanish Relations in Colonial California 1769–1850.* Williamsburg, Va.: University of North Carolina, 2005.

——. *Junipero Serra: California's Founding Father.* New York: Hill and Wang, 2013.

Heizer, Robert F., Almquist, Alan F. *The Other Californians: Prejudice and Discrimination under Spain, Mexico and the US to 1920.* Berkeley: University of California Press, 1971.

Hanson, Neil. *The Confident Hope of a Miracle: The True History of the Spanish Armada.* New York: Knopf, 2005.

Harrington, John P. "The Chumash Revolt of 1824: Another Native Account from the Notes of John P. Harrington." Travis Hudson, editor. *Journal of California and Great Basin Anthropology.* 6:2. 1980. In *Native American Perspectives on the Hispanic Colonization of Alta California (The Spanish Borderlands Sourcebook Vol. 26),* Edited by Edward D. Castillo New York: Garland, 1991.

Harrison, E.S. *A History of Santa Cruz County.* San Francisco: Pacific Press, 1892.

——. "Impact of Colonization on the Native California Societies." In *The Journal of San Diego History.* 24:1. 1978. In *Native American Perspectives on the Hispanic Colonization of Alta California (The Spanish Borderlands Sourcebook Vol. 26),* Edited by Edward D. Castillo New York: Garland, 1991.

Hittell, Theodore H. *History of California*, Vol. I. San Francisco: N.J. Stone, 1897.

Holterman, Jack. "The Revolt of Estanislao." In *The Indian Historian*. 3:1. 1970. In *Native American Perspectives on the Hispanic Colonization of Alta California (The Spanish Borderlands Sourcebook Vol. 26)*, Edited by Edward D. Castillo New York: Garland, 1991.

Hutchinson, W.H. *California: Two Centuries of Man, Land and Growth*. Palo Alto: American West, 1969.

Hunt, Rockwell D. *California The Golden State*. San Francisco: Silver, Burdett, 1911.

Hurtado, Albert L. *Indian Survival on the California Frontier*. New Haven: Yale, 1988.

Hyer, Joel R. *We Are Not Savages, Native Americans in Southern California and the Pala Reservation, 1840–1920*. East Lansing: Michigan State University, 2001.

Ibañez, Vicente Blasco. *El Militarismo Mexicano*. Mexico City: Gernika, 1995.

Jackson, Robert H. "Gentile Recruitment and Population Movements in the San Francisco Bay Area Missions." In *Journal of California and Great Basin Anthropology*. 6:2. 1989. In *Native American Perspectives on the Hispanic Colonization of Alta California (The Spanish Borderlands Sourcebook Vol. 26)*, Edited by Edward D. Castillo New York: Garland, 1991.

———, *Race, Caste, and Status: Indians in Colonial Spanish America*. Albuquerque, NM: University of New Mexico Press, 1999.

——— and Edward Castillo. *Indians, Franciscans, and Spanish Colonization: The Impact of the Mission System on California Indians*. Albuquerque, N. Mex.: 1995.

Jones, William Carey. *Report on the Subject of Land Titles in California*, Senate Executive Documents. No. 18, 31st Congress, First Session. Washintgon, D.C.

Kandell, Jonathan. *La Capital: the Biography of Mexico City*. New York: Random House, 1988.

Khlebnikov, Kirill Timofeevich. "Memoirs of California." Translated by Anatole G. Mazour. In *The Pacific Historical Review* 9:307. 1940. In *Documentary Evidence for the Spanish Missions of Alta California (The Spanish Borderlands Sourcebook Vol. 14)*. Edited by Julia G. Costello. New York: Garland, 1991.

Klar, Kathryn and Jones, Terry. "Scholars Paddle Upstream With Theory on Boat". By Steve Chawkins, *in Los Angeles Times*. Sept. 15, 2005. On web site: http://articles.latimes.com/2005/sep/15/local/me-poly15. Originally published in *American Antiquity*. Vol. 70, No. 3. July, 2005. Web site: http://www.saa.org/AbouttheSociety/Publications/AmericanAntiquity/Volume70Number3July2005/DiffusionismReconsideredLinguisticandArchaeo/tabid/511/Default.aspx

Krauze, Enrique. *Mexico: Biography of Power, A History of Modern Mexico, 1810–1996*. Translated by Hank Heifetz. New York: Harper Collins, 1997.

Kroeber, Alfred L. "California Place Names of Indian Origin." In *American Archaeology and Ethnology*. 12:2. Berkeley: University of California, 1916.

——. "Handbook of the Indians of California," in *Smithsonian Institution Bureau of American Ethnology*: Bulletin 78. Washington: Government Printing Office, 1925.

——. "The Language of the Coastal Indians of California South of San Francisco. In American *Archaeology and Ethnology*. 2:2. Berkeley: University of California, 1904.

——. "The Religion of the Indians of California." In *American Archaeology and Ethnology*. 4:6. Berkeley: University of California, 1907

Lands of Promise and Despair: Chronicles of Early California, 1535– 1846, Rose Marie Beebe and Robert M. Senkewicz, editors. Santa Clara, Calif.: Heyday, 2001.

Langsdorf, Georg Heinrich Freiherr von. "Voyage and Travels in Various Parts of the World during the years 1803, 1804, 1805, 1806, and 1807." London: Henry Colburn, 1813–14. In *Documentary Evidence for the Spanish Missions of Alta California (The Spanish Borderlands Sourcebook Vol. 14)*. Edited by Julia G. Costello. New York: Garland, 1991.

Laplace, Cyrille Pierre Théodore, "Campagne de Circumnavigation de la frégate l'Artémise pendant les années 1837, 1838,1839, et 1840 sous le commandement de M. Laplace, capitaine de vaisseau . . . Paris, 1841–54." In *The Works of Hubert Howe Bancroft*, Vol. XIX. *History of California*. Vol. IV, 1801–1824. San Francisco: Bancroft, 1886, p. 154.

Lasuén, Fermín Francisco de. *Writings of Fermín Francisco de Lasuén* Vol. I. Edited by Finbar Kenneally. Richmond: William Byrd. 1965.

Librado, Fernado. "Shovels and Stocks; Crosses and Bedsheets." *Breath of the Sun: Life in Early California as Told by a Chumash*, Fernando Librado to John P. Harrington. Travis Hudson, editor. Banning, Calif.: Malki Museum Press, 1979. In *Native American Perspectives on the Hispanic Colonization of Alta California (The Spanish Borderlands Sourcebook Vol. 26)*, Edited by Edward D. Castillo New York: Garland, 1991.

Lightfoot, Kent G. *Indians, Missionaries, and Merchants: The Legacy of Colonial Encounters on the California Frontiers.* Berkeley: University of California, 2006.

——, Wake, Thomas A., Schiff, Anna M. "Native Responses to the Russian Mercantile Colony of Fort Ross, Northern California." In *Journal of Field Archaeology* Vol. 20, 1993.

Mahr, August C., *The Visit of the Rurick to San Francisco in 1816.* Palo Alto: Stanford University, 1932.

Malcolm Margolin, Monterey in 1786, *Life in a California Mission, The Journals of Jean François de la Pérouse.* Berkeley: Heyday Books, 1989.

Maurice, Sullivan. *The Travels of Jedediah Smith.* Santa Ana, Calif.: Fine Arts, 1934.

Menzies, Archibald. "Archibald Menzies California Journal." Edited by Alice Eastwood. In *California Historical Quarterly.* 2:4. 1924. In *Documentary Evidence for the Spanish Missions of Alta California (The Spanish Borderlands Sourcebook Vol. 14).* Edited by Julia G. Costello. New York: Garland, 1991.

Merriam, C. Hart. *Studies of California Indians.* Berkeley, Calif.: University of California, 1955.

Milliken, Randall. *A Time of Little Choice: The Disintegration of Tribal Culture in the San Francisco Bay Area 1769–1810.* Menlo Park, Calif.: Ballena Press, 1995.

Mission Memories: The Franciscan Missions of California. Photographs by Vroman's, Pasadena. Los Angeles: Out West, 1903.

Missions of Southern California—Postcard History Series. Edited by James Osborne. San Francisco, CA: Arcadia, 2007.

The Missions of California, A Legacy of Genocide. Edited by Rupert Costo and Jeannette Henry Costo. San Francisco: Indian Historian Press, 1987.

Motolino, Torribo de. *Motolinas' History of the Indians of New Spain.* Translated and annotated by Francis Borgia Steck. Richmond, Va.: William Byrd, 1951.

Newcomb, Redford. *The Old Mission Churches and Historic Houses of California: Their History, Architecture and Lore.* Philadelphia: Lippincott, 1925.

Norton, Jack. *When Our Worlds Cried: Genocide in Northwestern California.* San Francisco: Indian Historian Press, 1979.

Nunis, Doyce B., Jr. "An Interview with Dr. Doyce B. Nunis, Jr." In *The Serra Report.* Thadeus Shubsada, editor. Unpublished press release. Monterey, Calif. In *Native American Perspectives on the Hispanic Colonization of Alta California (The Spanish Borderlands Sourcebook Vol. 26),* Edited by Edward D. Castillo New York: Garland, 1991.

Obregon, Marco Antonio Cervera. "El Sistema de Armamento Entre Los Mexicas." *Arqueología Mexicana*. 12:70. 2004. Mexico City.

Older, Fremont. *California Missions and Their Romances*. New York: Coward-McCann, 1938.

Orfalea, Gregory. *Journey to the Sun: Junípero Serra's Dream and the Founding of California*. New York: Scribner, 2014.

De la Pérouse, Count Jean François Galaup,. "A Visit to Monterey in 1786 and a Description of the Indians of California." In *California Historical Quarterly*. 15:3. 1936. In *Documentary Evidence for the Spanish Missions of Alta California (The Spanish Borderlands Sourcebook Vol. 14)*. Edited by Julia G. Costello. New York: Garland, 1991.

Palóu, Francisco. *Historical Memoirs of New California*, Vol. I. Translated into English from the manuscript in the archives of Mexico. Herbert Eugene Bolton, editor and translator. Berkeley: University of California, 1926.

———. *Historical Memoirs of New California*, Vol. II. Translated into English from the manuscript in the archives of Mexico. Herbert Eugene Bolton, editor and translator. Berkeley: University of California, 1926.

———. *Historical Memoirs of New California*, Vol. III. Translated into English from the manuscripte in the archives of Mexico. Herbert Eugene Bolton, editor and translator. Berkeley: University of California, 1926.

———. *Historical Memoirs of New California*, Vol. IV. Translated into English from the manuscript in the archives of Mexico. Herbert Eugene Bolton, editor and translator. Berkeley: University of California, 1926.

———. *Life and Apostolic Labors of the Venerable Father Junípero Serra*. Translated by C. Scott Williams. Edited by George Wharton James. Chicago: Lakeside, 1913.

———. *Palóu's Life of Fray Junípero Serra*. Translated and Annotated by Maynard J. Geiger. Richmand, Va.: William Byrd, 1955.

———. *Relación Historica de la Vida y Apostólicas Tareas del Venerable Padre Fray Junípero Serra, y de las Misiones que Fundó en la California Septentrional, y nuevos establecimentos de Monterey*. Mexico City: Zuniga y Ontiveros, 1787. La Vida de Junípero Serra. March of America Facsimile Series. Number 49. Ann Arbor, University Microfilms, Inc., 1966.

Payeras, Mariano. *Writings of Mariano Payeras*. Edited by Donald Cutter. Santa Barbara, Calif.: Bellerophon, 1995

Phelps, William Dane. Originally published as *Fore and Aft; or Leaves from the Life of an Old Sailor*. Boston: Nichols & Hall, 1871. Reprinted as *Alta California 1840–1842: The Journal and Observations of William Dane Phelps Master of the Ship* Alert. Briton Cooper Busch, editor. Glendale: Arthur H. Clark, 1983.

Phillips, George Harwood. "Indians and the breakdown of the Spanish Mission System in California." In *New Spain's Northern Frontier: Essays on Spain in the American West 1540–1821*. David J. Weber, editor. Albuquerque: University of New Mexico, 1979. In *Native American Perspectives on the Hispanic Colonization of Alta California (The Spanish Borderlands Sourcebook Vol. 26)*, Edited by Edward D. Castillo New York: Garland, 1991.

———. "Indians in Los Angeles, 1781–1875: Economic Integration, Social Disintegration." In *Pacific Historical Review*. 43(3):427-451, 1980. In *Native American Perspectives on the Hispanic Colonization of Alta California (The Spanish Borderlands Sourcebook Vol. 26)*, Edited by Edward D. Castillo New York: Garland, 1991.

Pitt, Leonard. *California Controversies, Major Issues in the History of the State*, Second Edition. Arlington Heights: Davidson, 1987.

Rawls, James J. *Indians of California: The Changing Image*. Norman: University of Oklahoma, 1984.

Reid, Hugo. *Letters on the Los Angeles County Indians. A Scotch Paisano: Hugo Reid's Life in California, 1832–1852, Derived from His Correspondence*. Susanna Bryant Dakin, editor. Berkeley: University of California, 1939.

Rivera, Fernando de Rivera y Moncada, *Diario del Capitan Comandante Fernando de Rivera y Moncada Vol. I. Coleccion Chimalistic*. Edited by Ernest J. Burrus. Madrid, Spain: José Porrua Turanzas, 1967.

Richman, Irving Berdine. *California Under Spain and Mexico: 1535–1847 A Contribution Toward the History of the Pacific Coast of the United States, Based on Original Sources (Chiefly Manuscript) in the Spanish and Mexican Archives and Other Repositories*. Boston: Houghton Mifflin, 1911.

Robinson, Alfred. "Journal on the Coast of California By A. Robinson, on Board of Ship Brookline Year 1829." In "Alfred Robinson, New England Merchant in Mexican California." By Adele Ogden. *California Historical Society*. 23:3. 1944. In *Documentary Evidence for the Spanish Missions of Alta California (The Spanish Borderlands Sourcebook Vol. 14)*. Edited by Julia G. Costello. New York: Garland, 1991.

———. *Life in California: A Historical Account of the Origin, Customs, and Traditions of the Indians of California*. First Published by Wiley and Putnam, New York, 1846. Unabridged republication of the first edition. New York: De Capo, 1969.

Rockwell, D. Hunt. *California the Golden*. San Francisco: Silver, Burdett, 1911.

Rogers, Harrison G. "Journal of Harrison G. Rogers, Member of the Company of J.S. Smith." In *The Ashley-Smith Explorations and the Discovery of a Central Route to the Pacific, 1822–1829*. Harrison Clifford Dale, editor. Cleveland: Arthur H. Clark, 1941.

"Selections from the Journal of Harrison G. Rogers, Member of the Company of J.S. Smith." Harrison Clifford Dale, editor. In *Documentary Evidence for the Spanish Missions of Alta California (The Spanish Borderlands Sourcebook Vol. 14)*. Edited by Julia G. Costello. New York: Garland, 1991.

Sacramento Union, July 31, 1860.

The Bay of San Francisco, The Metropolis of the Pacific Coast and its Suburban Cities—A History Vol. I. Chicago: Lewis, 1892.

Sandos, James A. *Converting California: Indians and Franciscans in the Missions*. New Haven, Yale University Press. 2004

———. "Junípero Serra's Canonization and the Historical Record." In *American Historical Review*. 93:5. 1988. In *Native American Perspectives on the Hispanic Colonization of Alta California (The Spanish Borderlands Sourcebook Vol. 26)*, Edited by Edward D. Castillo New York: Garland, 1991.

———. "Levantamiento!: The 1824 Chumash Uprising Reconsidered." In *Southern California Quarterly*. 67:109. 1985. In *Native American Perspectives on the Hispanic Colonization of Alta California (The Spanish Borderlands Sourcebook Vol. 26)*, Edited by Edward D. Castillo New York: Garland, 1991.

Séñan, José. *The Letters of José Séñan, O.F.M. Mission San Buenaventura, 1796–1823*. Edited by Lesley Byrd Siimpson, and translated by Paul D. Nathan. San Francisco: Howell, 1962. In *Documentary Evidence for the Spanish Missions of Alta California (The Spanish Borderlands Sourcebook Vol. 14)*. Edited by Julia G. Costello. New York: Garland, 1991.

Serra, Junípero. *Diario: The Journal of Padre Serra From Loreto, the Capital of Baja California to San Diego, Capital of the New Establishments of Alta California*. Translated and Edited by Ben F. Dixon. San Diego: Don Diego's Libreria, 1964.

———. *Writings of Junípero Serra*, Vol. II. Antonine Tibesar, editor. Baltimore, Md.: J. H. Furst, 1956.

———. *Writings of Junípero Serra*, Vol. III. Antonine Tibesar, editor. Baltimore, Md.: J. H. Furst, 1956.

———. *Writings of Junípero Serra*, Vol. IV. Antonine Tibesar, editor. Baltimore, Md.: J. H. Furst, 1956.

Shipek, Florence A. "California Indian Reactions to the Franciscans." In *The Americas*. 41:4. 1985. In *Native American Perspectives on the Hispanic Colonization of Alta California (The Spanish Borderlands Sourcebook Vol. 26)*, Edited by Edward D. Castillo New York: Garland, 1991.

Silliman, Stephen W. *Lost Laborers in Colonial California: Native Americans and the Archaeology of Rancho Petaluma*. Tucson: University of Arizona, 2004.

Simpson, Lesly Byrd. *The Encomienda in New Spain: The Beginning of Spanish Mexico*. Berkeley: University of California, 1950.

Soulé, Frank, Gihon, John H. and Nisbet, James. *Annals of San Francisco*. San Francisco: Appleton, 1854.

Stannard, David E., *American Holocaust: The Conquest of the New World*. Oxford: Oxford University Press, 1993.

Sullivan, Maurice. *The Travels of Jedediah Smith*. Santa Ana, Calif.: Fine Arts Press, 1934.

Tac, Pablo. *Conversión de los San Luiseños de la Alta California*, Messofanti Collection, Biblioteca dell'Archiginnasio di Bologna.

———. "Indian Life and Customs at Mission San Luis Rey: A record of California Mission Life Written by Pablo Tac, an Indian Neophyte." Edited and translated by Gordon Hewes and Minna Hewes. In *The Americas*. 9:1. 1952. In *Native American Perspectives on the Hispanic Colonization of Alta California (The Spanish Borderlands Sourcebook Vol. 26)*, Edited by Edward D. Castillo New York: Garland, 1991.

Temple II, Thomas Workman. "Toypurina the Witch and the Indian Uprising at San Gabriel." Southwest Museum. Masterkey 32:5. 1958. In *Native American Perspectives on the Hispanic Colonization of Alta California (The Spanish Borderlands Sourcebook Vol. 26)*, Edited by Edward D. Castillo New York: Garland, 1991.

Thomas, Hugh. *Rivers of Gold: The Rise of the Spanish Empire from Columbus to Magellan*. New York: Random House, 2004.

Vernard Foley, George Palmer, Werner Soedel. "The Crossbow." *Scientific American*. 252:1, Jan. 1985. pp. 106-107

To Toil in that Vineyard of the Lord: Contemporary Scholarship on Junípero Serra. Edited by Rose Marie Beebe and Robert M. Senkewicz. Berkeley: Academy of American Franciscan History, 2010.

Verger, Rafael. Letter to Manuel Lanz de Casafonda, dated August 3, 1771. Berkeley, Calif.: Bancroft Library, BANC MSS M-M 1847.

Visión De Los Vencidos: Relaciones Indígenas De La Conquista. Introducción, selección y notas: Miguel León-Portilla. Versión de textos nahuas: Ángel Ma Garibay K. Mexico, DF: Universidad Nacional Autónoma de México, 1992.

Voght, Martha. "Shamans and Padres: The Religion of the Southern California Missions Indians." In *Pacific Historical Review*. 36:4. 1967. *Native American Perspectives on the Hispanic Colonization of Alta California (The Spanish Borderlands Sourcebook Vol. 26)*, Edited by Edward D. Castillo New York: Garland, 1991.

Waters, Willard O. "Franciscan Missions of Upper California as Seen by Foreign Visitors and Residents: A Chronological List of Printed Accounts 1786-1848." In *Bookman's Holiday: Notes and Studies Written in Tribute to Harry Miller Lydenberg*. New York: New York Public Library, 1943. In *Documentary Evidence for the Spanish Missions of Alta California (The Spanish Borderlands Sourcebook Vol. 14)*. Edited by Julia G. Costello. New York: Garland, 1991.

Webb, Edith Buckland. *Indian Life at the Old Missions*. Los Angeles: Warren F. Lewis, 1952.

Weber, David J. Bárbaros: *Spaniards and Their Savages in the Age of Enlightenment*. New Haven: Yale, 2005.

———. *The Spanish Frontier in North America*. New Haven: Yale, 1992.

Wharton, James George. *In and Out of the Old Missions*. New York: Gosset and Dunlop, 1927.

Wright, Ronald. *Stolen Continents: 500 Years of Conquest and Resistance in the Americas*. Boston: Houghton Mifflin Harcourt, 2005.

Yenne, Bill. *The Missions of California*, San Diego, Calif.: Thunder Bay, 2004.

Index

About the Author

Elias Abundis Castillo is a three-time Pulitzer Prize nominee and has earned thirteen journalism awards in his career as a journalist. After working for the Associated Press and later the *San Jose Mercury News*, he left daily journalism in 1989 to devote himself to free-lance writing.

In 1991, under a grant from *National Geographic* magazine, he led the first scientific exploration of Mexico's vast Copper Canyon, a chasm that rivals the Grand Canyon in length and depth and is located in one of the most isolated areas of North America.

He is a recognized expert on Mexico and in 1997 was invited to speak before San Francisco's prestigious Commonwealth Club on Mexico and its future. He has also briefed California's Department of Investigation and the state's Bureau of Narcotics Enforcement on the future of Mexico and its criminal organizations.

He was born in Mexicali, Mexico, where his stepgrandfather, José Severo Castillo, a renowned newspaper publisher, exposed corruption in Baja California. After his stepgrandfather retired, the family moved to Santa Barbara. Castillo attended San Jose State University, where he earned a bachelor of arts in journalism and later a master's degree.

Fascinating California History

When the Great Spirit Died

An in-depth study of the tragic
destruction of the California Indians

$19.95 *$22.95 Canada*

When San Francisco Burned

Never-before-published photos of the
1906 Great Earthquake and Fire

$21.95 *$23.95 Canada*

Choose Your Weapon

When gunplay and politics mixed—the
history of dueling in 1850s California

$16.95 *$21.95 Canada*

Walking San Francisco's
49 Mile Scenic Drive

See the best of San Francisco on foot

16.95 *$21.95 Canada*

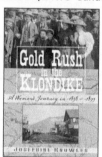

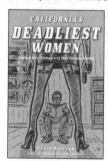

Gold Rush in the Klondike

A woman's journey in 1898–1899

$22.95 *$28.95 Canada*

California's Deadliest Women

A shocking look at women who kill

$14.95 *$18.95 Canada*

Available from bookstores, online bookstores, and
CravenStreetBooks.com, or by calling toll-free 1-800-345-4447.

9 781610 353045